Praise for
The Facebook Era

"Clara Shih has written a tour de force and one deeply rooted in actual experience. If you want to get past the theory and figure out how to harness the power of social networking in your business, read this book! And prosper."

—Don Tapscott, best-selling author of thirteen books,
most recently *Grown Up Digital: How the Net Generation is Changing Your World*

"With over 150 million active users and growing, Facebook is quickly becoming one of the dominant communication platforms of our time. However, as with any major advance in technology, most businesses are only beginning to leverage the game-changing opportunities that the 'online social graph' provides. As one of the leading innovators in this field, Clara personally has a unique perspective on how the benefits of these changes can be realized by companies across a gamut of industries. In *The Facebook Era*, she does an excellent job of explaining in detail how businesses can use Facebook and related tools to advance marketing, recruiting, business development, and customer service. *The Facebook Era* is a must-read for any professional who wants to understand how social networking will deeply transform business processes and relationships in the decade ahead!"

—Justin Smith, founder and editor,
Inside Facebook

"Today more than ever you need intimacy with your customers and a competitive edge, [both] of which you will potentially lose if you do not read this book. Your customers, employees, and stockholders are changing how they communicate, educate [and] socialize—are you prepared?"

—David Mather, President,
Hoover's, Inc.

"Clara leaves absolutely no stone unturned in this exploration of the world's most explosive social network. Her knowledge of the Web 2.0 industry and social networking combined with her understanding of today's selling power make for a fantastic book. If you own or are looking to start a business, read *The Facebook Era*. It will change the way you do business forever!"

—Chris Cranis, national account executive,
BT/Ribbit

"…A powerful book describing the power of networking for individuals and businesses, and how online social media sites are changing the rules."

—Shalini Govil-Pai, lead product manager,
Google

"Take a big breath—Clara Shih takes the reader on a deep dive into the big blue ocean that is Facebook, from both a consumer and business perspective. Before you come up for air, you'll be fascinated with all the strange-looking fish she finds in the vast new world of social networking which we are so completely and hopelessly addicted to…and loving every minute of it."

—Dave McClure, startup advisor and angel investor

"Companies are concerned about social networking—it feels like an area of business they don't have control over. Clara's book provides brilliant insight that dissolves that fear and provides business leaders the bottom line value to an era of innovation and collaboration that can only be reached by embracing Web 3.0…Clara's vision, as the creator of the first business app on Facebook, is transforming CRM and customer service technology space."

—Dr. Natalie L. Petouhoff, customer service and customer experience analyst, Forrester Research

"As an entrepreneurship educator, I know that the world of promoting your business has changed dramatically with the advent of Facebook. Clara Shih's book gives us a crash course on how to extract the value from this important new tool."

—Tina Seelig, executive director, Stanford Technology Ventures Program

"*The Facebook Era* provides practical information and advice on making the most of the social media phenomenon and does so in a highly readable style, with useful industry and organizational context. Whether tasked to integrate social media within their company's overall marketing, recruiting, or organizational development strategies or simply developing their personal brand, readers will gain valuable perspective on a rapidly evolving field, along with ideas and tips that can be put to work immediately."

—Steve Sieck, President, SKS Advisors, Inc.

"Clara Shih takes on one of the more difficult tasks in discussing any new technology or phenomenon: placing it in context and understanding how to engage to realize benefit. All too often the long-term implications are not the first consideration, we become too enamored with the sheer newness or frightened away. Social networking and specifically social CRM places the most critical commodity at the center of the discussion—relationships and trust. A breach in this most tenuous of human states could have significant consequences. As Clara points out, we are yet to know the broader implications, but this book thoroughly discusses what is social networking, its value broadly, and its potential for shaping the new social-centric enterprise. Organizations, heed Clara's advice; put in the work upfront, plan your strategy, understand your goals, and understand this new medium."

—Mary Wardley, Program VP, CRM and Enterprise Applications, IDC

the
Facebook Era

Tapping Online Social Networks to Build Better Products, Reach New Audiences, and Sell More Stuff

Clara Shih

PRENTICE
HALL

Many of the designations used by manufacturers and sellers to distinguish their products are claimed as trademarks. Where those designations appear in this book, and the publisher was aware of a trademark claim, the designations have been printed with initial capital letters or in all capitals.

The author and publisher have taken care in the preparation of this book, but make no expressed or implied warranty of any kind and assume no responsibility for errors or omissions. No liability is assumed for incidental or consequential damages in connection with or arising out of the use of the information or programs contained herein.

The publisher offers excellent discounts on this book when ordered in quantity for bulk purchases or special sales, which may include electronic versions and/or custom covers and content particular to your business, training goals, marketing focus, and branding interests. For more information, please contact:

> U.S. Corporate and Government Sales
> (800) 382-3419
> corpsales@pearsontechgroup.com

For sales outside the United States please contact:

> International Sales
> international@pearson.com

Visit us on the Web: informit.com/ph

Library of Congress Cataloging-in-Publication Data

Shih, Clara Chung-wai.

The Facebook era : tapping online social networks to build better products, reach new audiences, and sell more stuff / Clara C. Shih.

p. cm.

ISBN 978-0-13-715222-3 (pbk. : alk. paper) 1. Business enterprises—Computer networks. 2. Online social networks. 3. Facebook. I. Title.

HD30.37.S49 2009

658.8'72—dc22

2009000872

Bebo and the Bebo logo are trademarks of Bebo, Inc. AOL and the AOL Triangle Logo are registered trademarks of AOL LLC. Used with permission.

ISBN-13: 978-0-13-715222-3
ISBN-10: 0-13-715222-1
Text printed in the United States at RR Donnelley in Crawfordsville, Indiana.
Third printing August 2009

Editor-in-Chief
Mark Taub

Acquisitions Editor
Trina MacDonald

Development Editor
Michael Thurston

Managing Editor
Kristy Hart

Project Editor
Betsy Harris

Copy Editor
Karen Annett

Senior Indexer
Cheryl Lenser

Proofreader
Apostrophe Editing Services

Technical Reviewers
Chris Cranis
Shalini Pai
Steve Sieck

Publishing Coordinator
Olivia Basegio

Book Designer
Anne Jones

Senior Compositor
Gloria Schurick

To my parents James and Sophia Shih, my brother Vic,
and to finding the American Dream

Contents

Foreword

Ten years ago, I was an executive at a traditional enterprise software company. The industry had stopped innovating. Conventional wisdom said that "innovation was dead." I did not agree. I realized massive changes needed to be made in our industry, so I started salesforce.com with one simple idea: Make the software applications people use for business as easy to use as a Web site like Amazon.com.

Innovation was not dead; it was just emanating from a different place than we were expecting. The consumer Internet pioneers, like eBay, Google, and Amazon.com, were leading innovation. Taking advantage of the power of the Web, these companies were moving much faster and winning over much larger audiences than any of us had ever seen. Inspired by the Consumer Web, we developed a better way to serve business customers and ultimately transform the enterprise software industry.

Today, we still look to companies like Amazon.com and Google for inspiration, as well as a new generation of consumer companies, such as Facebook. Although we share similar philosophies with these companies, such as prizing intuitiveness and ease of use, the real power in this new era is not as much about learning from the consumer greats as it is about collaborating with them.

More than ever before, the lines are blurring between the consumer and enterprise worlds. It has become expected for people to use consumer applications such as Google Maps, Gmail, or eBay for business purposes. Bringing together social networking with enterprise applications represents the next phase in this evolution.

Relationships in today's competitive business environment are paramount, and Facebook's 150 million-user audience makes it an incredibly attractive community in which to conduct business. I realize that many in the business world have been leery of how this unknown frontier will affect their bottom line. But we are already seeing tremendous business value being unlocked on these social networking sites. And everything in this era is continuing to rapidly and profoundly change still.

We have entered a landmark new era in the maturity of the Internet. Web 1.0 revolutionized the transaction of goods and information and was marked by the killer apps from companies like eBay, Amazon.com, and Google. Web 2.0 gave rise to the next generation of applications, which allowed anyone to participate, such as through posting a video on YouTube or tagging photos on Flickr. Now, though, we have evolved to an entirely new level with Web 3.0—an era that is entirely about innovation and collaboration.

Cloud computing is enabling this new era by democratizing innovation. Today, anyone with an Internet connection can create even very complex and robust Web applications without any of the onerous infrastructure investment once required. Just look at the salesforce.com developer community, which now has over 450 independent software vendor (ISV) partners and 100,000 developers from around the world. Together, they have created more than 800 new applications now available on the AppExchange, our online marketplace for business Software-as-a-service apps and for which Clara Shih currently serves as product line director. On the consumer side, Facebook, too, is inspiring and empowering innovation with over 400,000 developers and entrepreneurs who have built 24,000 social applications on its platform.

When Facebook first launched its platform and application programming interfaces (APIs), developers clamored to build consumer applications, such as playing Scrabble, sharing photos, and "SuperPoking." Clara changed this when over a few days she developed Faceconnector (formerly Faceforce), the first enterprise social networking mashup that pulls Facebook profile and friend data in real time into Salesforce CRM. Clara had the vision that the next generation of enterprise software won't be about software at all. It will be about people and relationships, and social networking sites by design are all about relationships. Clara's breakthrough idea was that using Facebook, business professionals could get to know the person behind the name and title, and thereby build a larger number of richer, more personal, and longer-lasting business relationships with customers, prospects, business partners, and colleagues.

Clara built Faceconnector on the Force.com platform using Facebook's APIs and has made it freely available on the AppExchange, unleashing her innovation to our over 1 million subscribers worldwide.

Developers have taken notice and are following Clara's example in "mashing up" business with consumer social networking sites. It's a good thing, too, because times are changing. Increasingly, graduating college students entering the workforce and starting to take on leadership positions are shunning "antiquated" e-mail systems. (They say it's only for grown-ups.) They all use Facebook. Social networking and collaboration have become the expectation. They will be frustrated and unproductive, and even reject business applications that don't offer these features. Clara believes that five years from now, no enterprise application—CRM, recruiting, e-mail—won't be integrated with the social graph. She's right.

Recently, we announced a partnership with Facebook, led by Clara. Force.com for Facebook makes it easy for Facebook developers to build enterprise social apps on Force.com's global, trusted enterprise infrastructure. At salesforce.com, we've spent the last ten years building out enterprise-grade functionality like workflow, security, multilanguage and multicurrency, and integration services "in the cloud" so that developers can focus on innovation, not infrastructure. Both Sheryl Sandberg, the chief operating officer at Facebook, and I believe that this partnership will enable a whole new class of business applications inside Facebook, such as truly social CRM. The Service Cloud and Sales Cloud, our set of technologies that allow customer service reps and sales reps to tap the knowledge of customer conversations taking place on social networks, are proof that social CRM is real.

At salesforce.com, we have witnessed firsthand the power of connecting on Facebook. Early on, I encouraged everyone in our organization to sign up and required everyone on my executive team to do so as well. Many of our employees had already built huge personal networks—many of them with hundreds of friends, and the ability to reach into and touch millions. They were eager to use this platform in their professional lives, and we were eager to harness their energy and networks.

We immediately saw the benefits: Employees intimately knew the features of the site and offered suggestions about how we could use it to communicate with one another, reach prospective job candidates, and generate enthusiasm and support for our company's initiatives, such as new products and our nonprofit foundation. Employees, many who had recently joined us, or who were scattered across different departments or geographies, were able to easily communicate with one another as well as with previously hard-to-reach executives. The user profile—rich with information about one's family, hometown, or outside interests such as a passion for yoga or mountain biking—allowed individuals to get to know one another, foster connections, and establish deeper relationships. That was pivotal: Engagement helps us to retain our community spirit, continually inspire teamwork, and make us more aligned both internally with employees as well as externally with customers and partners.

In an age where traditional advertising influence is dropping like a rock, we have looked to social networking as an opportunity to become relevant in our customers' conversations, in their communities, where they want to be. We have a salesforce.com page to increase brand presence through sharing information about our company, posting photos from events, and uploading videos, such as a "trailer" to generate excitement for our annual user conference. We had exceptional success broadcasting our annual Dreamforce event through Facebook Events. As people registered, it was detailed in their News Feed, which further built viral awareness for our event. The result? We registered more Dreamforce attendees than ever before and did so more quickly. Hundreds of people have become "fans" of our page and their networks have been notified when they did so—thus further virally extending our reach and impact.

We don't just rely on our company page. I frequently contribute to my "status," in which I share what I am working on, convey my excitement for an upcoming event, or mention something great that was built on our technology. This information appears in my News Feed and reaches my entire network, which in turn, drives significant traffic to our site. The best part is the strength we have in numbers. Our employees update their profile with work-related information, and even mentioning that they work at salesforce.com magnifies our footprint.

Another real benefit has been in recruiting. The very best way to source new talent has always come from leveraging the relationships of our employees. With social networking sites such as Facebook or LinkedIn, this has never been easier. Our recruiters utilize these connections (*hint:* all young talented engineers are on these sites), and they also use social networks to actively keep in touch with former employees and interns. One of the most valuable features is the targeted search capability, which we use to find potential candidates based on their education (even specifying schools and majors), as well as by a particular past experience, area of expertise, or geographical location.

We are in the midst of a cloud computing revolution in which we are working, communicating, and collaborating in ways that are vastly different than ever before. *The Facebook Era: Tapping Online Social Networks to Build Better Products, Reach New Audiences, and Sell More Stuff* is the first book to reveal *why* these changes are important and *how* to take full advantage of them for your business. Author Clara Shih—the creator of the first business app for Facebook and an expert in this new blurry-lined world—articulately explains how the social networking phenomenon will fundamentally change how businesses fail and succeed.

Clara explores the crumbling walls between the consumer and enterprise spaces, and what this new era of collaboration and integration means for how all businesses can successfully build, market, and sell their products or services. Citing case studies from Victoria's Secret to men's clothing start-up Bonobos, Clara demonstrates that any company can adapt and thrive in the midst of these exciting changes. Most important, she reveals what everyone—from a CEO to an entry-level employee—must do to best prepare to compete, survive, and win in this revolutionary new era.

—Marc R. Benioff
Chairman and CEO of salesforce.com

Acknowledgments

I first need to thank my freshman-year roommate at Stanford and dear friend Kelly Bennett, without whose help this book would never have been completed. Kelly is blazing the trail for many of the concepts in this book through her role as COO of MightyQuiz, a social applications start-up. It was Kelly, in fact, who introduced me many years ago to Google search. I very reluctantly agreed to give it a try, and the rest is history.

I am indebted to my editors Trina MacDonald and Mark Taub, who found me on Facebook of all places and took a big chance on a first-time author. My reviewers Steve Sieck, Shalini Pai, and Chris Cranis were as generous with their time as with their thoughtful feedback and encouragement. They are the front lines of marketing, product management, and sales at some of the most successful and innovative companies of our time, and have kept this manuscript honest.

I owe this manuscript largely to the inspiration and support of my mentors at salesforce.com for whom I have tremendous admiration both professionally and personally: Marc Benioff, George Hu, Steve Fisher, Kendall Collins, Steve Lucas, Ariel Kelman, and Polly Sumner. Their leadership, vision, and passion for their people and our customers have changed my life and changed an entire industry.

I am grateful for the many lessons I learn each day from my AppExchange team at salesforce.com—Ryan Ellis, Ed Park, Sara Bright (Varni), Marie Laxague Rosecrans, Leyla Seka, and Eugene Feldman. I couldn't have asked for a better group of people in my first management role. Their great ideas and unwavering commitment to excellence are forging a new experience for customers to find and buy Web applications to run better businesses.

I would also like to thank:

My brother, Vic, who is a leading scholar on China's financial and political systems, real estate markets, and investment landscape. The guidance and inspiration he provided from his experience completing his first book have been invaluable.

My undergraduate and graduate advisors and professors at Stanford who with their passion, brilliance, and tireless mentorship helped me understand that the most interesting and worthwhile aspect of technology is how it can positively affect human lives—Armando Fox (now at UC Berkeley), Tina Seelig, Tom Byers, Randy Komisar (Kleiner Perkins Caufield & Byers), Tom Fountain (Mayfield Fund), Eric Roberts, Terry Winograd, Peter Fenton (Benchmark Capital), Rob McGinn, and Michele Tertilt.

Jonathan Zittrain and Chris Davies at Oxford, and the Marshall Scholarship.

Alberto Savoia, Shona Brown, Ming Wang, Jae Yu, and Magda Escobar for the inspiration and opportunity to work for them at Agitar, Google, the University of Illinois, Fermilab, and PluggedIn, respectively.

The loving and gracious support of my extended family, especially Chiu Wu, Susan K.L. Mok, Patrick Mok, Peter Mok, Rich Mok, and Otto Chan. The longest-standing, most wonderful friends one could have—Ally Russell (Basak), Bex Graciano (Seibert), Jill Starzyk Jeffe, Becky Wedel, Elizabeth Williams, Nathan Gettings, Larry Ozowara, John M. Tucker—who knew me before I knew myself and have always challenged me, stood by me, and believed in me no matter what. My dearest friends in San Francisco whose encouragement, enthusiasm, and patience kept me going during the worst bouts of writer's block—John Barkis, Mike Saldi, Kirsten Ziegler, Sylvie Patrick, Meredith Stanton, Elaine Kan, Cynthia Johanson, Pomme Ratanakanaka, Graham Rasmussen, Steve Garrity, Jenny Stefanotti, and Crid Yu. I look forward to spending time with them again now that the book is done!

The Camp Amelia team who first taught me in Ghana many summers ago that nothing can't be solved by the power of human connection and compassion, sometimes with the help of technology—Shirley Somuah, David Weekly, Katie Kollitz, Mel Burns, Nina Hsu, Sandy Yu, Julie Zhuo, Brandon Burr, Andy Szybalski, Camille Hearst, Shona Brown, Marina Remennik, Herb Walberg, Feliz Swapp, and the many thousands of kids around the world who have gone through our programs and curriculum.

Todd Perry, without whose help on Faceconnector (formerly Faceforce), none of this would have ever happened.

Dave Morin, Sheryl Sandberg, Elliot Schrage, Kelly Winters, and David Swain at Facebook for the historic partnership between our two companies that bring together social networking and enterprise applications and are making into reality many of the ideas in this book.

Charlene Li, Dave McClure, Don Tapscott, Kevin Efrusy, Sramana Mitra, Tony Perkins, and Timothy Chou for their wisdom, thought leadership, and willingness to help with this manuscript despite having some of the industry's busiest schedules.

Justin Smith, Nick O'Neill, David Mather, Jessica Lipnack, Ming Kwan, Matt Cohler, Gordon Evans, Bruce Francis, Jane Hynes, Chamath Palihapitiya, Tim Kendall, Net Jacobsson, Jeff Hammerbacher, Charlie Cheever, Jaemi Swope, Jeff Grosse, Bob Bickell, and the many loyal and vocal users of Faceconnector (formerly Faceforce), who are leading this social revolution!

Also, Carlye Adler, Paul Merage and the Foundation for the American Dream, Stephane Nakib, Denis Pombriant, Dan Chao, Kingsley Joseph, Ken Mah, Travis Bryant, Nathaniel Dean, Eric Silverberg, Dan Pastor, and Matt Gidney. My friend Ramit Sethi, who is an entrepreneur, blogger, and one of the most thoughtful and creative consumer marketers I know.

And last, but certainly not least, my grandmother Lau Kim Ping, who has spent her life breaking glass ceilings, inventing her own rules, and making sure that I do the same.

About the Author

Clara Shih is the creator of Faceconnector (formerly Faceforce), the first business application on Facebook. In addition, Clara is the product line director of AppExchange, salesforce.com's online marketplace for business Software-as-a-service applications built by third-party developers and ISVs. (Editor's note: Upon completing this book, Clara has created a new role and team at salesforce.com focused on enterprise social networking alliances and product strategy.) Previously, Clara worked in strategy and business operations at Google, and before that as a software developer at Microsoft. She is the founder and serves on the board of directors of Camp Amelia Technology Literacy Group, an East Palo Alto, California-based 501(c)(3) nonprofit that develops and distributes technology education software and curriculum. Clara holds B.S. and M.S. degrees in economics and computer science from Stanford, and has a master's degree in Internet studies from Oxford, where she studied as a United States Marshall Scholar. Clara is a frequently invited speaker at social media conferences around the world, including Web 2.0 Expo, Enterprise 2.0, Netgain, Social Ad Summit, and the Social Networking Conference.

Clara's first book, *Using New Media*, was commissioned by UNESCO to help teachers, parents, and school administrators in developing countries use digital media to adopt best practices and distribute high-quality content and curriculum. Clara is an immigrant to the United States from Hong Kong and learned English as a second language.

Introduction

"I am a firm believer in the people."
—Abraham Lincoln

I t was the spring of 2007. Smoking indoors hadn't yet been outlawed, though this place might not have cared either way. These two older men, clearly regulars, sat in the back corner, bare, lanky arms hanging out of their wifebeaters, cigarette dangling out one side of their mouth and a toothpick out the other. They were gesturing animatedly, laughing, eating, smoking, chattering away in loud Cantonese about this and that.

I tuned them out to focus on my steaming bowl of wonton soup. Just then, out of the corner of my ear, I heard them just barely: "...*blah blah blah Facebook.*" I instantly sat up to listen. I had not been mistaken—these two men slurping down their congee at an anonymous diner tucked away in a corner of Hong Kong where foreigners never go, and probably don't know about, were talking about *Facebook*. Their children who were in college abroad got them into it, and now they were hooked. I was floored. It was the moment I realized that if Facebook was not already mainstream, that it would become so very, very soon.

I flew back to San Francisco the following week and attended the first *f8*, Facebook's developer conference. There, they unveiled a new platform that would allow third-party developers and software vendors to build applications that Facebook users could add to their Facebook pages, such as their profile. The keynote presentation and product demonstrations were novel and interesting—new Facebook applications such as iLike for sharing music and concerts with friends, Slide for sharing photos and videos, and so on and so forth.

Still, I felt like something was missing. Photos and SuperPoking are fun, but where were the business applications? I was working (and still work) at an enterprise computing company, salesforce.com, which made its name developing customer relationship management (CRM) applications. But wasn't relationship management at the core of what Facebook was offering, albeit in a more fun and casual and modern way?

That night, I went home and sketched out an idea for bringing Facebook to business. As a product marketer, I had been spending a lot of time on sales calls and saw that the most successful reps established immediate rapport with their prospects and had the strongest personal relationships with their customers. Meanwhile in my personal life, I saw Facebook help establish faster and better rapport with people I had just met, and help me maintain closer relationships with my friends. So I decided to bring Facebook to CRM.

Facebook, I realized, *is* CRM. So I decided to try something bold: Combine Facebook with Salesforce CRM. With my friend Todd Perry's help, I developed Faceconnector (originally called Faceforce), which pulls Facebook profile and friend information into Salesforce account, lead, and contact records. Instead of anonymous cold calling, sales reps and other business professionals could get to know the person behind the name and title, and even ask for warm introductions from mutual friends.

Fortunately, Todd and I weren't alone. Enterprise start-up companies like WorkLight, InsideView, and Appirio evolved their products to include Facebook and other traditionally "consumer" social media. New companies emerged, like Telligent, Socialcast, and Small World Labs, to build enterprise social technology from the ground up. My employer, salesforce.com, brought voting, tagging, profiles, feeds, and other Web 2.0 capabilities into its IT platform and CRM applications. Oracle announced a strategy around "social CRM."

Our idea—bringing the power of community, trusted online identity, and user data on social networking sites to business—was a simple one, but has had powerful consequences. But it represented a paradigm shift: Facebook isn't just for kids anymore.

Why You're Reading This Book

This book is meant to help you understand online social networking and what it means for your company. Perhaps these situations sound familiar:

- You know online social networking is important but don't know what to do about it.

- You use Facebook in your personal life but aren't quite sure how it fits with your professional life.

- Your boss has asked you to create a Facebook presence for your company ASAP, but you don't know how or what to do.

- You *are* the boss and want to understand the social networking phenomenon and what it means for your bottom line.

- You want to hear how real companies are succeeding at sourcing leads, engaging new audiences, and transforming customers into a sales force on social networking sites.

- You understand that whether it's looking for a job, closing a deal, or advancing your career, a lot of it comes down to who you know in your social networks.

- Increasingly, you're being asked to do more with less, and want to leverage the power of your networks, your colleagues' networks, and your customers' networks to get the job done better, faster, and cheaper.

Three main premises motivate this manuscript. First, organizations are inherently social because organizations are only as good as their people and people are inherently social. Whether it's relationships between a sales rep and prospect, recruiter and candidate, vendor and procurement personnel, or other partners, business success has always come down to personal relationships. Second, recommendations and referrals from those you know and trust are powerful influencers of purchase decisions. Last but not least, research shows that weak ties, rather than your most intimate circle of friends and family, tend to carry the greatest amount of social capital in business contexts. It is precisely in weak ties where Facebook, Twitter, and other social networking services excel.

Welcome to the Facebook Era

We are witnessing a historic movement around the *online social graph*—that is, the map of every person on the Internet and how they are connected. It is the World Wide Web of *people*, a reflection and extension of the offline social graph—the friends, family members, colleagues, mentors, classmates, neighbors, and acquaintances who are important to us, who help shape us, and for whom we live. The online social graph empowers us to be better, more effective, more efficient, and more fulfilled doing what is inherent to our nature—communicating who we are, and transacting and interacting with others across the Web. Data from social networks, such as where people are from, what they are interested in, and who their friends are, with the right privacy controls in place can then be implicitly or explicitly mined to make business interactions more tailored, personal, and precise.

For succinctness, I call this "the Facebook Era," but am referring to the general social networking phenomenon emerging across the Web. With the lightning pace of technology, we are living in a very different world than a few years ago. Today's college students don't use e-mail except with "grown-ups" like professors and potential employers—they Tweet about what they had for breakfast and send Facebook messages. But it's not just college students. Although Facebook may have begun after office hours, its power extends far beyond our personal identities into our professional ones. Facebook statistics over the last year have consistently shown the greatest growth in audience numbers coming from people aged 35-49. According to Nielsen Online, by the end of 2008, social networking had overtaken even email in terms of global reach among Internet users.

200 Million and Counting

This very moment, on Facebook alone, over 200 million people around the world are logged in, updating their status, interacting with friends, interacting with brands, providing valuable information for you to be able to understand them better, and learning about you in return. As a business person, you *need* to be where your customers are, and increasingly, customers are spending time on social networking sites like Facebook and Twitter.

We can learn a great deal from Barack Obama's 2008 presidential campaign, which used social networking sites to rally millions of supporters and help raise nearly $1 billion in grassroots campaign contributions. According to the Pew Research Center, ten percent of Americans (and one-third of Americans under the age of 30) used Facebook or another social networking site to get information about the presidential election. How many people will use Twitter or Facebook to learn about or become engaged with your company and products?

It's All About the People

Perhaps the online social graph was inevitable. Technology shouldn't be—was never meant to be—an end in and of itself. It is only interesting and meaningful and valuable where and when it serves people. Technology-centric technology was the result of an immaturity of our systems and thinking. The online social graph provides us with a new way, a way to bring what most defines and differentiates each one of us—our history, our relationships, our memories—into all aspects of our lives, including the way we experience technology. This book started out about business and technology, but is equally about a paradigm shift underway that leaves us with different expectations, behaviors, and relationships.

What exactly the future holds is anyone's guess, but what we do know is that business will never again be the same—whatever your industry, wherever you work, whether you are in sales, marketing, product development, recruiting, or another corporate function. We were in a very similar place of anticipation back in the early days of the Internet, and the PC and mainframe computing before it. Then, as now, some companies jumped blindly on the bandwagon, investing a tremendous amount of time, energy, and capital to implement technologies they did not understand, with no clear strategy and, ultimately, little to show for it. Others dismissed the Internet as a passing fad and were gradually outcompeted by online businesses or companies that used the Web to achieve more efficient and effective sales, marketing, recruiting, product development, and operations. But the smart ones took notice and began preparing for what an Internet era might look like. They thought through the implications for their business, and they adapted and thrived. This book is here to help you be smart about online social networking so that this time around you, too, can adapt and thrive.

If it's true that we are separated at most by only six degrees, then you are not very far from any one of your customers or prospective customers. Read this book, and then go out and get them!

Welcome to the Facebook Era.

How to Use This Book

This manuscript is structured into three parts. Part I (Chapters 1 through 3) provides the bigger-picture framework from which we can develop a richer understanding and appreciation of the online social networking revolution—what is happening, why it's happening, and what we can learn and apply from past technology revolutions. Part II (Chapters 4 through 7) takes a tour across four major functions in a company—sales, marketing, product development, and recruiting—and explores how each is being affected by online social networking technologies. Part III (Chapters 8 through 12) of the book is a practical how-to guide around implementing the ideas and possibilities presented in Part II. In all, there are twelve chapters in this book:

Part I: A Brief History of Social Media

- Chapter 1, "The Fourth Revolution," talks about the significance of the online social graph in the context of the three digital revolutions before it: mainframe computing, the PC, and the Internet. It draws examples from Mutual of Omaha Insurance Company, JPMorgan bank, and Bloomingdale's department store to show how past technology revolutions changed industry landscapes and what business decisions helped these companies establish a competitive advantage. The chapter concludes with a brief history of online social networking, including the rise and fall of popular sites, discovery sites used mainly for sales prospecting, private networks, and online gaming.

- Chapter 2, "The Evolution of Digital Media," walks through the history of how our experience with and capabilities using media have changed as technology has improved. The PC Era enabled dramatic improvements in media creation and storage. The Internet transformed distribution capability, first with Web site communities and RSS readers, and then more recently with search engine marketing and behavioral targeting. Empowered by the online social graph, the future will be about "social filtering" and the ability to deliver precisely the right piece of content to precisely the right person at precisely the right time. The My Starbuck's Idea online community on Facebook is provided as an example of how social filtering can help improve relevance and engagement. Chapter 2 concludes with a discussion on what attributes of Facebook make it unlike any other media site we have ever seen.

- Chapter 3, "Social Capital from Networking Online," discusses the concept of social capital, how social capital is used to achieve business goals, and how online social networking transforms our ability to accumulate and exercise social capital to achieve our personal and professional goals. It explores how online interactions facilitate entrepre-neurial networks, the crossover between offline and online networking, organizational flattening, and value creation from network effects.

Part II: Transforming the Way We Do Business

- Chapter 4, "Social Sales," speaks to the power of the online social graph for a sales cycle, from prospecting and the first call through to customer references, navigating customer organizations, and enabling sales teams to more easily collaborate. It features a case study on how Silicon Valley start-up Aster Data Systems has used employees' collective MySpace, Facebook, and LinkedIn networks to source leads and build personal relation-ships with customers.

- Chapter 5, "Social Network Marketing," talks about the breakthrough new marketing techniques made possible by online social networks, including hypertargeting, enhanced ability to capture passive interest and conduct rapid testing and iteration on campaigns, social community engagement, and automated word-of-mouth marketing. Chapter 5 features two case studies, one from national retailer Victoria's Secret, the other from nascent start-up Bonobos, demonstrating that businesses both large and small are achieving marketing success with Facebook's new social advertising tools.

- Chapter 6, "Social Innovation," describes how the four stages of innovation—generating concepts, prototyping, commercial implementation, and continual iteration—become more effective and efficient with online social networking. Online social engagement transforms the relationship between companies and customers from one-sided "build it and hope they come" to a partnership model. Businesses feel more empowered to go after new markets and audiences. Customers feel more accountable for providing input and more grateful when their input is incorporated in the design of new products. This chapter features examples of how brands like Dell, Gap, and YouTube are tapping into the wisdom of their customer communities on social networking sites to source new ideas and keep getting better.

- Chapter 7, "Social Recruiting," applies these concepts to the ever-important task of find-ing, attracting, assessing, and closing job candidates. It features a short case study on how Joe, a Chicago-based headhunter, has used Facebook and LinkedIn to source new candidates, keep in touch with candidates who might not be ready yet to leave their current roles, and maintain personal relationships with successful placements. The chap-ter concludes with a short set of suggestions for job seekers on how best to use online social networking to find and land the right role at the right company.

Part III: Your Step-By-Step Guide to Using Facebook for Business

- Chapter 8, "Engage Your Customers," guides companies through the first steps of any enterprise social initiative. It explains why anyone who is serious about investing in social networking must first start with business objectives and define a clear set of milestones. Using the example of Sanrio's Hello Kitty brand, this chapter urges companies to first listen using tools like Twitter Search and Facebook Lexicon to what the community might already be saying about their brand, and then with that context establish a presence on the appropriate set of social networking sites to reach the right audiences.

- Chapter 9, "Get Your Message Across," is a step-by-step set of instructions on how to tactically execute on the social network marketing techniques described in Chapter 5. Featured examples include Wendy's national fast-food restaurant chain, the Crash television program series, and Green Works natural cleaners.

- Chapter 10, "Build and Manage Your Relationships," details how individuals set up a social networking account and provides tips for creating effective profiles, establishing friend connections, organizing contacts, and managing different identities across one's personal and professional contacts. It also talks about etiquette for initiating or accepting friend requests, using online networking in conjunction with offline networking, providing or requesting introductions, and other interactions. Most of the examples from this chapter are from Facebook but can be generally applied to other social networking services.

- Chapter 11, "Corporate Governance and Strategy," speaks to the challenges, obstacles, and realities of implementing social networking technologies in a corporate setting. Specifically, this chapter urges businesses to consider the risks around privacy, security, intellectual property, confidentiality, and brand misrepresentation, and the importance of partnering closely with legal and IT departments to put the right systems and policies in place to mitigate these risks.

- Chapter 12, "The Future of Social Business," likens the status quo of online social networking to where we were with the Internet in the late '80s. Though there are plenty of unknowns, such as which vendors and business models will prevail, certain trends are already taking shape: flatter organizations, stronger offline communities, more small businesses, greater collaboration across organizations, and tighter integration with mobile devices. Despite the uncertainty, companies can and need to start thinking now about how this revolution will affect their business so that they can take the necessary steps to thrive in the Facebook Era.

A Brief History of Social Media

1

The Fourth Revolution

Approximately once a decade, a radical new technology emerges that fundamentally changes the business landscape. In every case, regardless of prior competitive dynamics, businesses that understand and appropriately adopt the technology win, while those that fail to do so lose. In the 1970s, this was mainframe computing. In the 1980s, it was the PC. In the 1990s, it was the Internet. And today, it is the *online social graph* (see Figure 1.1).

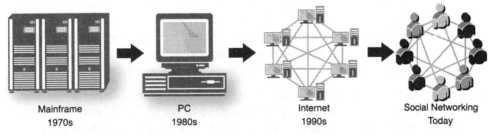

Mainframe	PC	Internet	Social Networking
1970s	1980s	1990s	Today

Figure 1.1
Every decade since the advent of computing, a new wave of technology sweeps across the business landscape.

But what exactly is the online social graph? Well, it is the World Wide Web of *people*—a map being constructed by social networking sites, such as Facebook, LinkedIn, and Hoover's Connect, of every person on the Internet and how they are interlinked. The social graph is for people what the World Wide Web is for hyperlinked Web pages: that is, for organizing, filtering, and association. Now that all of our machines and content pages are connected, the next digital revolution will be in capturing and using information about how we as individuals are connected. Metadata about Web pages, such as headings, keywords, and how they are linked, have been crucial for allowing us to manage and navigate through an eruption of content on the Web. Similarly, metadata from the social graph about individuals, such as where they work, how we know them, and who we know in common, will become crucial for allowing us to manage many different kinds of relationships with large numbers of people.

In order for us to better understand and prepare for the current transformation being brought on by social networking, it is instructive to see how past technology revolutions disrupted business practices. As you will see in the case studies and tables throughout this chapter, each wave of technology infrastructure is marked by a cycle of breakthrough innovation followed by commercialization, the emergence of a new class of applications, and, finally, business impact. As with the revolutions before it, the online social graph will give rise to a new, more nimble, and more efficient class of businesses that outcompetes those using technology from the previous era.

Mainframe Computing

The mainframe computer revolution rocked the '70s. IBM and the "Seven Dwarfs"—that is Burroughs, UNIVAC, NCR, Control Data, Honeywell, General Electric, and RCA—with roots in military and academic research labs, led the industry charge. Mainframes provided for those who could afford the million-dollar plus price tag—mostly in the airline, banking, and insurance sectors—unprecedented computing power. *Timesharing* allowed multiple users to simultaneously use a mainframe by dividing and alternately allocating computing power in small slivers of time. *Multitasking* allowed multiple different tasks to be performed concurrently by the mainframe, generally via batch processing. Thanks to these advances, mainframe computing was able to automate and greatly expedite existing tasks as well as enable previously intractable calculations and transactions.

In the late '70s, the advent of transistors and core memory enabled another generation of machines, called *minicomputers* because they took up only a corner of a room instead of filling an entire room like mainframes. Minicomputers from Digital Equipment, Data General, Tandem Computer, and other vendors made computing power more accessible for universities and medium-sized businesses, and were an important precursor to personal computers.

Table 1.1   CYCLE OF INNOVATION AND BUSINESS IMPACT FOR MAINFRAMES

Breakthrough Innovation	Burroughs Corporation invents and packages the first systems containing virtual memory, multiprogramming, and multiprocessing. Time-sharing was invented at Dartmouth College. Together, they enabled computation power and speed that were previously not possible.
Commercialization	IBM 360/370 sales to military, banking, and insurance industries help solve complex scientific, engineering, and business problems.
New Applications	Mainframes offer new capability to solve complex mathematics and science calculations.
Business Impact	Mainframes enable a new class of products and technologies across finance, military, and manufacturing.

Mainframe Computing at Mutual of Omaha Insurance Company

Mutual of Omaha Insurance Company was an early adopter of mainframe computing. The company's first computer—an IBM 705 mainframe—was deployed in 1957. According to the company, mainframe technology helped Mutual of Omaha grow relative to the competition by allowing much more rapid processing of insurance claims, speeding transactions such as benefits checks and premium payments, slowing the growth in number of clerical employees, and eliminating repetitious data handling. Mainframes freed Mutual of Omaha employees from manual processes and stacks of handwritten paperwork.

Mainframes also allowed Mutual of Omaha to streamline operations. Business processes that previously spanned multiple functions, with each function handled separately across the company, were gradually combined into one application, saving the company time, effort, and money.

The following excerpt, taken from an internal Mutual of Omaha document dated March 15, 1956, reveals the rationale and foresight of company executives in introducing mainframes.

****

What is the matter with our present system?

Present volume forces us to begin running notice and collection material 7 weeks prior to due date. Is it inconceivable that because of our ever-increasing volume we might be running a 9-1 notice before a 6-1 due was paid? The supplementary material now inundating our collection clerks is the result of early preparation of notices. But there is no other solution under our present system. **The speed of electronics will provide an answer.** Our closest estimate is that 60 hours before mailing time we will begin preparing notice and collection material…about 4 days compared to 35 days today. As a result, supplementary material will be reduced in proportion.

Increasing volume has always kept us alert for new methods of improving service to policyowners. Other companies in the insurance industry fighting the problems connected with volume are also turning to electronic data processing for the answer. Over 12 Health & Accident Insurance and Life Insurance companies have placed orders for an IBM electronic system. We will be the first Health & Accident company, and the 7th Life company, to have completed an installation.

The PC

In the 1980s, advances in integrated circuit technology and the first graphical user interface gave rise to the Personal Computer (PC) Era. Innovations from Intel, Xerox PARC, Microsoft, Apple, and others drastically reduced computer price and size while increasing capability, intuitiveness, and flexibility. For the first time, computing became accessible to the mass market. Businesses embraced spreadsheet software like Lotus 1-2-3 and VisiCalc to automate tedious, time-consuming, by-hand calculations. Word processors such as Corel WordPerfect and Microsoft Word replaced typewriters and eventually secretaries.

By enabling previously unimaginable levels of efficiency, automation, and advancement, PCs transformed how businesses were run and what people did at work. Mindless, manual tasks were replaced by a new Information Age where knowledge and higher-order thinking skills have become more valued than ever. In 1982, *Time* magazine named the PC as Machine of the Year, the first nonhuman ever chosen or nominated for its coveted Man of the Year award. Over the course of the decade, Microsoft emerged from unknown upstart to the first software company in history to exceed $1 billion in annual sales.

Table 1.2   CYCLE OF INNOVATION AND BUSINESS IMPACT FOR THE PC

Breakthrough Innovation	Xerox PARC invents the first graphical user interface (including icons and folders), the mouse, Ethernet networking, and file and print servers for the Xerox Star workstation.
Commercialization	Apple Lisa and Macintosh computers, Microsoft operating systems on IBM computers, and Intel x86 microprocessors are the defining commercial successes in the PC Era.
New Applications	PCs enable a new class of applications, including computerized spreadsheets, word processing, and graphics editing.
Business Impact	PCs result in huge efficiencies and cost savings in accounting, finance, and marketing/communications across all sectors.

The PC Revolution at JPMorgan

JPMorgan was one of the first investment banks to adopt PCs in the mid-eighties. Jean-Louis Bravard, who was a banker at the time and later became the company's first CIO in 1991, recalls how PCs enabled new transactions and financial products that were previously not fathomable. There were no IT processes or team in place, so Bravard purchased a PC with his personal credit card and expensed it.

- *Modeling complex transactions.* The economic downturn triggered by the savings and loan crisis left many clients in precarious financial situations that were difficult to grasp. One particular borrower who was at risk of defaulting had an especially complicated mix of short-term and long-term liabilities. Using Lotus 1-2-3 spreadsheet software on his PC, Bravard ran a simulation on what market conditions would be necessary for the client to remain solvent. He copied the financial model onto 5.25-inch floppy disks and sent them to the other banks in the loan syndication to secure their buy-in on how to address the situation at hand. No one contested his recommendation because none of the other banks knew what to do with the disk!

- *Navigating new financial climates.* When Bravard was put in charge of JPMorgan's Brazil office, the Brazilian *real* was undergoing hyperinflation of up to 6 percent a day. According to Bravard, mainframes were unable to keep up with the complexity of the environment. Spreadsheets were the only way Bravard and his team had of making sense of assets and value. While other banks were at a loss for how to operate in this environment, JPMorgan was able to manage its risk and thrive.

- *Creating new products.* The PC revolution contributed greatly to the liquidity and efficiency of financial markets by making it possible to create and value a host of new financial instruments, such as derivatives products.

Another company executive, John McColloch, was told that "not being facile on a PC would be like not having a driver's license from a career perspective":

I remember going to the Merrill Lynch training center in Princeton to go through PC 101. First thing we were taught was how to unscrew the case and expose the memory chip, and how to unplug the machine, all to convince us nervous executives that we were in total control (we weren't).

PCs provided the advantage JPMorgan's relatively less-established Investment banking business (the original investment banking business had been spun off in 1933 to form Morgan Stanley) needed to catch up and compete with Morgan Stanley and Goldman Sachs. The company was acquired by Chase Manhattan Corporation in 2000 and merged with Bank One Corporation in 2004.

The World Wide Web

The '90s were defined largely by the advent of the World Wide Web, developed by Tim Berners-Lee working with Robert Cailliau at CERN. E-mail, instant messaging, and Web conferencing applications dramatically improved communication capacity for businesses while drastically reducing costs. Web sites, online news, and search engines like Infoseek, Lycos, Yahoo!, Excite, and Google began providing affordable, real-time information for workers as well as a new medium for reaching customers. eBay, PayPal, and commerce sites like Amazon.com proved the feasibility and popularity of self-service transactions.

Within the enterprise software space, the Internet paved the way for the open source software and Software-as-a-service, or SaaS, movements, both of which have greatly democratized access to enterprise-grade software and services for small business and self-employed individuals. The Web made it dramatically easier and cheaper to start and run businesses. According to the U.S. government, thanks to technology, the number of small businesses in the United States alone ballooned to nearly 25 million by 1999.

Table 1.3   CYCLE OF INNOVATION AND BUSINESS IMPACT FOR THE INTERNET

Breakthrough Innovation	Hypertext system from CERN Research Laboratory, network infrastructure; National Science Foundation removed restrictions on using Internet for commercial purposes define the Internet Era.
Commercialization	Early commercial successes include the Netscape browser, dial-up access services from AOL, Prodigy, and CompuServe.
New Applications	The Internet enables new applications such as e-mail, instant messenger, Web sites, e-commerce, Web conferencing, online content and data services, and online ads.
Business Impact	The Internet Era results in cheaper, faster, democratized access to information, software services, communications, and transactions empowering businesses.

Internet Sales at Bloomingdale's Department Store, Take Two

In 1999, Federated Department Stores (now Macy's, Inc.), which owns Bloomingdale's, acquired e-commerce and online catalog company Fingerhut for $1.7 billion in what was seen as one of the most aggressive Internet plays in the industry. FDS planned to use Fingerhut's technology to create Bloomingdales.com, an online version of its Bloomingdale's By Mail paper catalog.

But just a few years later, they had very little to show. Customers did not see any benefit to shopping on the Web site, which was just an online replication of the print catalog. They were also not accustomed to making purchases on the Internet. Company executives decommissioned the e-commerce site, writing it off as a very expensive failure.

After a brief hiatus from Internet sales, Bloomingdales.com has been reincarnated with a new approach that takes advantage of the unique power and capabilities of the Internet. The new site is dynamic, engaging, and easy to search or browse in multiple different ways—by brand, by size, by genre, by color, by material, and by price. Sophisticated online search marketing and e-mail marketing campaigns drive traffic and track each Web visit. All of these were missing from the first version of the site and are simply not possible in a print catalog.

Now the fastest growing part of the business, Bloomingdales.com has allowed the company to better engage its traditional customer base and reach new audiences while reducing costs. It has been so successful that Macy's, Inc., has decided to discontinue the Bloomingdale's By Mail paper catalog, once a hallmark of the company, to focus the direct-to-consumer strategy entirely online.

There are a few important lessons to be learned. First, even a technology revolution as powerful as the Internet cannot in and of itself transform businesses. Success requires both a well-thought-out strategy and a market ready for the technology. Today, people are finally ready and willing to buy online. Bloomingdale's uses sales data and customer segmentation to determine what merchandise to sell via which channel. Second, you gain from the new technology only if you use it to accomplish something that was not possible before. Merely posting a digital version of a static print catalog on its Web site was not transformative. But creating a new catalog experience with dynamic images, hyperlinks, and related item recommendations has paid off with real results.

The Online Social Graph

Today, we are witnessing a fourth wave of "social" computing that stands to perhaps again challenge everything we know about what is meant by "business as usual." The online social graph is permeating across the Internet, connecting people and bringing context about relationships to every Web site and software application so that technology—finally—can be less about technology and more about people.

In previous eras, the workplace led adoption of new technologies. Online social networking is different. It is a movement that affects us personally first, professionally second. But the lines are blurring. More than ever, people are working for themselves, working from home, and taking care of personal business at work. Successful business interactions, whether in sales, recruiting, business development, or some other function, both define and are defined by relationships that increasingly blur the lines between personal and professional contexts. Important decisions, such as purchases of goods and services, are influenced by the recommendations and referrals of people we know, both personal friends and professional colleagues. More and more, these relationships, referrals, and rapport are crossing over from real life to social networking sites and vice versa.

Starting as early as 1995, online social networking pioneers Classmates.com, SixDegrees.com, and Friendster introduced the notion of profile pages and friend connections. These sites paved the way for today's popular sites, including Facebook, MySpace, LinkedIn, Orkut, Hi5, and CyWorld, each of which boasts tens or hundreds of millions of active members around the world.

Thanks to their viral nature, we have reached the tipping point in the mass adoption of online social networks, and they will only continue growing in prominence and pervasiveness. One would be hard-pressed to find a high school or college student today who doesn't use Facebook or MySpace, and what we're seeing as this demographic "grows up" is that the sphere of influence for these sites is expanding from social and dating life to professional opportunities and business interactions.

But social networking is not just for kids. According to Facebook, although it maintains an 85 percent or greater penetration among four-year U.S. universities, more than half of its users are out of college, and those 25 years and older represent the fastest-growing demographic. Between July and November 2008, Facebook grew from 90 million to 120 million users—it grew as much in those three months as it did in the first three years combined! The scale and scope Facebook now yields is unprecedented and profound. Yet it is only the beginning. Facebook, Twitter, MySpace, and an increasing number of other social networks now offer Web services application programming interfaces (APIs), which make it possible for other Web sites and Web applications to tap into profile and social data. These advances are extending the reach and impact of the online social graph beyond specific social networking sites to potentially every Web experience.

Besides the mainstream genre led by Facebook, Twitter, and MySpace, several other forms of social networking sites have developed in recent years that are important to note: discovery sites, affinity networks, and virtual world networks.

Table 1.4   CYCLE OF INNOVATION AND BUSINESS IMPACT FOR ONLINE SOCIAL NETWORKS

Breakthrough Innovation	Classmates.com, SixDegrees, and Friendster introduce concept of online profile pages and friend connections.
Commercialization	LinkedIn, Hoover's Connect, and the Forbes.com CEO Network are the most popular commercial social networks.
New Applications	Thanks to the social graph, information, communication, and transactions can be associated with individuals and shared socially.
Business Impact	Major business impact includes better user engagement, a powerful new method of market research, and capability for businesses to encourage socially influenced purchase decisions.

Discovery Sites

When people seek information on the Web, they typically go to a manually curated site like Wikipedia or to an automated search engine like Google. Similarly, the online social graph can be manually built up over time by individuals on sites like Facebook or approximated with algorithms. *Discovery sites,* such as Spoke, Rapleaf, ZoomInfo, Spock, and Wink and business/professional services, such as Generate, LexisNexis ExecRelate, and Collexis, construct a person database by crawling the Web for publicly available information and making associations. They are able to approximate user profiles and social graphs without any user participation.

This method is automated and scalable but has some drawbacks. First, automated discovery can be prone to error—data that is out of date, incorrect, incomplete, or redundant—simply because there is less public data about people and connections. Second, because we are dealing with people and not Web pages, discovery sites have generated a host of privacy concerns.

Still, discovery sites are growing in popularity. Data-mined biographical and contact data are being sold to salespeople and recruiters. For instance, Massachusetts-based company ZoomInfo has developed a product that allows Salesforce CRM users to access business information about sales prospects from its database of tens of millions of people and companies.

Instead of selling data about Internet users, sites like Rapleaf target the users themselves with a privacy and reputation management service. According to the Web site, Rapleaf's goal is to provide individuals with a way to manage their privacy and various online profiles as well as control what information is publicly available about them on the Web.

Hoover's Connect (formerly Visible Path), shown in Figure 1.2, is a corporate-sanctioned version of a discovery site. The application scans online communication content and frequency data from desktop applications like Outlook to map and assign weightings to connections based on the strength, frequency, and nature of interactions. Users seeking contact with a particular person, department, or company can use the tool to map the social path separating him or her from the target and to initiate the process for getting introduced.

Unlike the manual user-defined connections of Facebook and MySpace, autodiscovery has the advantage of being able to adapt to relationships as they change. That is, relationship strength is periodically updated based on how many e-mails are exchanged and how many joint meetings are scheduled, which can change over time.

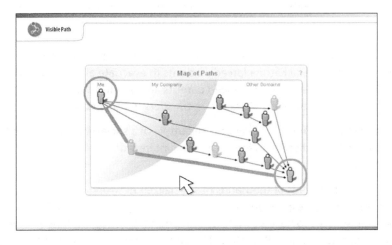

Figure 1.2
Hoover's Connect (formerly Visible Path), a corporate-sanctioned form of discovery social networking software, allows users to visualize their professional networks and chart the path of connections separating them from a potential target contact.

Affinity Networks and Private Networks

Many clubs and organizations, such as university alumni associations, have added online networking capabilities to their Web sites to reach and better engage their membership. Other affinity networks—perhaps the modern-day trade association—are entirely virtual. For instance, the Forbes.com CEO Network is an exclusive online community of senior executives from around the world who are given gated access to one another, in addition to specialized content, discussion boards, and polls. CEOs sign up to network with their peers and access news from Forbes, which benefits by cultivating a high-value network of global business leaders whom it can tap for interviews, focus groups, and targeted marketing campaigns for paid services.

"I love my dog/Dogs are people, too," Del Monte's invitation-only online community for dog lovers, is another good example of an affinity network, which Charlene Li and Josh Bernoff profiled in their recent book, *Groundswell*. By creating a place online for dog lovers to meet and discuss their passion for dogs, Del Monte has been able to effectively conduct market research and generate new ideas for their Snausages products while cultivating a loyal, passionate customer base.

Related to this notion of affinity networks, Ning is a service that allows users who perhaps have limited technical skills to easily create their own social networking sites around specific interests. For example, John F. Kennedy High School in New Orleans, Louisiana, has a comprehensive site for alumni, parents, and students featuring school news and events, the ability to connect with classmates and teachers, photos, videos, and fund-raising (see Figure 1.3). Thanks to Ning's Web site tools and ready-made templates, high school administrators were able to get a site up and running in a fraction of the time. The school's private social network has been especially important for the Kennedy community after Hurricane Katrina forced students to evacuate at the beginning of the 2005–2006 academic year. The site allowed parents and administrators to support one another, share information, and help facilitate transfers to other schools.

iDraw&Paint, shown in Figure 1.4, is another example of a social Web site on Ning. The site features tips and tricks, discussion forums, special interest groups, news, and an artwork showcase for amateur artists.

Today, Ning hosts hundreds of thousands of specialized networks on its free, ad-supported version. But despite the low barriers to starting a network on Ning, growth of new Ning sites appears to have slowed while the number of applications and audiences of Facebook continues to soar. Why should businesses choose specialized networks versus general-purpose networks containing specialized groups to reach their audiences? We will explore the pros and cons further in Chapter 11, "Corporate Governance and Strategy."

Figure 1.3
New Orleans, Louisiana-based John F. Kennedy High School's specialized social network community hosted on Ning.

Figure 1.4
iDraw&Paint, a specialized social network community for artists hosted on Ning.

Networked Gaming and Virtual World Networks

Networked gaming, led by social applications developers like Zynga and SGN, and virtual worlds like Second Life and Twinity are yet another form of online social networking. A small but growing number of businesses and professional organizations are being drawn by the lower customer acquisition costs and increased stickiness demonstrated by many of these sites. Business use of Second Life in particular has largely concentrated around four areas: point-of sale opportunities, advertising and promotion, recruiting job candidates, and virtual meetings:

- *Point-of-sale opportunities.* A growing number of businesses are setting up shop in Second Life to promote brand awareness and reach a new demographic of customers. For example, Playboy, the adult entertainment company, has created a rabbit head–shaped island with a retail store, events, and social opportunities. Staffed by virtual Playboy Bunny avatars, the virtual store offers merchandise from PlayboyStore.com that can be purchased for real-world wear or Second Life avatars. The Swedish Foreign Ministry, which is responsible for promoting tourism, has built a virtual "embassy" in Second Life to provide information about visa applications, Swedish culture and history, and recommended places to visit. In addition, "virtual only" businesses have emerged that exist only on Second Life, such as Prim & Proper, a retailer that provides virtual nineteenth-century clothing for Second Life characters.

- *Advertising and promotion.* Companies like Coca Cola and adidas are promoting their brands on Second Life with creative campaigns to drive customer awareness and engagement. In April 2007, Coca Cola issued a challenge to Second Life avatars to submit ideas for a portable virtual vending machine. The winning concept, as voted by Second Life residents of course, is profiled on a Coke microsite, VirtualThirst.com. Xbox, Microsoft's networked video game console, also features advertisements and the ability to purchase on-demand content, including movies, TV shows, music videos, and game videos. Players can log in to view which friends are online, see what games they are playing, and submit player reviews.

- *Recruiting job candidates.* The other major use of virtual worlds by businesses has been around recruiting job candidates, especially for technical talent. It has proven to be a more affordable way to provide personal attention to job candidates because recruiters can easily chat with multiple candidates at once. The Vancouver Police Department, for example, holds recruitment seminars for law enforcement officers in Second Life. In addition to being able to reach a new audience of potential candidates, the VPD is also hoping to target candidates who are web savvy and will be able to bring technology knowledge into fighting crime.

- *Virtual meetings.* Last, but not least, companies like IBM have invested heavily in Second Life, building out a large virtual campus for employee avatars to conduct meetings, product simulations, and training. For IBM, establishing a strong online community has been particularly important for creating a sense of unity across its several hundred thousand employees and many geographically dispersed offices around the world.

Although there has been increasing business activity in this realm of virtual world networks, in-depth analysis beyond the preceding real-world examples is beyond the scope of this book.

Empowering the End User

With each digital revolution, we are also seeing a change in *who* is making technology decisions for business. With mainframes, it was largely the CXO level and boards of directors—at the time there were no IT departments! The PC Era introduced IT departments into most mid- and large-sized companies, and by the late '80s, IT was making the vast majority of technology-purchasing decisions. In the '90s, the lines of business took control of software deployments in their respective departments. They were able to do so because with SaaS, they could get up and running without engaging IT. Today, more and more we are seeing end users themselves make and finance these decisions. Chapter 11 contains a more in-depth discussion of whether, when, and how to engage IT in business social networking initiatives.

Over time, technology is shifting from "command and control" to distributed, engaging, and empowering to the individual. Information, communication, and tools on the Web have given individuals not only a voice, but also the power to act and to own their own online identities. The online social graph accelerates this democratization of business by allowing individuals to more easily connect with one another and to bring the rich context of their relationships to accomplishing daily tasks and transactions. At its extreme is the notion of VRM, or vendor relationship management, which began as a research initiative out of the Berkman Center for Internet and Society at Harvard. VRM is the reverse of CRM. Instead of vendors managing data about customers in a unidirectional way, customers are given tools to manage and engage with vendors in a bidirectional way that is mutually beneficial. We are still in the very early days of VRM, but it poses interesting new possibilities for the online social graph and identity management across different web sites and applications.

"We help the Internet not suck."
—Jimmy Wales, Founder, Wikipedia

The Evolution of Digital Media

Each digital revolution enables new forms of media. Just look, for example, at how encyclopedias have evolved. In two decades, we have gone from heavy, leather-bound *World Book* volumes, to the Microsoft Encarta CD-ROM, to online, user-generated Wikipedia, to Aardvark.im, a real-time messaging service that connects people seeking information with knowledgeable experts in their network. Over time, new technologies are making it easier to deliver the right content in the right context at the right time while reaching larger audiences and reducing cost.

First, digitizing media made it vastly less expensive to store. Meanwhile, software on PCs made it easy for anyone to create personalized digital content. In the '90s, the Internet emerged as a powerful new distribution mechanism for media, which provided new incentives for people to get involved in creating content and publishing their work. This resulted in an information explosion. We have spent the last decade developing different ways of filtering down the massive amount of information, such as content aggregation, search, and behavioral targeting.

With the online social graph, we can do even better. Already, *social filtering* on social networking sites is making the content we come across more relevant, interesting, and personal than ever before. This chapter walks through the rise of Facebook and the more general history behind online social networking, platforms that have emerged around social networking sites, and how this latest step in the evolution of digital media is about creating a social experience across the Web.

Storage and Creation

The PC Era transformed media with digital storage capacity and tools for creating and editing content. Floppy disks, CDs, and later, DVDs and flash drives provided a much more efficient means of storing data and information, freeing businesses from having to maintain massive file cabinets and manually update records. One CD, for example, can store the equivalent of 300,000 pages of print text.

Media in digital form also became easier to copy and share and, therefore, more accessible to a greater number of people. Meanwhile, word processors, image editors, and later, video production tools drastically lowered barriers to media creation and editing. With PC publishing software such as Print Shop and Microsoft Publisher, suddenly anyone could make calendars, cards, and flyers.

Even still, the method of distribution did not fundamentally change. It was still by physical means. Although you could cheaply and easily make a newsletter, you still had to print and mail the newsletter (or at minimum, mail a CD containing your newsletter).

Media Distribution

The Internet turned media distribution on its head. As publishers, recording studios, and filmmakers quickly realized (often the hard way, as they saw pirated versions of their work eclipse company sales), the Internet is a powerful distribution mechanism facilitating public circulation of media. In the PC Era, anyone could become a producer. In the Internet era, anyone could become a publisher. In the early days, publishers used the Internet solely as a one-to-many channel to broadcast media. Although more people could become publishers, how they published was no more engaging for consumers than the prior model. Media publishers were still talking *at* media consumers in a one-to-many fashion. Meanwhile, through discussion forums, chat rooms, and Blue Mountain electronic greeting cards, individuals were having real conversations with one another.

In the late '90s, publishers finally took their cue and began engaging in conversations *with* consumers in a movement dubbed "Web 2.0." Businesses developed a more nuanced view of the Internet as a two-way, many-to-many communication channel to empower and engage audiences to contribute feedback, ideas, knowledge, answers, opinions, product ratings, reviews, and recommendations. Since then, user-generated media from blogs, wikis, and YouTube have helped businesses scale their online presence by shifting the burden of creating and updating content. The trend has even spilled over into traditional media, such as the user-generated video contest held by PepsiCo for its TV ad shown during the 2008 Super Bowl.

Four major developments in Internet media over the last decade have really laid the groundwork for the present opportunity with social graph media: Web site communities, content aggregation, search engine marketing, and behavioral targeting.

1995: Web Site Communities

An important precursor to modern-day wikis, blog sites, and online social networks were online communities of personal Web sites, like GeoCities, Tripod, and Angelfire. GeoCities led the pack with its easy-to-use and then–cutting edge publishing tools, which enabled nontechnical users to create a Web presence featuring their own design and content. At its peak, GeoCities was hosting over 3.5 million Web sites for free, serving 19 million unique monthly site visitors, and had a combined home/work reach of over 33.4 percent, making it the third most-trafficked site on the Internet in 1998. The following year, just before the Internet bubble burst, Yahoo! Inc. acquired GeoCities for $3.5 billion.

A few years later, amid speculation that GeoCities was still not profitable, Yahoo! introduced fees for hosting. Many believe this marked the decline of GeoCities. It has gradually become obsolete as new site-creation services such as Google Sites have emerged that are easier to use and administer, take advantage of the latest Web technologies and design, and are free. Despite this fact, GeoCities has left an important dual legacy: First, anyone can create a Web site and have a presence on the Internet. Second, businesses now have much more specialized mediums through which to advertise.

1999: Content Aggregation

With so many publishers on the Web, media consumers needed a way to manage all the content from their various Web sites of interest, particularly frequently updated content like news headlines, photos, and blog posts. RSS, which stands for *Rich Site Summary* and *Really Simple Syndication*, is a formatting standard developed to communicate Web content updates. RSS readers aggregate content (that is, RSS feeds) from multiple sources on the Web into a "custom newspaper" of sorts containing updated content from all subscribed-to Web sites. The RSS reader is programmed to regularly check these Web sites for updates so that consumers of content don't have to do so manually. RSS aggregation features are now typically standard in most browsers and e-mail programs. (In fact, I developed an RSS reader for Outlook in 2003 while working at Microsoft!) Bloglines and Google Reader are two popular Web-based RSS readers.

For publishers, RSS feed management tools like FeedBurner (acquired by Google in 2007) provide automatic formatting, traffic analysis, and optional advertising services. Although people were initially unsure whether ads would be suited to RSS, over two-thirds of FeedBurner publishers now opt in to feed advertising, suggesting that it might be a viable model after all.

2003: Search Engine Marketing

As helpful as aggregation can be in consuming content, it still does not address the fundamental problem of too much content. Search makes content more manageable with a "just in time" approach that returns content matched to interest based on keywords.

This, of course, has allowed ads to be returned "just in time" as well. The first successful search marketing model, pioneered in 1998 by Overture (acquired by Yahoo! Inc. in 2003), was pay-for-placement, which ranked search results based on advertisers' willingness to pay. Google adopted a similar model for its AdWords paid search product but with an added relevance component. Google also dedicates a special section for paid ads that is separate from organic search results based solely on relevance. Relevance, as measured by clickthrough rate, effectively shifts the burden of determining search quality to users because people implicitly vote by clicking on certain search results over others. High-quality organic search results have won Google a large global user base. Highly relevant paid ads have resulted in greater ad clicks, translating into greater sales for the businesses who advertise. As evidenced by countless stories of small businesses reaching new audiences halfway around the world and the over $20 billion-dollar-a-year industry that has formed around it, search marketing is a powerful action-based targeting mechanism that can catch people at the moment they are ready to buy.

2008: Behavioral Targeting

One shortcoming of keyword search, however, is that it doesn't consider context. For instance, Google search doesn't take into account different types of Web data—is the search term referring to a person, place, song, clothing brand, and so on? Although that works fine in certain cases (for example, "Canon 5 megapixel digital camera"), it might be ill-suited to others. Homonyms are especially difficult to disambiguate. For example, "Paris Hilton" might refer to the person or the hotel. Among references to the person, "Paris Hilton" might mean heiress, reality TV show star, or ex-girlfriend of Greek shipping heir Stavros Niarchos. Terms often carry multiple meanings and have multiple contexts.

As the amount of information on the Web continues to explode, disambiguating these meanings and contexts will be paramount to keeping the Web navigable and relevant. Recognizing this, both established media players like Thomson Reuters as well as Internet upstarts like Metaweb are investing in efforts to define a "semantic Web." These initiatives seek to classify Web content in a way that is understandable by computers so that the tedious work of linking information on the Web can be automated. For example, say there is a semantic Web system for selling used books over the Internet. The first time someone visits the site, she will be asked to identify herself with information such as name, address, e-mail, and phone number. The data provided is stored in a Resource Description Framework (RDF) file to provide context about this person for future visits to this site and any other semantic Web site. Similarly, any data provided about a particular book, such as title, publisher, ISBN number, cover image, and description would be stored in an RDF file about the textbook to provide context for any future references to this textbook. In this way, a universal knowledge database is gradually built about different people, places, and objects based on their meaning, references across the Web, and relation to one other.

In addition to metadata about Web content, the unique characteristics, preferences, and history of people searching also provide important context for the search. Today's search engines more or less assume that all people who search are identical. That is, the same search result or ad that is relevant to me will also be relevant to you—and to your 90-year-old grandmother, to your 12-year-old neighbor, and to a sweet-potato farmer in Nairobi.

Behavioral targeting tries to fill this gap by creating a profile on each Internet user based on demographic information and Web activity history, and then targeting ads and a custom experience to each user based on his profile. Ad networks and some portal sites like AOL and Yahoo! have been using behavioral targeting for nearly a decade to serve up ads and content deemed relevant for a user based on her past activity, such as sites visited, length of visit, clicked ads, and purchases. DoubleClick (acquired by Google) has been a leading driver of cookie-based ad targeting. Recently, companies such as Tacoda (acquired by AOL), Revenue Science, Front Porch, NebuAd, and Phorm have revived these techniques for use by broadband Internet service providers, who have access to far greater amounts of Web activity data because they process all site traffic for their users versus only a subset of participating sites. But behavioral targeting has sparked a wave of controversy over privacy issues because for most of these systems, users do not explicitly opt in, might not have the choice to opt out, and cannot control what information is collected about them or how it is used.

The Future: Social Filtering

Today's age of "everyone a publisher" has fueled an explosion of content online. As human beings, we can't possibly process all of this information. From any individual's perspective, most of what's out there at any given time is junk. Although search engines and behavioral targeting have been important first steps in making the abundance of online media more manageable, it remains an uphill battle to wade through the volume of information and distractions on the Web. We fight a seemingly endless battle against spam in our e-mail Inboxes. When searching for information, we wade through pages of search results that are out of context. Annoying floating banners that are irrelevant to us block the screen showing the online article we are trying to read.

But all hope is not lost. With the online social graph, there might be an opportunity for the first time to align what publishers and advertisers want to show with what users want to see (see Figure 2.1).

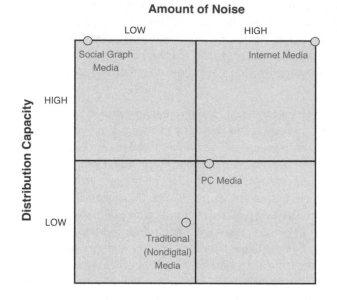

Figure 2.1
Prior to the social graph, greater distribution resulted in more junk. With the social graph, we can use our friends as filters for finding the right content and data at the right time.

For *push* content—that is, content actively pushed out to Internet users—people on Facebook and Twitter are already seeing *socially filtered* feeds, notifications, and SMS messages about Web pages, articles, photos, and blog posts—that is, content created or recommended by friends. These push alerts are perceived as being less invasive not only because recipients can specify the frequency and format of these updates, but also because the information is about people they know and care about. You would be less likely to consider something spam if it were recommended by a friend or someone you chose to "follow" on Twitter. On the contrary, most people appreciate discovering content and information that their friends find interesting and relevant.

FriendFeed, founded by former Google employees, is a feed-of-feeds that aggregates updates across the Web, including blogs, micro-blog sites like Twitter, social networking sites like Facebook, and any other RSS and Atom feeds. FriendFeed members can customize and share their feeds with friends, creating for the first time a comprehensive and systematic way to experience content on the Web through social filters. Social networking sites are becoming the new Web portal. From a user's perspective, everything on a social networking site is highly personalized and personal. Contrast this to today's experience on other sites. Anyone who goes to YouTube, Yahoo!, or BBC.com sees the same content. Even Amazon.com, which is highly *personalized* based on products purchased and viewed, does not feel *personal*. Amazon.com has no idea who we are, where we're from, or who we're friends with. On Facebook, no two experiences are identical. Once logged in, users feel they are among friends—and for all intents and purposes, they are.

For *pull* content—that is, content out on the Web for people to proactively access—a combination of social filtering and use of opt-in profiles created and managed by users themselves could provide a higher-quality, more personalized Web experience. Search, for example, might more heavily weight the preferences and opinions of friends or others with similar profiles in calculating which results are relevant. As Table 2.1 shows, we could start using our friends to help filter out junk and find content that is useful and relevant to us. It doesn't feel like a violation of privacy if content or ads appear as recommendations by friends and we have control over what information is shared and used about us—unlike the stealthy profiling behind most behavioral targeting systems.

Table 2.1   IMPACT OF NEW TECHNOLOGIES ON CONTENT CREATION AND DISTRIBUTION

	Content Creation	Content Distribution
Mainframes/ Precomputing Era	Not applicable	Physical distribution
PCs	Tools for content creation	Increased storage efficiency, but no change in underlying distribution method
Internet	Primitive targeting, content aggregation, and search marketing	Virtual distribution with near-zero marginal cost
Social networking	Advanced content targeting based on profile information, friend activity, and recommendations	Social distribution spread from friend to friend and, therefore, not viewed as spam

Music to My Ears, Junk to Yours

The tools in place today on Facebook help its members manage information about friends to provide good insights into how effective filtering might be applied more generally to all ads and content online.

First, it's important to observe the sociological movement under way. Today's teenagers and twenty-somethings, far from valuing privacy and boundaries like earlier generations, embody a new kind of self-obsessed, YouTube broadcast culture. The typical high school student today posts her photos on Facebook or Flickr, and tells the world where she is, what she is doing, and how she is feeling on her Facebook status message or Twitter. College students admit that e-mail is reserved for professors, prospective employers, and other "grown-ups" only. With one another, Facebook messages, pokes, and wall posts are the preferred forms of communication.

Without social filtering, the constant stream of status updates, messages, posts, and other broadcasts would be unmanageable and overwhelming. To a stranger, a random update such as a blog post or status message is not relevant and, therefore, viewed as junk. But to a friend, this might be extremely relevant and interesting. The online social graph brings the richness of user-generated content and self-expression with a ready-and-willing audience—namely people we know. For businesses, *social filters* might mean being able for the first time to effectively target ads without annoying audiences or triggering privacy concerns.

Changing Communities, Relationships, and Interactions

Whereas earlier-generation Web communities like GeoCities and Usenet groups centered around shared interests among strangers, today's popular communities center around friends who often happen to have shared interests. But in addition to chatting with strangers who have shared interests, high school students through twenty-somethings are increasingly spending their online time interacting with people they already know from the offline real world. As the number of Internet users grows, people are choosing to use the Internet as much for meeting new people as for strengthening relationships with people they have already met in person. Especially for those out of college, many of the new acquaintances (potential friends or dating partners, perhaps) that people do meet online today are typically friends of friends or separated by at most a few degrees, within a trusted network.

The major difference between the Chicago Bears fan page on GeoCities and a typical Facebook group for Chicago Bears fans is that the latter is smaller and bridges—if not includes exclusively—people who are friends offline. We are no longer satisfied chatting online about sports or other interests with just anyone. We want the comfort of knowing who we are talking to or at least knowing that we know the same people in common. Social networking sites provide context not only for content, but also for the people with whom we interact online. The "MyStarbucksIdea for Facebook" prototype detailed in the following case study is a good example of social filtering at work in online communities.

MyStarbucksIdea for Facebook

MyStarbucksIdea is an online ideation community (powered by the Salesforce Ideas application) for Starbucks Coffee Company customers to post, vote, and comment on suggestions for how Starbucks could be improved. Less than a year after it was started, MyStarbucksIdea has resulted in hundreds of thousands of ideas, users, and comments (see Figure 2.2). The widespread adoption of MyStarbucksIdea has been celebrated as the industry model for what's possible with Web 2.0, but has not been without its set of challenges. Specifically, the site's sudden growth has caused some community members to feel less influential, important, and engaged. Fortunately, the online social graph has come to the rescue.

Figure 2.2
MyStarbucksIdea is an online ideation community for Starbucks customers that boasts hundreds of thousands of ideas, comments, and users.

As part of the Force.com for Facebook platform partnership between Facebook and salesforce.com, a prototype was built that takes the original Salesforce Ideas application and brings it inside Facebook. This new application, called MyStarbucksIdea for Facebook, applies social filtering to how each individual user experiences the online community (see Figure 2.3). Instead of equally weighting all ideas, votes, and comments, those from friends rise to the top, helping each person feel more directly connected to what is happening in the community. In effect, people are given an opportunity to engage with their friends around the Starbucks brand. To the individual, the ideas and comments, even if she does not agree, are not junk because they come from friends. Thanks to the online social graph, Starbucks is able to maintain a personal feel to its community even as the size of the community grows.

Figure 2.3
MyStarbucksIdea for Facebook takes the original application and applies social filtering from the friend graph to make the ideas and comments shared more relevant and engaging.

Online social networks have changed the nature and relevance of Web communities by adding a layer of identity and relationships. As Harvard Berkman Center Fellow Danah Boyd points out, the popularity of social networking sites signifies a behavioral shift online from interest-driven practices to socially driven practices.

An interesting twist to this is celebrity-fan relationships that might be more one-sided, for example adding a band as your "friend" on MySpace, "following" a movie star on Twitter, or becoming a "fan" of a politician on Facebook. By definition, these are more interest- or affinity-driven versus socially driven because most of us are not personal friends with Britney Spears or Barack Obama. In this case, online social networking is used primarily to help broadcast individual identities and rally friends to the cause.

Why Facebook Is Different

Many of the early social networking sites, like SixDegrees.com and Yahoo! 360°, were short-lived fads because users lost interest. Facebook, thus far, has been different. Three early decisions and innovations helped set it apart from the rest: trusted identity combined with clearly defined networks, exclusiveness, and providing continual engagement.

Trusted Identity and Clearly Defined Networks

Owing either to great foresight or a great coincidence that the founders happened to be Harvard undergrads at the time, Facebook's decision to go after the university student population first has proven to be a good one. University networks are clearly defined and have well-understood offline analogies to Facebook in the form of student directories and yearbooks. Most freshmen arrive on campus in the fall not knowing anyone, so rapid networking is critical. Even after the initial acclimation, student life revolves around social networks for everything from study groups and project partners to clubs, parties, and sororities. Facebook also wisely used school e-mail domains to authenticate that those signing up were really students, for instance limiting University of Michigan network registrations to @*umich.edu* e-mail addresses, which brought an important element of trust to the site.

Aided by this effective means of confirming online identity, Facebook has become a clear extension to the offline world. Peer pressure helps achieve near-total adoption across the student population at schools because no one wants to miss out. Postgraduation, geographically dispersed alumni need a way to stay in touch with one another. By design, everyone in a Facebook network has something in common. In contrast, users of many earlier social networking sites lost interest when the quality of their networks became diluted with strangers. Without trusted identity and a clear protocol for when to accept or reject friend requests, friend networks degraded to strangers, spam, and junk.

Exclusiveness

Second, Facebook's decision to initially limit the number of schools on the service and only very gradually grow as it was able to get new servers online had the added benefit of creating a certain cachet of exclusiveness. Facebook started at Harvard, spread across the Ivy League, and gradually expanded to other schools. By design or coincidence, the order in which schools were added bore an uncanny resemblance to the prestige of university rankings, and at least to some degree the elitism of Facebook schools already on the service helped draw in other schools to participate. Although Facebook is now open for anyone to join, its early positioning as an exclusive service helped make it seem more desirable and drive a critical mass of users. Early on too, it was only possible to search, browse, and view profiles within one's own network (that is, your school), which further helped to reinforce the sense of trust on the site. Meanwhile, Orkut and MySpace members were getting bombarded by message spam and connection requests from random strangers.

Adding just one or a few schools at a time also allowed Facebook to plan for and control jumps in site traffic. In comparison, service hiccups and outages around the same time on Friendster and Orkut due to inability to keep up with unexpectedly rapid growth turned off many of their users.

News Feeds

The final secret to Facebook's success has been figuring out how to keep members engaged on a continual basis. Like other sites before it, Facebook provides incentives for people to come back to the site. For example, you must log in to view Facebook gifts or wall posts, see photos and videos tagged of you, or respond to messages. But what really has set Facebook apart have been feeds that broadcast updates about your friends' recent activities, such as new friend connections, wall posts, photos and videos tagged of the individual, and event RSVPs. A summary of updates across all of one's friends, called News Feed, is shown on the Facebook home page once logged in, and a summary of activity updates specific to each Facebook user appears on that individual's profile page wall.

Ironically, the News Feed feature, which has proven so instrumental to Facebook's longevity, was initially a big source of controversy. When News Feed appeared suddenly on the site in September 2006, it sparked a public outcry over privacy. Thousands of people filed complaints with the company. A Facebook group was formed called "Students Against Facebook News Feed," which grew to hundreds of thousands of members overnight. Students across the country banded together to boycott the site. But Facebook recovered, and then some. An apology on the Facebook Blog from CEO and founder Mark Zuckerberg together with user privacy controls and a promise to conduct market testing next time placated the concerns. Feeds are now one of the top reasons why members keep returning to Facebook. The continual sense of recency about the information has transformed Facebook from novel thrill to repeat destination. The concept of activity feeds has even become a best practice copied by other Internet sites to sustain site traffic.

Social Network Ecosystems

Facebook's spectacular growth and loyal base of users have resulted in an unprecedented social graph charting the relationships, interactions, and histories of 200 million people on the Internet. But what does it mean to be the biggest online social graph?

First, success begets more success: the more people on Facebook, the more people join Facebook. Almost by definition, social networking sites are subject to network effects. If all of your friends are on Facebook, you feel pressure to be on Facebook, too, to view photos, videos, event invitations, and interact with your friend group. You are less likely to join a different social network where you know fewer people.

Facebook is the largest globally, but other social networking sites have hit important tipping points among certain audiences that will make them difficult to topple completely—for instance, Bebo® (acquired by AOL) in Great Britain, Orkut in India and Brazil, Hi5 in the Caribbean, and Friendster in Asian countries like Singapore and the Philippines (see Appendix A, "Snapshot of Top Social Networking Sites, March 2009," for a

more complete list). Being the first to reach and sustain a critical mass of users in a particular market has cemented these social networking sites' place in history. Over time, their
social graph just becomes more valuable and harder to displace.

But the value proposition is not just to users—advertisers, software developers, and IT
departments also stand to benefit from large, well-established social graphs. The larger
the social graph, the more attractive the distribution opportunity.

History of Social Networking Platforms

Before platforms were introduced, social networking sites were simple communication
utilities that let people send messages to one another and share photos and event information. But social network members wanted to be able to do more with their friends
online. Similarly, the online social networks wanted their members to spend more time
on their sites to maximize ad impressions and clicks so that they could make money. For
this reason, just about every major social network has unveiled a *platform* to enable new
applications. Social networking platforms expose data, tools, and placement on social
networking sites to third-party developers, allowing them to create new functionality
that sits on top of the social network. In an ideal scenario, the platform ecosystem is a
win-win-win for everyone: *Users* have access to more functionality, *software developers*
have access to data and users, and *the social network* becomes more interesting, valuable,
sticky, and engaging.

The rise of YouTube is a good example of how this works. An important precursor to
social platforms was the ability to embed YouTube videos on MySpace pages. Prior to
MySpace, YouTube struggled to hit a tipping point and really take off. It had a small and
scattered community of fans that used its video-sharing service as one-offs. Joining
forces with MySpace changed everything. Overnight, YouTube found itself with a large
global audience and infrastructure for word-of-mouth distribution. MySpace saw Web
traffic go way up and its pages come to life with rich, multimedia video.

Facebook took this idea of embedded video further when it created the first social networking platform in May 2007, which allows any type of application (not just video) to be
embedded as a widget in Facebook. According to Facebook, over 24,000 applications
were developed on its platform in just the first year, and more than 95 percent of
Facebook members have installed at least one platform application in their Facebook
profile. MySpace, Bebo, Hi5, Friendster, and the others shortly followed suit announcing
their own platforms.

It was an exciting time for social networking platforms, but was not without its set of
challenges. With so many different platforms emerging, developers faced a difficult decision: Tie your destiny to one (or a handful of) social networking platform(s), or rewrite
your application a dozen times to run on all of them. The developer community began to
call for industry standards.

In autumn of 2007, product managers at Google responded. They led an effort, called OpenSocial, to define a set of open source social APIs that could work across any social networking site or other Web site. Having a standard set of APIs would theoretically enable developers to write an application once and have it work on any OpenSocial site. OpenSocial has since spun off from Google as its own independent nonprofit organization and is supported by an industry consortium of social networking sites, including MySpace, LinkedIn, Hi5, Bebo, Orkut, and Ning. Over 7,500 applications were developed on OpenSocial in its first year.

Platform Applications

Internet users want applications that are "socially aware" of their identity and relationships, but don't want to reenter profile information and reestablish friend connections on every new site they visit. Social networking platforms allow developers and businesses to tap the existing social graph for their applications and Web sites instead of having to reinvent the wheel. When people install a platform application into their social network account, they can automatically interact with all of their friends who have also installed the application.

When social networking platforms first emerged, the applications developed were largely around entertainment—such as games and sharing media with friends. For example, social gaming companies such as Zynga, SGN, and Playfish have created applications that let people on Facebook challenge one another to chess, backgammon, bingo, trivia, and other games. Another company, iLike, has an application that lets Facebook members share music playlists and concert information. Slide and RockYou, the leading application developers on social networking platforms, specialize in photo and video sharing, quizzes, and virtual gift applications. RockYou's applications—such as Super Wall, Likeness, and Vampires—and Slide's applications—including SuperPoke, Slideshow, and Top Friends—are used by tens of millions of people across MySpace, Facebook, Hi5, Friendster, Orkut, and Bebo to playfully engage with their friends.

As social platforms have matured, developers are setting their sights beyond just fun and games. Applications now span categories like fashion, music, sports, finance, travel, food, and even philanthropy. For example, Causes (see Figure 2.4) is a popular application that lets Facebook users promote their favorite charities. When users install Causes, a widget appears on their profile page featuring the nonprofit organizations of their choosing. Anyone who visits that person's profile can learn more about the charities, donate to the charities, or add the charities to her own Causes. In its first year of operation, the application raised over two million dollars for nearly 20,000 nonprofit groups.

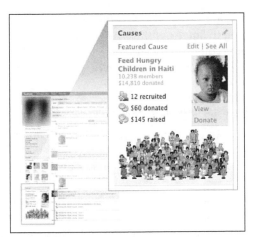

Figure 2.4
Causes is a popular Facebook application that allows users to promote their favorite charities on their profile page.

With Force.com for Facebook, its platform partnership with salesforce.com, Facebook hopes to take social platform applications even further into the realm of business and productivity applications. For example, application developer Appirio used Force.com for Facebook to build a social recruiting application that lets companies tap employees' friend networks to source job candidate referrals (see Chapter 7, "Social Recruiting," for more details).

It's not just stand-alone applications companies like RockYou and Appirio building apps for social networking sites. Stanford University has a class dedicated to teaching students how to build applications for Facebook. Traditional businesses, too, are starting to explore the benefits of plugging into the online social graph with their own platform applications. Pizza Hut just developed an application that Facebook members can install on their profile page. Visitors to the page can order pizza delivery directly from within Facebook!

Another example comes from FamilyLink, a genealogy database company that provides ancestry tracking tools to 17,000 or so subscribers. FamilyLink developed a Facebook app, We're Related, that lets people show whom on Facebook they are related to and create family tree visualizations. In just several months, over six million Facebook members have signed up for We're Related, allowing FamilyLink to promote its brand to a far greater audience than its original customer base. Chapter 9, "Get Your Message Across," describes in detail when companies should consider investing in social networking apps and the options for doing so.

Pizza Hut and FamilyLink might view Facebook merely as a nice extension to their marketing efforts, but for iLike, Slide, and the million or so other social application development companies, the social networks can make or break their business. The social gaming companies, like Playfish, are more shielded because they offer premium services for which people are willing to pay. But the companies with free apps who are betting on ad-based revenue models are increasingly finding themselves at odds with the social networks, which are trying to figure out their own ad-based revenue models. The following sidebar provides some commentary into the co-opetition taking place between social networks and their application developers.

Co-Opetition Between Social Networks and Application Developers

It is a love-hate relationship these days between social networks and application developers. On the one hand, they need each other to succeed. On the other, they are increasingly going after the same limited pool of advertising dollars.

There are three particular areas of contention between the social networks and application developers, all tying back to the question of monetization: placement, promotion, and value-add. First, how apps appear on social networking sites (for example, size, placement, prominence) has a tremendous impact on how often the apps are used and the extent to which they spread virally to other users. Facebook's summer 2008 redesign changed the appearance of the profile page, including where apps appear. The new design tended to favor certain kinds of applications over others.

Second, how applications are promoted and where users go to find them strongly influence app adoption. Facebook, MySpace, LinkedIn, Hi5, Friendster, and Bebo all have application directories that their members can search and browse. Depending on which applications and categories the social network features on the front page and how search results are returned, certain apps can get disproportionately favored or hurt.

Separate but related to this, there has also been a precedent for social networks completely removing applications from their site when the apps pose a security threat. For example, MySpace suddenly started blocking slideshows and videos from Photobucket in April 2007, citing advertisements embedded in the videos violated its terms of service. (Ironically, MySpace acquired Photobucket one month later.)

Finally, there has been some concern over what functionality the social networks provide versus what application developers provide. For example, many felt that Facebook subsumed Slide's Top Friends application when it introduced a similar feature to the Friends bar on its profile pages in July 2008. Application developers want to provide value for social network members, but if the functionality is *too* valuable, it can be tempting for the social network itself to co-opt.

The monetization struggle between platforms and developers is not a new one—just as Microsoft in the 1980s began offering its Office suite of applications to help proliferate Windows, it might be in the best interest of social networks to offer their own core set of applications to bolster their platforms. Some believe Facebook is the new operating system for the Web. Only time will tell.

Taking Applications Beyond Social Networking Sites

So far, we have talked about social applications that appear inside social networking sites. While these continue to grow in number, the reality is most applications are not on Facebook or MySpace. They live on their own servers and Web sites. Social network APIs (how different services on the Web talk to each other), such as the MySpace API, Facebook Connect, and Google Friend Connect, take the online social graph beyond social networking sites to external Web sites and applications. *Mashup* applications that call these social APIs allow users to view and interact with their social network identities and contacts when on other sites.

For example, Faceconnector (originally called Faceforce) is a mashup I developed that pulls Facebook profile information and friend data into the Salesforce CRM application. Depending on the individual's privacy settings and degrees of separation, a sales rep viewing a lead or contact record in Salesforce might now see that person's Facebook profile information as well as who they know in common. Instead of having to make a cold call with no basis for striking up a conversation, the sales rep might be able to talk about something they have in common or ask their mutual friend for an introduction. Chapter 4, "Social Sales," delves more deeply into this use case.

Another good example is the Red Bull Energy Drink Web site, which uses Facebook Connect to let site visitors engage with their Facebook Friends on blogs, videos, and contests (see Figure 2.5). Instead of developing its own login system, Red Bull taps into the Facebook social graph. Facebook members can log in to the Red Bull site using their Facebook username and password, and see what their friends like and view friends' comments. Conversely, if the Facebook member consents, actions taken, such as blog commenting and sharing, appear as feed stories on the member's Facebook profile and News Feed. Social filtering makes the Red Bull content more interesting and relevant to Facebook members even when they are not on the Facebook site. Hundreds of other Web sites, including Citysearch, CNN.com, and the University of Toronto alumni association site, have similarly implemented the Facebook Connect API to allow visitors to interact with their Facebook Friends while on these sites.

What the Social Graph Means for Digital Media

Digital media is getting smarter. Instead of blasting out content and praying people will find it, the online social graph is reshaping our Web experience to deliver the right content to the right person at the right time. Already, more and more people are using social networking sites as their main entry point to the Web. And why not? We manage our relationships and identities on Facebook, MySpace, and LinkedIn. Why not use the social graph as our filter to make sense of the abundance of information on the Web?

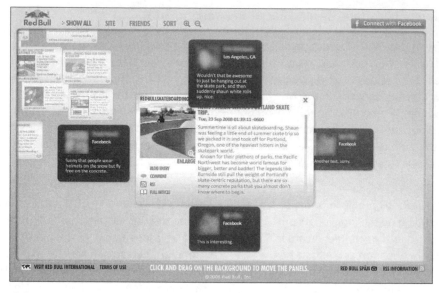

Figure 2.5
Red Bull's Web site uses the Facebook Connect API to bring the social graph to its blogs, videos, contests, and other content. The social filtering provides a more relevant and engaging experience for Web site visitors.

For businesses, social platforms present an exciting opportunity to engage more meaningfully with customers, prospects, partners, and employees in ways that simply weren't possible before. Enriching existing Web sites with social data from the Facebook and MySpace APIs allows a new dimension of personalization to seamlessly emerge for site visitors. Suddenly, an anonymous product review site like Epinions can be taken to the next level by showing product reviews from *your friends*, similar to what MyListo does. Web communities like MyStarbucksIdea come alive when ideas, comments, and votes *from people you know* rise to the top. It all ties back to the Holy Grail we have been seeking of relevance and trust.

We are at the cusp of a massive paradigm shift. We are moving from technology-centric applications to people-centric applications that conform to our relationships and identities. The social graph is enabling a new Web experience that allows us to bring our online identities and friends with us to whatever site or application we choose to visit on the Internet. It is the death of the anonymous Web, and it is transforming the way we work, learn, and interact across every aspect of our lives.

3

Social Capital from Networking Online

The online social graph reaches far beyond technology and media. It is one of the most significant sociocultural phenomena of this decade. By inventing more casual modes of interaction and thereby making possible new categories of lower-commitment relationships, social networking sites like Facebook, MySpace, and LinkedIn are fundamentally changing how we live, work, and relate to one another as human beings.

One important way the online social graph is manifesting itself in the sociology of business is in facilitating the accumulation of social capital.

As individuals, we have two sources of personal competitive advantage: human capital and social capital. Human capital, which includes talent, intellect, charisma, and formal authority, is necessary for success but often beyond our direct control. Social capital, on the other hand, derives from our relationships. Robert Putnam, a professor of political science at Harvard who coined the term in his seminal work in the mid-1990s, defines social capital as the collective value of all social networks and the inclinations that arise from these networks to do things for each other. According to Putnam, social capital can be measured by the level of trust and reciprocity in a community or between individuals, and is an essential component to building and maintaining democracy. More recent work on social capital has focused on the individual. Studies such as those by Deb Gruenfeld at the Stanford Graduate School of Business and Mikolaj Piskorski at Harvard Business School have shown that social capital is a powerful source of knowledge, ideas, opportunities, support, reputation, and visibility that is equally if not even more influential than human capital.

Individuals with greater social capital close more deals, are better respected, and get higher-ranking jobs. Online social networks offer access to social capital, empowering those who are well connected with private information, diverse skill sets, and others' energy and attention.

Early research already shows that bringing networks online makes people more capable and efficient at accumulating, managing, and exercising social capital. Consciously or unconsciously, people are using sites like Facebook and LinkedIn as tools for maximizing their social capital from relationships:

- *Private information.* Frequent, informal communication that occurs on social networking sites, such as Facebook messages, can sometimes contain private information. Even when that is not the case, emotional rapport between individuals on social networking sites carries over into their offline relationship, increasing the likelihood of information exchange.

- *Diverse skill sets.* Hiring managers, recruiters, and others can easily search on LinkedIn or Facebook for member profiles that match desired skills, and then reach out directly or see how they are connected and request an introduction from mutual friends. Because online social connections are lower-commitment and more abundant, chances are higher that someone in the friend-of-friends network fits the bill or at least knows someone who does.

- *Others' energy and attention.* Instead of spamming your network with a mass e-mail, online social network members can passively broadcast opportunities on their profile or status message, and allow interested parties to come to them. Without online social networks, these otherwise-interested parties might never hear about the opportunity either because they are not closely connected enough to be part of the e-mail distribution or the individual does not notify them out of social protocol and not wanting to bombard their network with mass messages.

Social capital is the currency of business interactions and relationships. This chapter provides an important conceptual framework around social capital that will be repeatedly referenced in subsequent chapters on social sales, marketing, product innovation, and recruiting. In particular, there are four important implications for business: First, social networks establish a new kind of relationship that is more casual than what was previously acceptable. Second, online networking is able to fill important gaps in traditional offline networking. Third, the resulting social economy, which has been made more efficient by online networking, is helping accelerate the flattening of traditional organizational hierarchy. Last, but not least, net-new value is created for everyone on the social graph because networking online magnifies network effects.

Establishing a New Category of Relationships

For people you see every day, your close friends and family, your boss, coworkers, and neighbors, Facebook and MySpace—although perhaps an important part of your interactions—don't make or break your relationships. No matter what, these people will be a part of your life—they will still be your friend or daughter or coworker, as it were.

For your weak ties, it's a different story. It is for relationships *on the fringe* that online social networking can make a world of difference. Weak ties include people you have just met, people you met only a few times, people you used to know, and friends of friends. Prior to the online social networking era, most of us just didn't have the capacity to maintain these relationships, nor sufficient knowledge or prescience to know which ones might become valuable in the future.

Yet as sociologist Mark Granovetter established in his seminal work in the 1970s, it is precisely our weak ties that carry the greatest amount of social capital. Weak ties act as crucial bridges across clumps of people, providing an information advantage to network members.

Online social networks have defined a new kind of relationship—like the Facebook Friend and LinkedIn Connection—that is more casual and, therefore, makes it possible to maintain a greater number of connections. Thanks to Facebook, MySpace, and LinkedIn, it has become socially acceptable to initiate lower-commitment relationships with people we would not have kept in touch with in the past. A Facebook Friend might be someone you met at a party last weekend over a couple of beers. A LinkedIn Connection could be someone you met at a conference or on a plane with whom you established a good rapport. Instead of letting that momentary rapport go to waste, you can "file it away" for later. Instead of losing a large, potentially valuable pool of fringe contacts over a lifetime, it is now possible to accumulate these lightweight relationships as social capital "options" you might want—but are not obligated—to exercise later. Twitter takes this even further by allowing one-sided relationships: Person A can "follow"—that is, subscribe to updates from—Person B without Person B having to return the favor. Person B may not personally know any of her followers, but it doesn't matter. She still has a very intimate way of communicating and connecting with her fans.

How is this possible? Before, the notion of "keeping in touch" was hard work. It required one if not both parties to actively pursue contact on an at least somewhat regular basis. Communication required time and planning. Social networking sites, on the other hand, are designed for easy, lightweight, ad hoc communication. Two important innovations in particular have reduced the cost of staying in touch. First, social networking sites provide an easy-to-use database for managing contacts. Facebook is CRM for the masses. It is fun and intuitive, visual, active, searchable, and self-updating:

- *Fun and intuitive.* Far from fitting the stereotype of traditional databases as being boring and complicated, social networking sites bring games, multimedia, and intuitive design to managing contacts. A simple design and the help wizard that appears when you first register for sites like Facebook enable people to start using these sites right away, reducing the barriers to joining the online social graph.

- *Visual.* The visual aspect of social networking sites is especially important. Most people in the world aren't very good at remembering names, especially when we have just met a large number of people over a short amount of time. After a party, conference, wedding, or the first day on a new job, profile pictures act like flash cards to help us put the face to the name and better remember people we meet. Seeing people's photos and videos from different aspects of their lives that they choose to share, such as pictures of their dog, also helps us get to know and understand them better.

- *Active.* Most databases are passive in the sense that they wait for you to query them for specific kinds of data. Social networking sites go beyond passive data queries. Every time we log in to Facebook, we are shown News Feed updates—such as new status messages, profile pictures, friend connections, videos, gifts, and so on—about a different, random subset of our contacts. We are, in effect, reminded to think about people we know who might not otherwise have crossed our mind that day. News Feed (introduced in Chapter 2, "The Evolution of Digital Media") and Upcoming Birthdays on Facebook are, in effect, timely, proactive suggestions about whom we might want to reach out to and what we might want to say. Compared with before, communication with our contacts requires less work, planning, and remembering because we can count on social networking tools to tell us who, when, and what we want to communicate.

- *Searchable.* Social networking sites make it easy to find contacts within your network. Almost all of the sites allow you to search and filter contacts based on various criteria of interest, such as name, employer, school, city, hobbies, gender, relationship status, and other profile information. This search functionality is useful both when you want to establish a new online connection as well as when you want to search from among your existing connections, for example, if you want to know which of your friends have a particular area of expertise.

- *Self-updating.* Last, but not least, the advantage of social networking sites over traditional contact databases is that everyone is responsible for maintaining and updating her own profile. This means that information is much more likely to be current and accurate.

In addition to providing an easy-to-use contact database, social networking sites, like Facebook, have invented new modes of interaction that make it faster, easier, and more efficient to communicate with contacts. The following list details a few examples, including photos, status messages, and Facebook pokes, that are replacing and augmenting our traditional communications arsenal (Chapter 10, "Build and Manage Your Relationships," provides a more comprehensive overview of all Facebook interaction modes):

- *Photos.* If pictures are worth a thousand words, then the ability to post, share, and tag photos on social networking sites represents an important advancement in our ability to communicate. Before, if you wanted to share digital photos, you had to e-mail everyone to let them know. With social networking sites and feeds, when you post new photos on Facebook, your friends get automatically notified in their News Feed (unless you have restricted them from viewing your photos). People can also see the photos on your wall and "Photos of [You]" when they visit your profile.

- *Status messages.* As in the case of photos, status messages are broadcast out to your network, making it easier to update a large group of people you know all at once. By posting a photo or a status message, you are effectively saying to everyone in your network, "Hey, look at what's new in my life" and creating opportunities for them to think about you and potentially reach out for more interaction. Compared with the kind of news or content that was needed to justify a traditional message, status messages such as Facebook Status and Twitter Tweets tend to be more casual, spontaneous, temporal, and personal. It's a lower bar for what qualifies as a message. Often people express feelings, likes, dislikes, what they are doing at the moment, where they are, or where they are headed—for example, "Clara is… working on her book." In the pre-Facebook Era, many of these thoughts and feelings that people had were simply never communicated. For example, I would never e-mail or write a letter to someone just to say that I am working on my book. It's not big enough news to warrant an e-mail or letter.

It has become acceptable because social networking sites reduce the cost of both sending and processing information. Feeds provide opportunities to send information in a one-to-many fashion (information about you broadcast to your friends' News Feeds) and process information in a many-to-one fashion (your News Feed updates about your friends).

- *Facebook pokes.* The fun part about Facebook pokes is that no one really knows what they are or what they mean. Like real-life pokes, they could be playful, flirtatious, or just a neutral way of calling attention to yourself. Poking is an easy way to let someone know you are thinking about him or her without having something specific to say. Typically, people respond by poking back or sending a Facebook message.

For most people, social networks are characterized by few strong connections (such as with parents and best friends) and many weak connections. The exact number and type of connections vary by individual, but we all have a threshold beyond which we choose not or simply are unable to maintain relationships.

At their core, social networking sites are relationship tools that allow us to be both more aware and better able to engage with our outer networks. By reducing the cost of interaction and the cost of maintaining a relationship, sites like Facebook and LinkedIn help increase our network capacity to include otherwise-foregone fringe relationships. As a result, we can capture more of the full value of our cumulative lifetime social network (see Figure 3.1).

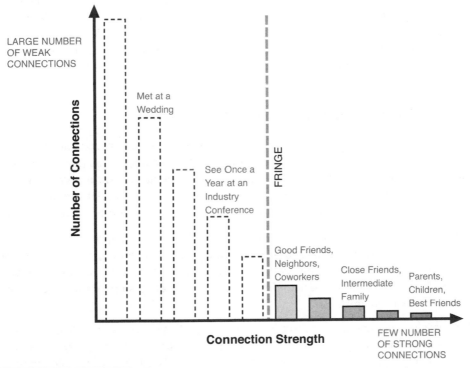

Figure 3.1

Online social networking sites like Facebook are like contact databases that increase our capacity to maintain relationships. We potentially no longer have to forego as many fringe, "long tail" relationships.

Discovering Which Relationships Are Valuable

In addition to increasing our relationship capacity, social networking sites also provide important information that can help us better assess the potential relevance and value of a relationship. Instead of waiting for time or happenstance to reveal common ground, mutual friends, or overlapping interests, we can glean more of this information sooner from viewing profile information our new contacts have chosen to share. Having access to this information makes us smarter about which relationships to invest in, prioritize, and potentially escalate from the fringe.

For example, it might never have come up during your brief conversation and business card exchange with the guy you met at a medical conference last month that he also plays soccer. If, say, your league team is seeking another member, that new information could be enough for you to decide to become more than just fringe friends. There might be any number of reasons why you would actually want to stay in touch, but you just wouldn't have had a chance to discover this the first time you met—and as a result, you might decide not to stay in touch at all.

Online social networking gives serendipity extra chances. First, you are more likely to stay in touch with people you have just met because the bar for establishing an online social networking connection is lower compared with traditional relationships. Second, once you've established the connection, you are empowered with information to decide sooner whether this is a relationship worth pursuing. Information helps us qualify early and reduce false positives and false negatives: We waste less time on relationships that likely won't go anywhere, and we miss out less often on relationships that likely will go far.

Latent Value: When Options Come in Handy

Friend options come in handy when life circumstances change and new unmet needs emerge. If you are laid off, tap your social network to find a job. If you are moving or traveling to a new city, see who in your network is local and perhaps they can show you the ins and outs. If you are starting a company, hire employees from your network. If you have a sudden need for advice or expertise, find answers and experts from your network.

Fringe relationships can carry immense latent value. Who knows, maybe that friendly gal who sat next to you on the flight to New York ends up introducing you years later to your new job or business partner. She might not have seemed "valuable" at the time when you met, but she could become "valuable" later. Online social networking extends serendipity across time and circumstance.

Especially for younger generations of people who are starting to use Facebook at earlier ages, there are interesting implications of having a database containing every person you have ever met. My friend's younger brother, Tyler, is a good example. Tyler is thirteen (the minimum age for joining Facebook) and registered for an account several months ago. The first thing he did was search for all of his elementary school classmates and add them as friends. If Tyler wants, he could be Facebook Friends with these people forever. In fact, Tyler is going to be able to keep in touch with everyone he meets from now on, accumulating a lifetime of latent social capital. In twenty years, perhaps Tyler will find that his friend from kindergarten has become an important business partner.

Of course, Tyler might not want to stay in touch in every instance. (Who among us hasn't wanted to "start over" at some point?) When relationships or life circumstances change, it sometimes makes sense to reflect these changes in our online social networks. We have several options: adjusting privacy settings to limit what information is visible to a contact, "de-friending" a contact, blocking a contact, or committing "Facebook suicide." The following list describes each option, ranging from most subtle to most drastic:

- *Limiting profile visibility.* Using Privacy Settings and Friend Lists, you can change who has visibility into your profile (including photos, friends, contact information, and wall posts), who can search for you, how you can be contacted, and what stories about you get published to your profile and to your friends' New Feeds.

- *"De-friending" a contact.* You could decide to remove a contact from your friend network altogether by de-friending him. When you do this, the person will not be explicitly notified. However, he will see your name and be able to initiate a Friend Request if they search for you or view the Friends section of any mutual friend's profile.

- *"Blocking a contact."* Blocking a contact takes de-friending even further by removing your presence completely from the person's Facebook experience. You will not show up if they search for you or view the Friends section of mutual friends' profiles.

- *Committing "Facebook suicide."* There are a small but growing number of Facebook members who are committing so-called Facebook suicide by deactivating their accounts. Three reasons are most often cited: Facebook addiction, not wanting certain people from the past to reemerge in your life, and wanting to start over. Several college students I interviewed mentioned they have temporarily deactivated their Facebook accounts around midterm and final exam time to focus on studying, and then reactivated once the exams were over. But as Chapter 11, "Corporate Governance and Strategy," explains, canceling your account might not be the best way to get off the Facebook grid because other members could still tag you in photos and videos or, worse yet, create fake profiles pretending to be you.

Supporting Entrepreneurial Networks

Yet not all social networks are created equal. Ronald Burt at the University of Chicago Graduate School of Business has laid much of the research foundation for modern social capital theory. Burt depicts two types of networks: clique networks and entrepreneurial networks. Clique networks are typically characterized by strong, mutual, and redundant ties, with few ties to other networks. Entrepreneurial networks tend to be broader and shallower, with many connections to other networks. Although clique networks might feel more secure, they can be isolating and limited in scope.

In contrast, entrepreneurial networks empower their members with access to a wider range of knowledge, people, and opportunities. By providing access to new networks and supporting weak ties, online social networking, in effect, encourages entrepreneurial networks and maximizes social capital.

Online Interactions Supplement Offline Networking

One common objection to online social networking is that it sacrifices relationship quality for quantity. Although this might have been true of first-generation sites, it is becoming less the case as people become more sophisticated about the connections they accept and establish. As we discussed in Chapter 2, interactions on social networking sites tend to augment, rather than replace, offline interactions. One of the reasons why Facebook has been so successful compared with its predecessors is the focus on supporting offline networks over online-only relationships.

To test this assumption, I surveyed 100 of my own friends to ask whether they initiate or accept friend requests from strangers on social networking sites. A *stranger* is defined as someone whom you have never met in person. I tried to get representative coverage across different age groups, professions, and geographies, but admittedly many of my friends tend to reflect my own demographic. Also, this is not strictly an apples-to-apples comparison because not everyone I surveyed belongs to all four sites.

Still, the results are illuminating. First of all, most (73%) had never received a friend request from a stranger on Facebook. Even among those who had, most did not accept these requests. They either clicked "ignore request" or did not respond at all (see Table 3.1). The results for LinkedIn follow a similar pattern.

Table 3.1   SURVEY OF FRIEND REQUESTS INITIATED AND ACCEPTED FROM STRANGERS ON FACEBOOK, LINKEDIN, ORKUT, AND MYSPACE

	Facebook	LinkedIn	Orkut	MySpace
Received friend request from a stranger	27%	34%	100%	100%
Accepted friend request from a stranger	5%	18%	66%	94%
Initiated friend request with a stranger	0%	7%	3%	47%

The respondents' experience on Orkut and MySpace was markedly different. Without exception, everyone had been solicited by a stranger. More tended to accept strangers' requests on MySpace than on Orkut. There was also a higher incidence of initiating friend requests with strangers on MySpace, presumably because it is common practice to befriend bands and celebrities on MySpace.

I dug a little deeper. Most people who accepted requests from strangers said they did so because it's not clear what the protocol is for acceptance or rejection, and they didn't want to appear rude. Many told me that after awhile, their Orkut networks degraded into largely random connections. Spam started drowning out interactions with real friends; as the site became less relevant, people stopped logging in and interacting, which made it even less relevant for their real friends who were on the site. Pretty soon, entire groups of friends stopped logging in.

Compared with Orkut or MySpace, Facebook and LinkedIn established a clear friend request protocol and culture of trust for their networks. Facebook did so through e-mail-based identity confirmation (talked about in Chapter 2) and modeling their online networks off of real offline networks. For example, when you join Facebook, one of the first things you must do is choose one or more networks with which to be associated. Your options include schools, employers, cities, and other real offline networks that have real offline trust. LinkedIn took a different approach to establish protocol. By accepting a LinkedIn connection request, you implicitly agree to share your network and to professionally vouch for this person. Most people aren't willing to vouch for strangers, so they are more careful about accepting LinkedIn connection requests from strangers.

Even when people meet for the first time on Facebook or LinkedIn, they are usually friends of friends or at least belong to the same network versus complete random strangers. In the case of LinkedIn, there is generally a business objective being driven that would result in a real offline relationship.

Far from signaling the end of traditional relationships, Facebook's success is a testament that nothing is stronger than in-person rapport. Protecting the quality of online networks and focusing them on supporting offline relationships keep the Facebook experience relevant and valuable.

One interesting trend I did notice in the surveys, however, is that teenagers are more willing to initiate and accept requests from strangers. As I investigated further, it became clear this is due to competition over who has the most Facebook Friends. Fortunately, it is now possible on Facebook to classify and tag your relationships using Friend Lists, and to accordingly limit interaction and how much data is visible to each connection. For example, you could create a "Never Met" Friend List for strangers and hide all of your photos, wall posts, and contact information for all connections on this list. Relationship tagging and tiering using Friend Lists can be extremely helpful in maintaining high-quality online networks. Chapter 10 describes in detail how Friend Lists work.

With perhaps the exception of teens, we are seeing that online interactions tend to support rather than replace offline rapport, strengthening relationships you already have and laying the groundwork for future relationships you might not otherwise have enough context and capacity to pursue.

The Flattening Effect

At the end of Chapter 1, "The Fourth Revolution," we discussed the general trend with each digital revolution toward corporate decentralization. It is interesting to think about this in terms of social capital, or privileged access to resources, in an organization. The Internet democratized privileged access to information. Online social networking takes this further, democratizing privileged access to people.

Because there are fewer barriers in place, people are empowered to build social capital in more informal, entrepreneurial, and ad hoc ways. On most social networking sites, registration is open to anyone, and every member more or less starts on level footing. Sites like Facebook were designed without hierarchy, so real-world social structures that are hierarchical don't translate well. They tend to flatten out. Take corporate communication, for instance. Something the CEO says is more likely to spread across the company's informal word-of-mouth networks compared with something said by an entry-level worker. But to Facebook, these statements look identical.

Say the CEO posts a link on her profile to a news article annotated with her comments, and the entry-level employee does the same with a different article. Before, likely the CEO's comments would propagate across the company and the employee's would not. But on Facebook, both messages might have equal opportunity to propagate the company network. In the truly flat Facebook Era, entry-level workers potentially have the same opportunity as the CEO to have their voice heard.

Using online social networking, employees might also be able to bypass traditional organizational hierarchy and boundaries to network directly with senior managers or colleagues in other departments, units, and geographies. Just like blogging democratized who had a voice on the Internet, someone who is really active on Facebook and posts interesting links and commentary might win visibility in the company in ways which would simply not have been possible before.

Creating New Value from Network Effects

Metcalfe's Law provides a good explanation behind the power and value of the online social graph. Originally used to describe telecommunications networks, it states that the value of a network increases exponentially with the number of members. This is because for n members, there are roughly n^2 possible connections. Among these n^2 connections forms a social economy of mutual trust, favor, and contribution. Over time as new members join, the value of the each individual's network increases as well as the value of the overall social economy.

The Reciprocity Ring

I experienced Metcalfe's Law firsthand in spring 2008 during a somewhat contrived but nevertheless convincing offline experiment. It was the last day of a weeklong leadership course I was taking at the Stanford Graduate School of Business, and in our final session together, we created a reciprocity ring to demonstrate how social networking can create value for everyone who participates.

The first step was coming up with a request to put forth to the group. Each one of us wrote down our request along with our name on a Post-it Note and placed it around a large circle that had been drawn on the whiteboard (see Figure 3.2). Next, we were handed a pad of blank Post-it Notes and given ten minutes to survey the circle of requests. For each request where we could contribute, we wrote down our name and how we might be able to help on a Post-it, and placed it below the request on the whiteboard (see Figure 3.3).

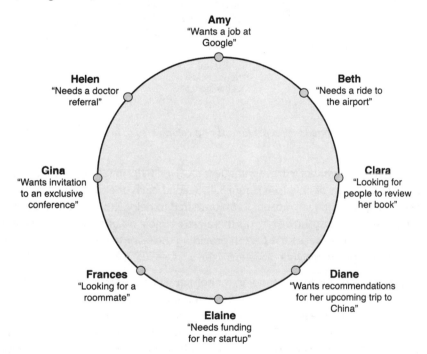

Figure 3.2
The first step in the reciprocity ring exercise was to write down your name and a request to put forth to the group, and then place these in a circle.

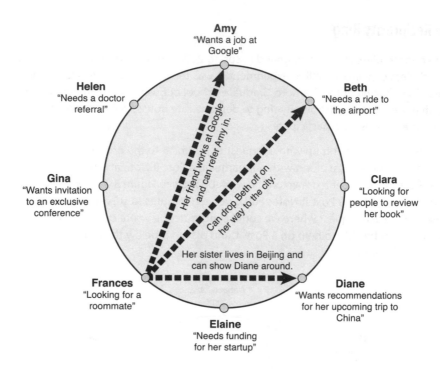

Figure 3.3
Next, each participant scanned the set of requests and volunteered to help where they could provide value.

The results were impressive. First, every request received help; in fact, most requests received multiple offers of help (see Figure 3.4). Second, each one of us could contribute to at least one request; in fact, most of us volunteered to help with multiple requests. What was most interesting, however, was there were almost no one-to-one exchanges. That is, in the majority of cases, the person providing the favor to you is not the same person to whom you are providing a favor.

For example, Elaine needs to find funding for her new start-up. Amy volunteered to help because she knows several of the partners at a venture capital firm. Amy, in turn, is looking for a job at Google. She receives help on this request, but not from Elaine. It is Frances, who receives help from Gina, who receives help from Elaine, who actually can help Amy. The reason this works is that the cost of helping is generally miniscule compared with the benefit of being helped. To Elaine, receiving an introduction to a venture capitalist is worth a lot because it could make or break her new start-up. But to Amy, providing the introduction is no big deal. It takes her just a few minutes to do so over e-mail. In the end, new value is created for each individual as well as for the group collectively. Everyone wins.

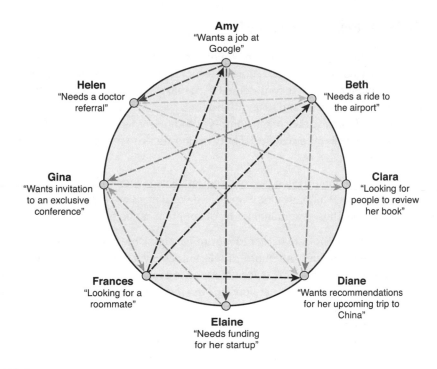

Figure 3.4
The result was every request received help and every participant helped provide a favor.

The Online Social Graph Reciprocity Ring

For the Stanford experiment to work, we all had to be there at the same place and same time for the same purpose. In real life, this is extremely rare. Offline, such explicit networking feels too utilitarian and contrived. And you would never physically assemble a large group of people for the purpose of asking each other favors. But in Facebook, Orkut, and LinkedIn, these large groups of people are already assembled and ready to be mobilized when you need a favor.

Social networking sites take the rapport we have established offline and bridge them into a system that you can call on in times of need. Online social networking extends the notion of the reciprocity ring across time, geography, and networks and is, therefore, capable of generating a tremendous amount of social capital for participants. Ultimately, efficiency gains from bringing technology to the intrinsically human activity of social networking create net-new value for individuals as well as to the collective community.

Easier to Ask a Favor, Harder to Say No

In fact, social networking sites might even be making it easier to ask for favors while making it harder to say no. Because interactions feel more casual on Facebook or LinkedIn, there is a lower bar for when it is considered OK to make a request. Picking up the phone or visiting someone in person and asking them for a favor puts them on the spot and, therefore, carries a higher social cost. In contrast, sending someone a Facebook message is no big deal. By reducing the cost, social networking sites can make people feel more comfortable asking for favors.

What about being on the receiving end of a request? Even when they contain legitimate requests you should actually consider, e-mails and voice mails are easy to ignore or let get lost in the shuffle. These traditional forms of communication feel too impersonal.

Requests made on Facebook are harder to ignore. Facebook messages do not come in isolation—you see the requestor's photo, profile, and who you know in common. The request feels personal, so you think twice before saying no. Especially if you have strong mutual ties or belong to the same networks (or the requestor belongs to a different network that has value to you), the social and mental cost of ignoring the request is higher. This ties back to the earlier discussion on how information on social networking sites helps people qualify the potential value of relationships earlier on. If you receive a request on Facebook and can quickly identify that the requestor might be a valuable contact, it is much harder to ignore the request. If you received the same request on e-mail, in our age of rampant spam you might never have even given it a chance.

In certain cases, asking favors is made even more effective when requests are passively broadcast to your network using a status message, say *"[Clara is…] looking to hire an engineer,"* versus a directed one-to-one message. Because the request hasn't been directed toward any one person specifically, no one feels annoyed or obligated to respond. It feels serendipitous that your status message happens to show up in their News Feed, or if they visit your profile page where your status message is visible, then that was their choice to look at your profile in the first place. In this case, your entire network is given an opportunity without the obligation to respond, which frees you to make more requests more often because you are not expending any social capital with any one individual contact.

Because it feels more personal and there is more information about who is making the request, online social networking both makes it more casual and acceptable to ask for favors while making it harder to say no. As a result, more requests tend to get made and tend to get fulfilled, increasing the amount of social capital in circulation and overall value of the social economy. In a sense, social networking sites extend the notion of the reciprocity ring across time, geography, and networks and might, therefore, have the potential to generate a tremendous amount of new value for everyone involved.

Blurring the Lines

The lines are blurring between our personal and professional lives. We refer friends to our employer. We befriend colleagues, clients, and business partners. We work from home, we exercise at work, we work for ourselves. The added social capital from our personal relationships and fringe relationships are empowering us with broader networks that give us access to more information, people, and resources than ever before. Meanwhile, e-commerce and Web 2.0 have given us as individuals not only a voice, but also the power to act. By using online social networking tools to keep in touch with fringe networks, discover valuable relationships, transcend traditional hierarchy, and ask more favors, we can maximize social capital, enjoy more satisfying careers, and ultimately be more effective at achieving our goals.

Transforming the Way We Do Business

"Sales IS social networking!"
—Geoffrey Moore

Social Sales

As anyone who has ever bought or sold something knows, sales is an intrinsically social activity based on mutual trust. Even in the case of commodity products and services, relationships can sometimes even trump price as the deciding factor in purchase decisions. Ultimately, people like doing business with people they like, and refuse to do business with people they don't trust.

One major result of the democratization of business described in earlier chapters has been unprecedented market competition. In today's business landscape, companies are faced with a greater number of competitors and savvier buyers empowered with information. More than ever, sales reps must strive to maximize the lifetime value of their customer relationships versus maximizing the value of a single transaction.

With fewer unfair structural advantages for reps to count on, timely insights into customer needs and interpersonal communications in the sales process have become requirements for closing the deal. Online social networks are emerging as critical business tools to help facilitate these insights and communications.

Although many of the best salespeople are just natural instinctive relationship builders, certain sales methodologies have been proven in recent years to help the rest of us learn to emulate their success. Customer relationship management, or CRM, attempts to capture the science of sales with software and processes to handle all of a company's interactions with its customers. Sales force automation, in particular, builds in processes like forecasting, territory management, e-mail templates, dashboards, activity management, and deal alerts so that managers have visibility and sales teams can be more productive (see Figure 4.1). Online social networking adds another dimension of possibility to CRM by enriching critical sales practices with contextual information and relationship-building tools.

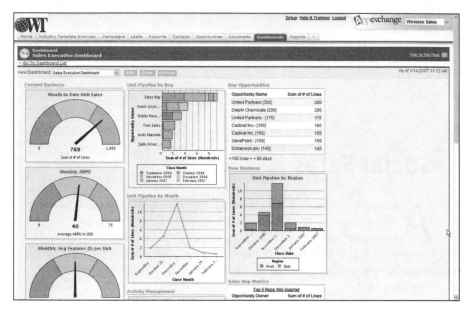

Figure 4.1
CRM systems like this one from salesforce.com offer business visibility for managers, improved rep productivity, and effective selling processes.

This chapter is divided into three parts. First, it walks through a typical sales cycle and suggests ways in which the online social graph might be leveraged to increase sales effectiveness. Next, this chapter resumes discussion on network structures, first introduced in the previous chapter, and how they apply in sales. It concludes with a short discussion on the implications for CRM, and how the future of information contained in CRM will likely be bidirectional between companies and their customers. Many of the techniques in this chapter are exploratory as social sales tools are still very nascent. Chapter 10, "Build and Manage Your Relationships," provides concrete instructions on how individuals can build and manage relationships on Facebook for sales or otherwise.

Transforming the Sales Cycle

Sales reps can use online social networking to become more productive in two ways: to glean insights about customers and to engage in casual communications with customers. From the customer's perspective, the sales call has the potential to become more personalized and relevant. It's no longer acceptable for reps to generically push every product and service. Today's reps are expected to have "done their homework" based on the information available on the Internet and on social networking sites. Customers, for their part, are responsible for managing and maintaining what information they choose to share with whom. Chapter 10 explains how to use Facebook privacy controls to manage online identities, and Chapter 11, "Corporate Governance and Strategy," speaks to more general issues and concerns around privacy and security.

Based on the sales deals I've participated in as well as interviews with my colleagues in sales, I have identified eight aspects of the sales cycle that stand to benefit from the online social graph: establishing credibility, sales prospecting, getting your foot in the door, navigating customer organizations, collaborating across sales teams, providing customer references, building ongoing rapport, and ensuring ongoing customer success with postsales support. These are also very much in line with the general techniques advocated by popular sales methodologies such as Miller Heiman and CustomerCentric Selling.

Before we delve into the sales cycle, I would first like to call out some differences between B2B (business to business) and B2C (business to consumer) sales, and discuss how these might affect social sales strategy.

B2B Versus B2C Sales

Selling to consumers, or business to consumer (B2C), tends to be more straightforward, transactional, and driven by product and marketing. Because of a lower price point and fewer people involved in making the purchase decision, B2C typically has a shorter sales cycle. For many items, especially those below $100, it is usually more about marketing than about sales. Often there is no salesperson involved. As far as online social networking, these goods and services stand to benefit more from social merchandising, targeted advertising, and viral marketing tactics, which we discuss in Chapter 5, "Social Network Marketing."

As we go up in price and complexity, B2C begins to resemble business to business (B2B). Especially when "intangibles" like warranties, customer support, authenticity, and service quality factor into a sale, trust and relationships become critical differentiators (see Figure 4.2). B2B selling into organizations is often a multistep process involving multiple stakeholders and levels of decision making, resulting in a longer sales cycle. The upcoming sections on sales team collaboration and navigating customer organizations are directed especially at B2B sales. Finally, B2B deals tend to be custom transactions. These typically involve negotiation, as there is a higher markup to begin with and imprecise information about the value of the good or service being offered.

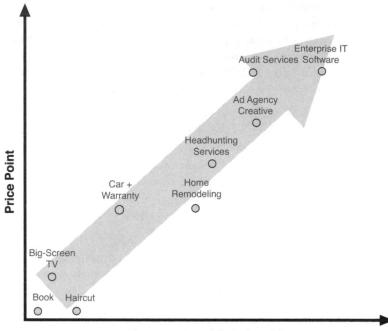

Figure 4.2

Relationships and trust play a bigger role in purchase decisions of higher-priced items that are more difficult to value and require greater expertise to understand. Credit: Timothy Chou, cofounder of Openwater Networks and lecturer at Stanford. He whiteboarded a similar concept for me in his office in June 2008.

But why use a person-to-person tool like Facebook for selling to an organization? The important thing to keep in mind is that individuals are at the heart of any organization. Purchase decisions are made by individual people, not entire companies. Transactions succeed or fail because of a few key such individuals—your customer champion, executive decision maker, customer reference, sales rep, product expert. By strengthening the bond and improving information flow among your internal deal team as well as with key customer stakeholders, social networking sites can help your company create a more productive selling machine.

Establishing Credibility

First, sales reps need to establish credibility that they are competent and committed to delivering customer success. Traditionally, reps had to rely on the brand reputation of their company and products, and their Rolodex of customer relationships slowly built up over many years.

Today, sales reps and others can accelerate the process of building trust by using social networking sites to convey qualifications. A typical LinkedIn profile, for example, contains four types of information that would have been awkward or more difficult to provide in the past: public testimonials, list of connections, professional experience, and education pedigree. Just like Amazon.com has customer reviews on books and Zagat has customer reviews on restaurants, social networking sites are becoming the de facto place for reviews on business professionals. If you have satisfied customers, it might not be a bad idea to ask them for public testimonials on LinkedIn or the Testimonials application on Facebook. Chapter 7, "Social Recruiting," goes into greater detail about LinkedIn recommendations in the context of job candidate references.

Bidirectional visibility helps foster mutual trust. With this information on hand (which you have chosen to share), prospective customers are empowered to "check you out" as a sales rep and hopefully gain confidence in your knowledge and competence in helping them find the right solution for their needs.

Sales Prospecting

As we cover in the next chapter, marketing is responsible for generating leads en masse. But great salespeople are able to source their own leads, too. As Tupperware party hosts and Mary Kay and Cutco Cutlery salespeople have known for decades, sometimes your best prospective customers are right in front of you: friends, family, and acquaintances.

Most people, however, wouldn't feel entirely comfortable calling down the list of contacts in their phone book. Fortunately, as we talked about in Chapter 3, "Social Capital from Networking Online," online social networks have created a new set of interaction modes and relationship types, like Facebook Friends and LinkedIn Connections, that make it less invasive, more comfortable, and easier to ask favors of your network.

Prior to social networking sites, it was both less efficient and less socially acceptable for a sales rep to directly prospect into her network. It was inefficient because there was no easy way to tell who among your contacts might be interested in your product. It was invasive because the sales rep burned through social capital each time she tried selling to someone who was not interested.

In the Facebook Era, it is a different story. LinkedIn and to a lesser extent Facebook typically have employment information (that is, location, employer, and role) for each contact. The sales rep can search on the exact profile of the ideal target prospect and qualify the lead earlier in the cycle. The sales call feels less invasive because the interaction feels more casual, and the pitch is targeted specifically to the prospective customer's profile. The following case study profiles how one company, Aster Data Systems, successfully sourced its initial wave of customers using social networking sites.

Social Graph Prospecting at Aster Data Systems

Aster Data Systems, a start-up software company located in Silicon Valley, has dramatically grown its business through creative use of LinkedIn. As a small start-up, Aster lacked brand recognition and did not have the budget for large marketing or advertising campaigns.

To source early customers, Aster instead tapped into the company's collective social network on LinkedIn, MySpace, and Facebook. Senior management asked all employees, not just sales reps, to tap their networks for potential prospects who had keywords like "data warehousing" in their title or functional expertise.

In just a few months, the resourcefulness of this strategy has already begun to pay off. LinkedIn and other social networking sites are used to identify who among those contacts connected to Aster employees might be interested in the database product. Then a sales cycle is initiated through a combination of LinkedIn and traditional communication modes. Thanks to the power of the social graph, Aster has successfully signed on more than a dozen customers.

And it's not just immediate contacts. As Figure 4.3 shows, social networking sites also allow you to reach friends of friends and greater extended networks, expanding your addressable prospecting audience.

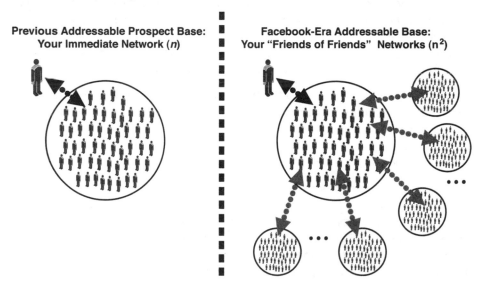

Figure 4.3

Using a service like LinkedIn grows the prospect base from n contacts to n^2 or more contacts because of the "friends of friends" effect. This gets multiplied even further if more employees (including nonsales functions) tap their networks in this way.

In addition to their own networks, salespeople can tap discovery sites (introduced in Chapter 1, "The Fourth Revolution") to access larger pools of contact data. Popular services include Hoover's, OneSource, ZoomInfo, JigSaw, Spoke, and ActiveContacts.

LIONs are an interesting phenomenon that tries to combine the reach and access offered by discovery sites with the data accuracy and user opt-in offered by social networking sites. Traditional social network philosophy says that people should only invite and accept connection requests with people they personally know. This approach is both what I generally advocate as well as what I found in surveying my friends about their usage of Facebook and LinkedIn, as we talked about in the previous chapter. However, some LinkedIn members view this as overly restrictive and have adopted a policy of accepting connection invitations from strangers. These individuals, known as LinkedIn Open Networkers (or LIONs, for short) are mostly sales professionals who have chosen to sacrifice network quality for network scope and optimizing for weak ties.

The biggest LION network, which was also the first, is www.metanetwork.com. It has a corresponding LinkedIn Group called "LI Open Networkers." To get around LinkedIn's requirement that you need to know a person's e-mail address to invite the contact, most LIONs publicly post their e-mail address in their profiles.

The First Call

Traditionally, most first calls do not meet with a high success rate. The prospective customer dreads them because they are usually irrelevant and, therefore, can feel insincere and like a waste of time. The salesperson dreads them because the recipient is annoyed by the call.

In the Facebook Era, the first call looks very different. There is much more lead qualification and preparation that can occur beforehand, saving both the rep's time and the prospect's time. Many of the traditional discovery questions can be answered by poking around on the prospect's social networking profile, such as his tenure at the company, key responsibilities and accomplishments, and past experience with solutions in your space, to name a few. Prospects are far more willing to take that first call if the pitch is tailored to their needs, versus just a generic push of every product and service. Data from the social networking sites allows sales reps to qualify out early, or if they decide it might be a good fit then formulate the right introductory pitch and even involve mutual contacts who can serve as references. The basic expectation has become that a salesperson has "done her homework" given the wealth of information available, and even the first call should reflect an initial level of effort.

The salespeople I interviewed said they are increasingly using LinkedIn for prospecting and making initial contact. They find that, surprisingly, the simplest e-mails solicit the most responses. Figure 4.4 shows a sample e-mail one of my friends was kind enough to share. Tying back to the notion of bidirectional visibility, the sales rep in this example provides a link back to her own social networking profile so that the prospect can glean more information without sales pressure. The rep also calls out some commonality shared with the prospect (college alma mater in this case) to differentiate herself and establish early rapport. Often, profile data such as shared company or industry experience, sports teams, hometowns, or fraternities and sororities are used to establish common ground and get one foot in the door. To prospects, the call feels less invasive because this is all information they have opted to share on public social networking sites, compared with the old model of marketing lists that might get bought or sold without their consent. This also ensures that the profile data and contact information being used by reps are more accurate and up to date.

Subject: Quick question re: LinkedIn

I am looking at your LinkedIn profile right now and have a quick question for you.

My name is *Jane Sales* and I am on the *Prospective Customer X* account team here at *Vendor Y*. Check out my LinkedIn profile <u>here</u>. I see that you are a fellow *Arizona State* alum!

Let me know when you have a few minutes to discuss.

Thank you,

Jane Sales
Vendor Y
222-222-2222

Figure 4.4
A sample sales prospecting e-mail sent to a social network contact. It's a good idea to keep initial contact short and simple, and if possible, find common ground to establish early interpersonal rapport.

Another great benefit of social networking sites is the ability for sales reps to see who they know in common with the prospect. Instead of a cold call, reps might consider requesting a warm introduction from a mutual friend or business colleague. The warm intro increases the chances that the rep will rise above the spam, and at least get to make her initial pitch. Before social networking sites, even if there were mutual contacts, it was hard to know that they were there!

I believe Facebook is CRM. I created Faceconnector (originally Faceforce) in the autumn of 2007 to help reps connect the dots between the leads they were getting and the *real people* behind the leads. Traditional leads are a name, title, and company. *People* are far more complex and interesting. They are defined not just by their current title and employer but also by the rich set of past experiences that have collectively shaped who they are, their interests, hobbies, where they're from, and who their friends are. More and more, people are getting comfortable with sharing at least some of this information on their social networking profile. Faceconnector pulls real-time Facebook profile and friend information—such as schools attended, past employers, favorite books, interests, and friends in common—into Salesforce CRM so that reps viewing a lead or contact record inside Salesforce can see more than just the title and company (see Figure 4.5). They can begin to know the *person* and try to tailor a sales call that is more *personal* and relevant. They might even ask mutual friends for introductions.

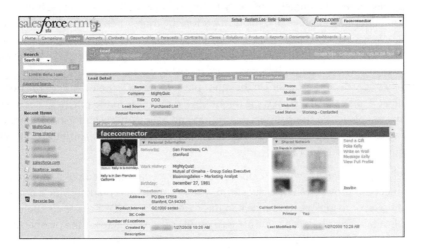

Figure 4.5
Faceconnector (originally Faceforce) pulls real-time Facebook profile and social graph data into Salesforce CRM account, contact, and lead records so that sales reps can tap into the insights of the online social graph to make their pitch more personal and relevant.

Of course, not every first call will result in a closed deal. There is little reps can do if the product is just not a good fit or the buyer does not have the necessary budget. Still, social and profile data from social networking sites can go a long way in increasing the first call success rate by enabling reps to qualify early, tailor their pitch, add a personal touch, and tap mutual contacts for references and introductions.

Navigating Complex Customer Organizations

In addition to helping facilitate one-on-one relationship building, data from social networking sites at a high level can also be used for B2B deal strategy—that is, how to approach a deal, which individuals at the buyer can be connected with, and who has influence in the deal. Sales methodologies like TAS, Miller Heiman, and Solution Selling emphasize the importance of navigating customer organizations and identifying key decision makers. There is powerful data contained in the online social graph to help aid this exercise.

Online social networking sites reveal a wealth of information about people's title and role, status in the company, working relationship with other contacts, and decision-making status. One high-tech account executive who has successfully sold into many IT departments told me that whenever he gets a new contact, he immediately goes to LinkedIn to understand how the individual fits into the bigger picture. There are a few subtle but critical pieces of information for which he is always on the lookout that greatly affect his strategy on a particular deal:

- *Political strength and tenure.* Almost always, people specify on their profiles how long they have been working at a company. If they are new, perhaps they have less political capital but more to prove, and might, therefore, be more open to bringing in a new vendor or way of doing things. You can usually also view their connections. Is the CIO connected to the CEO and CFO? Is she connected to her own IT directors? If not, this could be a sign that there might be some internal politics at play and could be a good opportunity to divide and conquer. On the other hand, if the CIO is seasoned and all her subordinates are new, that signals she might have greater say in the purchase decision. If many people in the company are connected and have publicly endorsed one another using LinkedIn Recommendations, then it is likely a tight-knit organization that will require a different approach.

- *Likelihood of being a champion or roadblock.* Past experience, stated skills, and external connections provide valuable clues as to whether someone could become a potential champion or roadblock to your deal. In this case, the account executive competes against Microsoft. He once came across a profile of an IT director at the prospective buyer that showed this person had extensive experience implementing Microsoft solutions, had been certified in several Microsoft technologies, and had many LinkedIn connections to Microsoft employees, resellers, and consultants. This raised a red flag in the rep's mind, and sure enough this IT director became a big roadblock in the sale (that went through despite this). Similarly, someone who had been successful using the account executive's product at previous companies is likely to be a champion. Your prospects want to do the right thing for their companies, but often this is in the context of what is the right thing for their careers and where their skill sets and comfort zones lie.

- *Organizational structure.* The account executive also told me he always searches on company name to get a list of the prospective buyer's employees. Not only does this generate valuable contacts to whom he might want to reach out, he can also glean information like offices and subsidiaries, departments, titles, and how the company is organized. For example, the title of "vice president" might signal a powerful decision maker in one firm but be meaningless in another. One prospective buyer had 20 vice presidents out of 50 total employees! Once you have a lay of the land, you can formulate the overall sales plan and start spending time winning over individual decision makers.

- *Commonality with deal team members.* Last, but not least, this account executive recommends seeking commonalities not only between yourself and prospects, but also between other members of your account team and prospects. That way, you can strategically assign different people in your company to the various individuals at the prospective buyer to maximize rapport. For example, say a key technical executive at your prospect company is originally from Texas and graduated from Rice University. If you have a team of sales engineers and one happens to be a fellow Texan who also attended Rice, then that's the person you want to staff on the account and assign to this prospect. As we talked about in this previous section, shared personal experiences, even if they are small coincidences, can go a long way in establishing rapport and differentiating your deal. This extends beyond individual reps to entire sales teams.

Hoover's, which provides a popular database containing tens of millions of business contacts, is another company that has set its sights on providing online social networking tools to help reps navigate to the right decision makers. Hoover's acquired social networking company Visible Path in January 2008, and launched Hoover's Connect, a professional social networking service that bundles Hoover's contact data with Visible Path's social mapping functionality. With Hoover's Connect, sales reps can identify and connect to the right stakeholders in a prospect organization through people with whom they already have a relationship (see Figure 4.6).

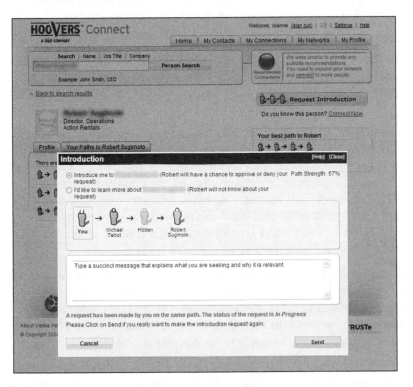

Figure 4.6
Social networking tools like Hoover's Connect (formerly Visible Path) help sales reps navigate complex organization structures and map out critical connections to key decision makers.

Building on the previous chapter's discussion, social capital is the currency of influence in sales, too. Valuable information from social networking sites can arm reps with social capital for deals. Those with accurate maps of the social networks inside their prospective buyer know whom to talk to, are better known by others, know who gets along and who doesn't, and uses this knowledge to drive deal strategy and tactics.

Sales Team Collaboration

Especially in B2B transactions, there is often an entire sales team rather than one individual rep working on a deal. In addition to the account executive, there might be various product specialists, sales engineers, consultants, auditors, training staff, and others internal and external to the vendor company all working together to address a customer's needs in the sales cycle and close the deal.

In addition to collaborating to assign the right account team members to the right prospect, sales teams can use online social networking to communicate, collaborate, and coordinate across their different functions as well as to log individual interactions with prospect stakeholders. According to the reps I interviewed, if team members are geographically dispersed, the personal connections facilitated by social networking sites can be invaluable for establishing rapport and coordinating group effort.

Another important use of enterprise social networking is for discovering expertise within the selling organization. Especially in large vendor companies with vast product portfolios and high employee turnover, it is often a challenge for account reps to find the right product experts internally to involve in the deal. Chapter 6, "Social Innovation," goes over expertise discovery in greater detail.

Not only can online social networking help reps collaborate within deals, but it can also aid collaboration across deals, too (see Figure 4.7). Sales Rep A might find herself in a deal that is very similar along certain dimensions to another deal that Sales Rep B worked on six months ago—for example, by industry, customer size, product interest, or competitors. Perhaps Rep B found certain customer references, product demonstrations, and collateral especially useful in closing the deal. Rep A can be much more productive if she can leverage the combined experience and expertise of Rep B and all the other reps in her company instead of reinventing the wheel.

Of course, reps don't and shouldn't provide deal information on public social networking sites. Rather, this informal deal collaboration is happening within enterprise systems like CRM, wikis, and intranet sites. Salesforce.com is investing heavily in this area with new sales collaboration features in its sales force automation application that allow reps working on one sales opportunity to search for similar past opportunities.

ePeople TSmail is another popular team selling solution that enables rep collaboration in identifying expertise and other resources, building sales proposals, leveraging account insights for future deals, and providing management visibility (see Figure 4.8).

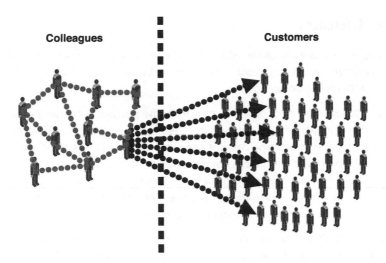

Figure 4.7

In addition to tapping social connections between sales reps and prospects, sales organizations can achieve greater productivity from collaborating within and across account teams. Internal social networking fosters collaborative coordination and collective wisdom.

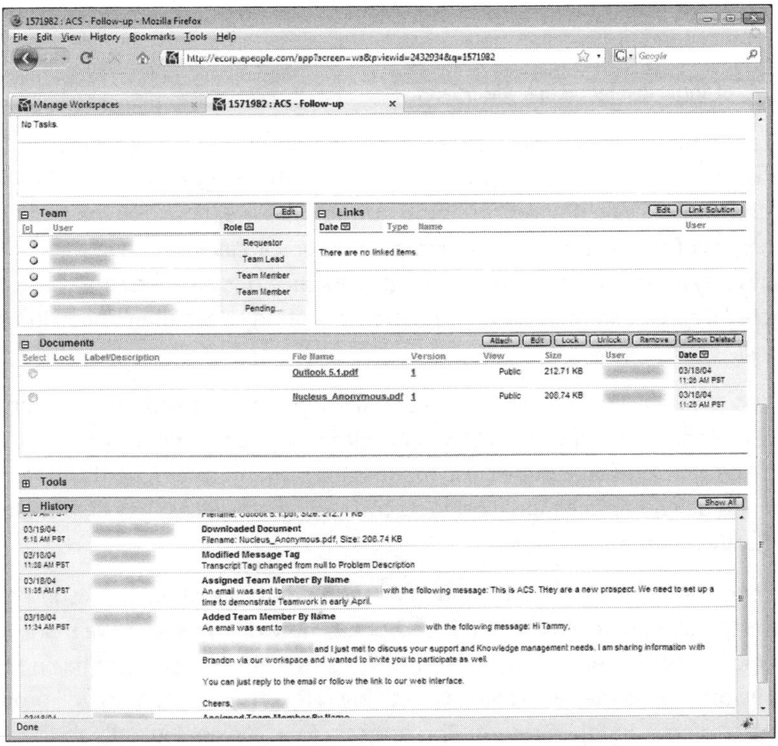

Figure 4.8

TSmail helps account teams coordinate across the life cycle of sales deals.

Customer References

Customer references are critical for establishing trust to close deals. Testimonials from existing customers provide the most convincing social validation of your product. They have voted with their money and time.

Traditionally, salespeople track down references in the prospective buyer's region or industry to demonstrate competence serving the buyer's unique requirements. But in today's competitive environment, chances are other vendors have similar references. The online social graph provides valuable insight into who knows whom that can help set your references apart from the rest. Especially in situations where you happen to be one of the lesser-known vendors, providing your prospect with references from *their* trusted friends and colleagues can be a powerful differentiator.

Why does this work? Well, for any more complex, noncommodity sale, there is an inherent degree of ambiguity in evaluating the product or service. Ultimately, differentiation means that a buyer is comparing apples to oranges, and at some point needs to make a "leap-of-faith" decision in spite of the uncertainty. Customer references provide valuable information, both real and perceived, to mitigate this uncertainty. With social networking sites, it has become possible to take this further and find exactly which of your customers is connected with a prospective buyer. The following sidebar provides an example from medical sales.

The Power of Social References in Medical Sales

Rob is a top medical equipment sales rep, having achieved over two times his sales quota each of the last five years. According to Rob, the biggest challenge in his job is getting and keeping doctors' attention during sales meetings. Having been in different types of sales prior to his current role in medical sales,
Rob says physicians are an especially tough audience because they are constantly distracted by crises and typically have patients waiting to see them following his sales call.

Rob's secret to success? He relies on personal referrals from existing customers. He believes this has worked especially well for him because the medical community is a tight-knit group. People forge close friendships from medical school and residency, and develop professional contacts through conferences they are required periodically to attend.

These personal referrals used to happen on a one-off basis when an existing customer was willing to reach out to a friend. Social networking sites have made it much more efficient for Rob to discover who knows whom. Instead of having to ask each customer who they are willing to actively refer (often customers will promise to make a referral and then forget), Rob goes on Facebook or LinkedIn to the prospect's profile page and views their mutual contacts. Sometimes these include some of Rob's existing customers. During sales meetings, Rob name-drops. Rob says his prospects become instantly engaged, often recounting stories from medical school about the existing customer who is their friend. Rob's sales win rate and average deal size has gone way up as a result of this valuable information from social networking sites.

Although medical professionals as a group have been slower to adopt social networking, younger generations of doctors are joining Facebook en masse, and even more seasoned physicians are seeing the value in keeping in touch with people they meet at conferences.

Trust is transitive, to a degree. Because Rob's customer trusts Rob (that's why he's a customer after all!) and Rob's prospect trusts his friend who is Rob's customer, Rob's prospect is more willing to trust Rob. Reps like Rob, in a sense, are tapping the social capital of relationships between their prospect and existing customer to help close the deal (see Figure 4.9). From the prospective buyer's perspective, she is getting a referral from a trusted colleague. This carries far more weight than an anonymous referral.

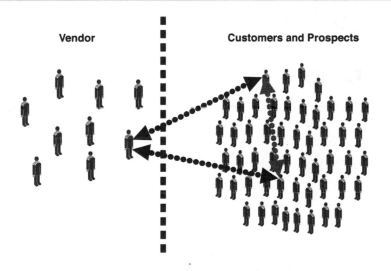

Figure 4.9
Customer references are much more powerful when they are from someone the prospective buyer knows personally. Online social networking services can allow the sales rep to discover which of her existing customers might be connected to a prospective buyer.

Building and Sustaining Rapport

Because B2B sales cycles tend to take longer, reps often find themselves working multiple overlapping deals at once. As sales reps start new deals and shift focus from deal to deal, it is imperative they sustain rapport with prospects so that progress can continue to be made. Traditionally, this was difficult for most account executives to juggle.

Fortunately, Facebook can help. Casual interaction modes, like Facebook pokes and messages, together with proactive updates in the form of News Feed alerts and Birthday Reminders (both described in Chapter 3) on social networking sites help reps save time staying in touch with their portfolio of customer and prospect contacts.

One account executive I interviewed swears by a combination of CRM calendar alerts and Facebook. For contacts at all of his key accounts, he sets monthly reminders in his company's CRM system to reach out and say hello. When a reminder pops up, he visits the person's profile on Facebook to find something interesting and personal to say, sometimes completely unrelated to the deal. For example, last month the Facebook status message of a prospect CEO indicated she was en route to Tokyo. The account executive sent a (virtual) Facebook gift of sushi along with recommendations of his two favorite restaurants in Tokyo (Figure 4.10 gives you an idea of what this might look like).

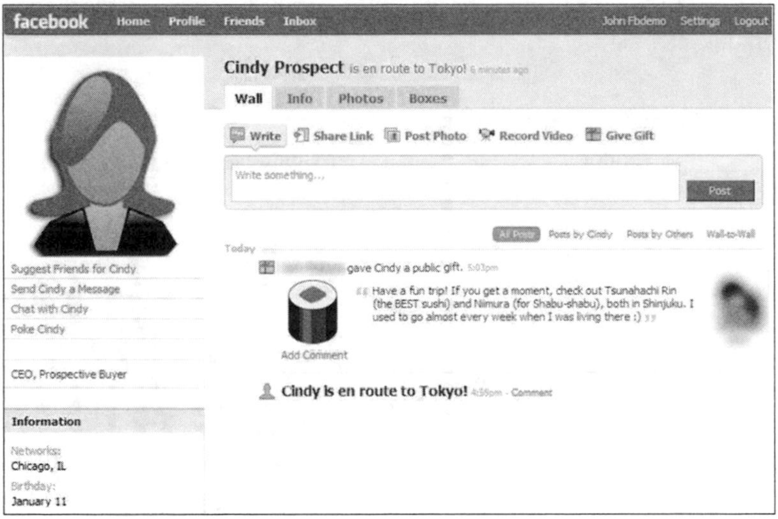

Figure 4.10
Playful, casual interaction on Facebook is an easy way for reps to stay in touch and sustain rapport with contacts. For example, an account rep might respond to this prospect's Facebook status message with a Facebook gift and Wall Post.

Periodic casual communication enabled by social networking sites can also help keep leads warm when the timing is not right for a prospect. Company reorganizations, budget cutbacks, and other competing projects are all too common reasons why deals get put on the back burner. Instead of walking away completely, reps can use online social networking to stay engaged without expending a lot of their time. Updates from social networking sites provide the perfect excuse to check in on prospects and remind them in a friendly way that you still exist without being so explicitly pushy about closing the sale.

Postsales Customer Support

Some say in B2B, the relationship only really begins once the deal closes. But for many vendors, offering quality customer service and support to ensure postsales success is extremely expensive and a frequent source of concern and distraction from their core business.

It's still early, but social networking seems to be coming to the rescue along three dimensions. First, just like their employees collaborate using social networking systems to do team selling, companies are realizing their employees can collaborate to offer team support. ePeople Teamwork is a popular team-based support tool that uses social networking within a company and its network of support partners to handle case escalation, expertise discovery, and cross-functional collaboration for resolving customer issues.

Second, companies are encouraging their support reps, not just sales reps, to invest in customer relationships especially on strategic, marquee accounts. Unlike sales account executives, support reps are typically not dedicated to specific accounts. But that doesn't mean they can't get quickly up to speed on the person calling in for help. Putting the customer at ease is especially important because by the time the customer calls, she has experienced a certain level of frustration, not to mention likely having been put on hold by the call center system. Increasingly, support reps are making small talk using personal information about a customer from social networking profiles and CRM systems. That way, reps can start calls on a more positive note and keep the customer engaged if she needs time, for example, to look up a solution or ask a colleague for help.

Some firms are using Faceconnector, first introduced in the sales prospecting context, in customer service scenarios to help support reps establish quick rapport. Instead of pulling in Facebook profile information for leads, they are accessing profile information for existing customer contacts. From the customer's perspective, the call feels more personal and engaging. In addition to traditional CRM information such as products purchased and case history, reps can speak to lighter topics like sports teams, hometowns, and hobbies. As a result, support reps are achieving higher customer satisfaction and greater success with attempts at cross-selling and upselling.

Last, but not least, companies have realized they can *crowdsource*, or outsource to the "crowd," a substantial portion of support questions by encouraging customers to talk to one another, troubleshoot for one another, and share tips and tricks in online forums. For instance, a number of such customer self-support groups have sprung up on Facebook, often to vendors' surprise and delight as these greatly alleviate the burden on their own reps and call centers.

To better understand this phenomenon, I monitored the YouTube discussion boards on Facebook for several weeks. A few individuals in particular were extremely active in helping answer questions posted by other community members. I contacted these individuals to ask what motivated them to volunteer their time in this way. Most cited a passion for the product and a desire to demonstrate their knowledge and be viewed as an expert in the community.

In addition to discussion boards on social networking sites, Get Satisfaction, Lithium, and FixYa are popular vendors that specialize in crowdsourced support tools. Get Satisfaction is used by companies like Whole Foods, Adobe, and Apple to facilitate support-related conversations among customers and between customers and employees (see Figure 4.11).

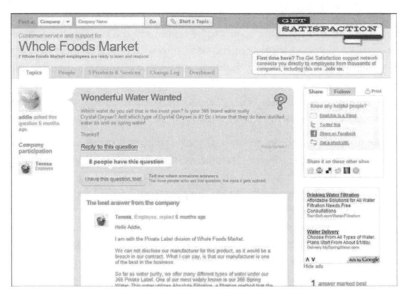

Figure 4.11
Get Satisfaction helps alleviate companies' support volume by tapping into customers to help answer each other's questions.

Salesforce.com hopes to tackle all three dimensions with Service Cloud, a set of technologies that augment traditional knowledge base solution data with crowdsourced knowledge. Service Cloud weaves together disparate silos of conversations across Facebook and Internet blogs and forums, and then relies on user voting and tagging to incorporate high-quality knowledge from the community into the corporate knowledge base. Over time, the system gets smarter, and the growing body of knowledge becomes available to any support rep who logs into the system as well as to partners and customers who visit a self-service knowledge portal.

Even the online social networks themselves have turned to the community to help translate and localize their sites into different languages. For example, Facebook created a platform application, Translations, that allows members to translate, review, and vote on translations in 63 different languages, similar to the Wikipedia submission process. Thanks to help from its members, Facebook has already been translated into 20 different languages, including most recently Chinese and Russian, and has its sights set on many more.

The Need for Multiple Network Structures

The notion that weak ties are generally more valuable for business than strong ties, as we discussed in Chapter 3, is an oversimplification in sales. Success in B2B sales, in particular, demands a more nuanced view of social networks. Tuba Üstüner and David Godes from Cass Business School and Harvard Business School, respectively, did an excellent job of distilling these nuances in their 2006 *Harvard Business Review* article, "Better Sales Networks."

We can gain new insights by revisiting the different stages in a typical sales cycle from the perspective of optimal network structures. The primary tasks required of a sales rep change, often significantly, at each stage in the sales cycle. The networks called upon by the sales rep to fulfill these tasks change, too. Different tasks require different kinds of networks:

- During sales prospecting, it holds true that entrepreneurial networks of weak ties are paramount for identifying and accessing opportunities. LION networks are, therefore, ideal during this initial stage.

- When it comes to winning buy-in across the prospect organization, the rep must focus on understanding the organizational map and who the key influencers are. As discussed earlier, a lot of this information can be gleaned from social networking sites, but ultimately the rep will need to rely on one or a handful of internal customer champions. In terms of network structure, these relationships are characterized by clique networks of strong ties.

- Assembling the dream deal team is very much an exercise of internal networking at the rep's company. The rep needs internal entrepreneurial networks of strong ties with colleagues and solution partners to identify, mobilize, and coordinate the right resources for the account.

- Finally, customer references require external entrepreneurial networks of strong ties not only between account executive and existing customers but also between existing customers and prospects.

In sum, if information matters, then "hole-rich" (that is, with sparse contacts) entrepreneurial networks are ideal; if consistency and coordination matter, dense networks are ideal. Salespeople need both types of networks to close a deal. Generally speaking, the importance of strong ties increases as we advance in the sales process.

There are several different strategies reps can adopt to accommodate the need for multiple network structures. One option is to create multiple profiles. For example, a rep might have two LinkedIn profiles: One is a LION profile for prospecting; the other is a higher-quality exclusive profile for valuable customer and prospect contacts only. A second option is to use different systems for different networks. For instance, a rep might maintain a LION profile on LinkedIn for sales prospecting, use Facebook for personal relationships with high-value customer contacts, and leverage ePeople for networking with coworkers at her company. Lastly, a rep could use advanced identity and relationship management tools, such as Facebook Friend Lists, to segment contacts within a social networking system and treat different connection types differently. (Chapter 10 talks about how to do this.)

CRM—The First Social Network?

In many ways, traditional CRM was an important precursor to many of today's social networking sites. At its most basic level, CRM is a fancy contact database. It is a one-way social networking tool that lets sales reps view "profiles" of their accounts, capture deal information, track performance, communicate with contacts, and share information internally with sales managers and other members of their account team.

The main difference with social networking sites like LinkedIn and Facebook is that these offer bidirectional visibility and interaction. This transforms the sales dynamic into much more of an even-sided partnership (see Table 4.1).

Table 4.1   COMPARISON OF CRM AND MODERN SOCIAL NETWORKING SITE

	CRM ("One-Way Social Networking")	Social Networking Site
How new connections are established	Buy a marketing list, scan trade show badge, or post Web lead form	Either party can initiate, but decision to connect must be mutual.
Where is contact/personal information displayed?	Account, lead, and contact records	Profile page.
Data, updates, and alerts shared with…	Sales team, sales manager	By default, friends and networks but can adjust privacy settings.
Communication mechanisms	E-mail templates, notifications, alerts	Message, Wall Posts, Notes.
Data updated by…	Sales rep or admin only	Bottom-up approach; everyone responsible for updating their own information.

Already, many of the innovations from social networking are making their way into CRM systems, as evidenced by the new deal collaboration features mentioned earlier and the partnership between Facebook and salesforce.com. Next-generation CRM tools will be even more bidirectional between vendors and customers—for example, Salesforce Ideas introduced in Chapter 2, "The Evolution of Digital Media," and Get Satisfaction described in the earlier section, both of which take customer contributions to a user community and capture them directly inside of CRM. By making the customer an active participant in CRM, not only will companies benefit from more accurate data and better engagement, but they will also finally achieve a true 360-degree view of their customers across every touch point—whether it is online, on the phone, presales, mid-deal, post-sales, or beyond.

*"Facebook advertising doesn't feel like advertising
because it comes from your friends."*
—Tim Kendall, Director of Monetization at Facebook

Social Network Marketing

Marketers need to be where their customers and potential customers are, and increasingly, this is on social networking sites. There are hundreds of millions of active users across sites like Facebook, Hi5, and MySpace. 2.6 billion minutes are spent on Facebook each day. Social networking is a rapidly growing global phenomenon sweeping across every continent. According to Alexa, two social networking sites (Facebook and MySpace) are among the top-five trafficked sites in the United States, and four social networking sites (Facebook, MySpace, QQ, and Hi5) are among the top-twenty trafficked sites in the world.

Meanwhile, enhanced distribution on the Internet has resulted in information overload, making it difficult for businesses to differentiate their marketing messages and regular people to find what they're looking for (as we talked about in Chapter 3, "Social Capital from Networking Online"). *Hypertargeting* and social filtering solve this problem. These aspects of online social networking are enabling brands to engage the right people in the right conversation at the right time. They are enabling people to take greater control over their Web experience and use friends to find content that is interesting and important.

Social networks are emerging as a powerful and sophisticated new kind of marketing channel. Marketing is becoming precise, personal, and social: Social networking sites are giving marketers new abilities to hypertarget campaigns using profile information, engage community members by tapping into social capital within friend groups, and systematically cultivate word-of-mouth marketing across their existing customer base. The opportunity for social network marketing can be equally compelling for B2B. Just like anyone else, B2B decision makers have social networking profiles that can be targeted and advertised to. For many products and services, recommendations and referrals from trusted friends and colleagues are important factors in deciding whether to buy.

From the users' perspective, when they log in to a social networking site, many feel they are among friends. The content they see is tailored just for them, and there is a level of implied trust. Social network advertisers are, in effect, given access to a direct, customized portal for each individual audience member. The challenge has been that although advertisers might be catching their audience in a more trusting mind-set, social networking sites thus far have largely been about communication, not purchase intent. It is still an open question of whether high context from friend and profile data will be able to overcome low intent, or whether online social networks will be able to successfully incorporate elements of online marketplaces, search, and product comparison sites (all high intent). This chapter talks through the high-level concepts and possibilities around social network marketing. Chapter 9, "Get Your Message Across," provides the step-by-step guide on how to get started with creating ads and communities.

Hypertargeting

"Half the money I spend on advertising is wasted; the trouble is I don't know which half."
—John Wanamaker, Department Store Merchant

John Wanamaker's famous saying seems to ring as true today as it did a hundred years ago. But especially as budgets are getting squeezed, more and more advertisers are saying enough is enough. As tools and technologies for tracking campaigns have improved, we are seeing a fundamental shift in the online advertising industry toward performance marketing. With the exception perhaps of the biggest brands, advertisers increasingly are willing to pay only for hard-and-fast results.

Hypertargeting (also called *microtargeting*), the ability on social networking sites to target ads based on very specific criteria, is an important step toward precision performance marketing. Facebook and MySpace are leading the charge with sophisticated targeting tools. Their advertisers can target member profiles based on filters like location, gender, age, education, workplace, relationship status, relationship interests, and interest keywords. For example, MySpace members who recently changed their relationship status to "engaged" might be shown ads for wedding planning services.

Here is another example. If your company's product is meant only or mainly for men in California between ages 40 and 55 who are interested in golf, you can for the first time design an ad campaign that gets shown to exactly that profile of person only. In effect, both you and the social network waste fewer ad impressions because the targeting is so precise.

Hypertargeting is possible because of the information social networking members elect to share on their profiles. To establish their presence, express identity, and emotionally connect with friends, people reveal a tremendous amount of demographic and psychographic information. For example, it is standard to share gender, birthday, hometown, employer, college, and high school information, and not unusual to share relationship status, political views, religious beliefs, activities, interests, and favorite music, TV shows, movies, and books. All of this information is fair game for ad hypertargeting. Even if certain information, for example birth year, is hidden based on privacy settings, Facebook and MySpace still use the information for targeting ads. As a result, ad campaigns are reaching a new level of precision and efficiency.

Stop Wasting Ads on People Who Will Never Buy

Prior to social network marketing, advertisers had no choice but to show ads to everyone who visited a Web page they sponsored or searched on a keyword they bought. There was no way to turn ads on for some people and turn them off for others. This was less efficient for both search marketing and display ads because some (at times substantial) portion of the ads paid for were invariably shown to and wasted on the wrong audience — people who weren't the right age, gender, religion, or didn't have the right occupation, marital status, or stated interests to ever be likely to demand your product. With hypertargeting, advertisers can cut out audience segments from their campaigns that are unlikely to buy or have lower probability of buying (equates to lower ad return on investment [ROI]) and focus on probable buyers.

Let's revisit the previous example about reaching male golfers 40 to 55 in California. Before, advertisers had no direct way to access this group. They had to access by proxy, either with brand advertising in men's golf publications or search advertising from California IP addresses on the term "golf." In either case, the targeting is incomplete, imprecise, and expensive: There are still ads wasted while demand is left on the table (see the upcoming section "Cost-Effectively Reach Passive Buyers"). As Figure 5.1 shows, social network hypertargeting lets advertisers minimize the number of wasted ads by going after desired audience segments only.

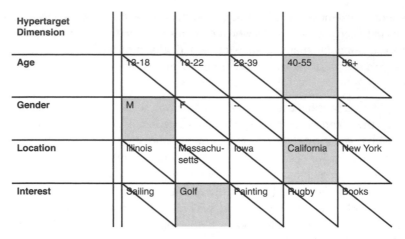

Figure 5.1
It's hard to capture the full power of hypertargeting in this two-dimensional figure, but here is the basic idea. Hypertargeting lets advertisers for the first time specify audience profile, in this case men in California ages 40–55 who mention "golf" in their profile. No ads are wasted on anyone who does not fit all of these criteria.

Tailor Specific Campaigns

Not only can advertisers cut out undesirable audience segments, among the people they do want to target it is now possible to segment and tailor what ads are shown to whom. Before hypertargeting, advertisers had no choice but to show more or less the same ad to everyone. If different ads were shown, it was usually random who got shown what. Hypertargeting makes it possible to run very specific ad campaigns; ad copy can be customized for the exact segment of individuals being targeted. Better tailored, more specific ads, in turn, result in higher clickthrough rates and, ultimately, increased returns on advertising spend.

Social network hypertargeting, therefore, provides a new ability to "think global, act local." Advertisers can use what they know about a particular hypersegment to make ads feel more personal. The advertiser knows the exact demographic and psychographic attributes of the audience because he has chosen them as the hypertargeting criteria. This allows advertisers to make their ads less about the generic features of their product and more about what's important to the person viewing the ad.

Bonobos, Inc., a global online retailer of colorful men's pants, uses hypertargeting to "act local." Its ads on Facebook hypertarget audience segments based on gender, age, and stated interest in a sports team. Bonobos' marketers use knowledge about sports team colors to determine which pant-color style to promote and tailor ad copy. For example, men 18 and older in the United States who have "Red Sox" in their profile are shown the ad in Figure 5.2. As you can see, the main message of the ad is not about Bonobos pants. It's about being a loyal fan and looking good when you attend a Boston Red Sox game at Fenway Park.

Ads like this one have done well because Bonobos is able to tap into the positive feelings and emotional connection sports fans have with their team to sell its pants. Instead of showing the same ad to every male sports fan 18 and older in the United States, Bonobos hypersegments its audience by college and hometown sports teams, and then displays customized ad copy and the right pant color to each audience segment. The result? Higher clickthroughs and higher sales! The case study at the end of this section goes more in-depth into Bonobos' success with advertising on Facebook.

Figure 5.2
Bonobos' ads on Facebook have done well because they appeal specifically to the hypersegment. For example, this ad is meant for Boston Red Sox fans.

Test with Greater Precision

Hypersegmenting also enables greater precision in measuring campaign performance. If an ad campaign fails, did it fail for everyone or only certain audience segments? Advertisers can now get very granular about whom they're showing what ads to, continually test new ads, and experiment with different ways of slicing and dicing their audience. Are males more responsive than females to an ad? Are these ads not working on people under age 20? What about if the image and wording of the ad are altered? Hypertargeting gives advertisers more levers to test and optimize: location, gender, age, education, workplace, relationship status, relationship interests, and interest keywords.

Instead of having to optimize campaigns globally across all audience segments collectively, marketers can hypersegment, test, and iterate to optimize for each individual segment. The ads that Bonobos would develop if it had to show everyone the same ad are not the same as if they can tailor ads for each segment. If advertisers are underperforming with a particular audience segment, they can focus on testing new messages with that segment, or even cut out the segment altogether from their campaigns, without affecting strategy elsewhere. This results in more optimal performance across the entire portfolio of campaigns. There are no more weakest links.

But not only are companies like Bonobos getting valuable feedback about ad campaigns, they are also able to quickly learn which audiences are demanding (or not demanding) their products and services. Demographic and psychographic information on social networking sites are helping companies better understand who their customers are beyond traditional purchase history information as well as prioritize limited resources across audience segments. Are high school students in the Midwest fanatical about clicking on your ads and buying your product? You could inadvertently have tapped into a bigger trend. Why not jump on the opportunity and concentrate your marketing efforts on this niche where you are seeing the greatest return?

The implications of these new insights reach far beyond marketing; they can be used to drive the overall strategy of the business, including decisions around research and development, sales, and operations—such as what kinds of products to develop, which products to push through which channels, and where to locate inventory.

Cost-Effectively Reach Passive Buyers

Search advertising is so effective because it catches people at the moment they are ready to buy. There is high intent, and the timing is right. But investing in search advertising alone can be expensive while leaving money on the table. It's expensive because everyone else also wants to access a high-intent audience; for some keywords like "real estate" and "casino," advertisers have bid up prices upwards of $50 *per click!* Yet money is left on the table because search advertising captures only a small portion of the total number of people you might want to advertise to.

There is value in showing ads to "passive buyers"—that is, people who aren't proactively seeking out your product *per se* but might be interested in buying if encouraged. An offline example of passive buyers is people at the grocery store who make impulse purchases in the checkout aisle—for example, gum, magazines, sodas, or gift cards. People might not have gone to the store expressly to buy the current issue of *US Weekly,* but seeing the item in front of them makes them realize they want it. Similarly, Bonobos might want to show its ads to people even if they haven't gone to Google to search for "colorful men's pants." In fact, the vast majority of people Bonobos has sold pants to probably did not search on Google. They were passive buyers who had latent demand.

Well, how do companies reach passive buyers? Display ads reach everyone, including passive buyers, but they are on the whole even more expensive than search advertising. There is less inventory because they tend to occupy dedicated ad slots. Because there is no targeting of any kind, display ads tend to overshoot, often resulting in wasted ad spend. Not only are some impressions wasted on people unlikely to buy, similar to search advertising (see previous section on this topic), but these ads also suffer from low audience intent. It's a double whammy. For example, a small start-up company like Bonobos might not be able to afford display ads because not enough people would find the ads relevant enough to click on. Traditionally, it only made sense for big brands to adopt the "spray-and-pray" approach of display ads. Fewer of their ads are wasted because they might appeal to a greater percentage of people viewing them.

But even the big brand advertisers are demanding greater precision and better results. For them and other advertisers, hypertargeting might for the first time offer a cost-effective way to reach passive buyers and capture latent interest. By layering key demographic and psychographic filters that correspond to their ideal customer profile, social network advertisers can capture latent demand without wasting ads on the wrong audience segments. They can access passive buyers without spending a fortune (see Figure 5.3).

This is not to say, of course, that social network advertising will displace search engine marketing or display ads. On the contrary, the online social graph will likely be used—is already being used—to make these models better. Both MySpace and Facebook already offer hypertargeted display advertising. It is not unreasonable to expect social networks will try to incorporate search marketing as well sometime in the near future.

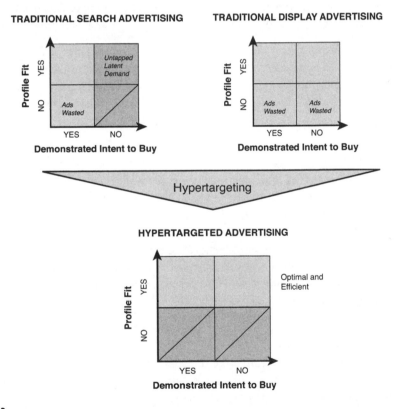

Figure 5.3
Hypertargeting allows advertising precision that can uncover latent interest from passive buyers while minimizing wasted ad impressions. The result is a more optimal and efficient ad campaign.

The following case study describes how Bonobos, Inc., has used hypertargeting on Facebook to achieve impressive sales results.

Bonobos' Success with Hypertargeting on Facebook

Bonobos, Inc., is an innovative men's clothing company started by Brian Spaly and Andy Dunn while they were MBA students at the Stanford Graduate School of Business. Bonobos specializes in fashionable men's pants in colorful styles that are only available online through its Web store. As a start-up company, Bonobos lacked brand awareness and distribution. But creative campaigns run through Facebook Ads helped Bonobos overcome these hurdles and achieve a $2 million sales run rate less than one year after launching the company. According to CEO Dunn, Facebook Ads are the only form of advertising he has seen that is cost-efficient.

Facebook's targeting capabilities have given Bonobos greater control over ad development and optimization. By hypertargeting very specific audience segments by geography, college, and interests, the marketing team is able to quickly tailor, test, and optimize advertising messages while improving traction in new markets.

For example, the month of July is summer in the Northern Hemisphere but winter in the Southern Hemisphere, so Bonobos targeted ads for shorts to American and European audiences, and targeted ads for pants to Australian audiences. Another successful hypertargeted campaign previously mentioned has been around promoting colored pants to fans that match their favorite sports team colors. For instance, ads for Nantucket red pants (the "Capertons") are shown to Facebook profiles in the Boston regional network who have "Red Sox" in their list of interests; ads for orange pants ("Orange Crush") are shown to profiles in the Clemson University network, and so on. Hypertargeting has allowed Bonobos to expand the brand's relevance and sphere of influence by relating to prospective customers in personal ways that are important to them.

Moreover, the flexibility to start ad campaigns at any time of day has allowed Bonobos to successfully launch timely promotions that drive higher clickthrough rates and immediate sales. Returning to the sports team example from earlier, one time-sensitive ad strategy that worked particularly well was messaging pants "perfect for attending baseball games" just as the season was about to begin. Hypertargeted ads and timed ads have driven as much as 10 percent of Bonobos' site traffic volume.

Loyalty and Engagement

Beyond advertising, there is a large opportunity on social networking sites for marketers to engage audiences and build loyalty in ways that weren't possible before. As many before me have said, social media is a commitment, not a campaign.

People participate in social networking sites to express themselves and socialize with their friends. Smart marketers are inserting themselves into these conversations with dynamic and memorable interaction opportunities with their brands. This is happening largely in two ways: communities and "appvertising." Social network communities allow members to identify themselves with your brand, learn more about your brand, and share their interests and opinions. Appvertising is the use of platform applications (usually games) by companies to get social network members engaging with their brands.

Social Network Communities

Online social networking sites provide an ideal medium for engaging with existing customers and building loyalty. Social network communities, such as MySpace groups, Hi5 groups, Facebook groups, and Facebook Pages, can be a great way to supplement or even replace existing stand-alone online communities. Communities on social networking sites have better distribution, feel more personal, and make it easier to reach noncustomers.

Generally speaking, it is just a lot faster, easier, and more sustainable to tap into existing real-world networks and communities than building one from scratch. From a distribution point of view, many if not all the people you are trying to reach are likely already on social networking sites. When someone new becomes interested in engaging with your brand, the barriers to do so on Facebook or MySpace are very low. Instead of having to visit a new Web site and sign up with all their information, people can just go to your community page and join with one click. Very few brands can sign up nearly 200 million of their own registered users. (YouTube, with 100 million, is the only one I can think of that even comes close.) It's very hard to unite people who would otherwise not be connected. Even "cult brands" that do have that capability, including YouTube, Apple, Prius, and the Barack Obama presidential campaign, have created a presence on social networking sites to spread the word and recruit new fans. Why reinvent the wheel?

Second, communities on social networking sites feel more real and more personal. Every post is accompanied by someone's profile picture, name, and what network the person belongs to. Depending on individual privacy settings, you can click on a name and view the person's full profile, send a message, or request to add him as a friend. Because no one is anonymous, people tend to feel more engaged and accountable, and act more responsibly when they participate. On Facebook, you can see which of your friends are members of the community. For people you don't know, you can see who you know in common. Posted videos and photos are tagged of real people. Facebook Events can also be associated with the community, which show who is planning to attend. Social networking sites can help foster a personal, welcoming feel to your community initiatives that would otherwise be difficult to sustain as your community grows. In contrast, many stand-alone online communities fall victim to their own success: As the number of members grows, each individual member feels more anonymous and, therefore, less engaged. By bringing friends and identity to community, social networking sites help brands create a personal experience even inside very large communities that is more meaningful to members.

Third, traditional stand-alone communities have had difficulty reaching noncustomers. Generally, anyone who joins your community is part of a self-selected group who already loves your brand. But they might or might not talk about your brand outside of your isolated community. Few noncustomers likely ever visit your Web site. Social networking sites, however, include everyone, whether they are your brand advocates or have never heard of your product. As we discuss later in the section on social distribution and word-of-mouth marketing, online social networks provide a unique opportunity to use existing customers as a bridge to access noncustomers.

All of these factors contribute to a more engaging experience for community members, usually your biggest fans and best customers. This is important as existing customers are some of your greatest assets. They are why you are in business today and why your business continues to grow tomorrow. They are the easiest and least expensive to sell to; you have already won them over and gotten through the initial, highest hurdle. Most important, customer advocates are the fastest and cheapest way of creating positive brand association and acquiring new customers.

Why do customers participate? It all goes back to people's desire for expressing their identity and socializing with friends. Social networking sites are the ideal place for these brand conversations, as both of these incentives disappear when companies try to encourage the conversations to take place on their stand-alone Web communities. First, in dedicated brand communities people don't feel special anymore. The person is not expressing anything unique about herself by being a customer advocate for Company X because everyone else on Company X's Web site is also a customer advocate. Second, the audience to whom people want to express their identity and socialize are not present in isolated brand communities. Social networking sites give people a semipublic forum surrounded by friends where not everyone has the same interests and affiliations. By becoming a fan of Bonobos' Facebook Page, for example, a Facebook member might be asserting that he stands for attributes of the brand, like fashionable, youthful, and fun. Along with the other information he has included in his profile, this helps the Facebook member communicate his identity to his friends and acquaintances.

Just about all of the online social networks have some sort of group capability, which typically includes four things: basic information (date founded, company Web site, group administrators, number of members), blog, discussion board, and list of members. Facebook and MySpace have the most developed capabilities for brands to establish communities. Beyond this baseline group functionality, these two social networks also allow brands to have profiles that are more customizable and extensible than groups.

What's the difference between the two community types? MySpace brand profiles and Facebook Pages are the official communities for a brand. (Only brand representatives are allowed to create and administer these.) MySpace groups and Facebook groups are unofficial communities that can be started by anyone.

First, let's talk about MySpace, which is famous for helping connect fans with the entertainment industry. For example, musicians like Grammy award-winner T.I. and movies like *X-Men 3* have millions of MySpace Friends. Musicians, comedians, and filmmakers get their own special profile type to help promote their work. But nonentertainment brands are starting to create profiles, too. Just like with bands and celebrities, MySpace members can add company brands as friends, post comments, and participate in discussion forums. Compared with other social networking sites, there is a high degree of customization allowed with HTML and CSS (JavaScript is not permitted for security reasons), including embedding video, music, and Flash content. Jack in the Box, profiled in the following sidebar, is one company that has successfully built a social network community on MySpace.

Jack in the Box on MySpace

Jack in the Box, a popular American fast-food restaurant, has a successful community on MySpace with nearly 140,000 friends. Working with the MySpace advertising team, the restaurant chain created a profile for its fictitious owner and founder character, "Jack," who has a ping pong-ball head and dresses in a business suit (see Figure 5.4).

It is a simple page following the traditional MySpace profile layout and features an entertaining fictional biography. It turns out Jack is married, is from a cattle ranch in Colorado, has one child (Jack Jr.), is 7'2", and is on MySpace "for friends." Hilarious.

Jack has a MySpace Blog. Most entries are short one-line requests asking people to share their thoughts on Jack in the Box. For example, in February 2007, Jack asked, "Will one of you hopeless romantics out there please write a poem about my ultimate cheeseburger?" Over 60 people responded.

continues...

People seem genuinely engaged and enthusiastic about the brand. Several people wished Jack a Merry Christmas. There are comments like "See you next week :)" and "We need you in Tulsa!"

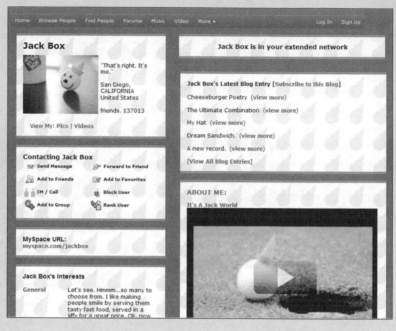

Figure 5.4
In 2006, Jack in the Box created a humorous, sarcastic MySpace profile that has become very popular and successful at engaging over one hundred thousand community members.

Unlike MySpace, Facebook clearly distinguishes between brands and regular members. Instead of profiles, brands establish communities using Facebook Pages. Only the official representative of an artist, business, or organization is allowed to create the Facebook Page for that brand. Rather than becoming friends with a brand as on MySpace, Facebook members can choose to become fans of the brand's Page.

Like MySpace brand profiles, Facebook Pages are designed to be dynamic and media-rich, and also allow HTML, Flash, and embedded applications. They support updates from external blogs and can be promoted with Facebook Ads that take advantage of social distribution, which is covered in the next section.

Facebook groups, on the other hand, are unofficial brand communities started by social network members. How do Facebook groups differ from Facebook Pages? First, groups can be created by any user about any topic. Second, there is little customization allowed in groups; for example, external blogs and platform applications can't be added. Third, there are different communication policies. For groups that have fewer than 5,000 members, group administrators can send messages to all members that will appear in their Inboxes. Page administrators can't do this. (They can send updates to fans that appear in the "Updates" section of the Page.) The final difference is that administrators can restrict access to a group (they can set it up to approve each new member) but not to a Page. Facebook Pages can only be restricted by certain ages and locations.

There is only one officially sanctioned Victoria's Secret community on Facebook (the Victoria's Secret PINK Page) but over 500 unofficial communities that have been formed with groups. Although brands have less control over groups, these unofficial communities are an important and valuable part of the brand experience on social networking sites. Besides their official Page, companies will need to think about groups as part of their overall social network community strategy—for example, when to bridge between Pages and groups, and when to create their own groups.

The sidebar that follows describes the official and unofficial communities Victoria's Secret has on Facebook.

Victoria's Secret PINK

Victoria's Secret, a well-known U.S. retailer of sleepwear and lingerie, has a successful Facebook Page for its PINK line targeting high school and college students. Less than a year after establishing its official community on Facebook, PINK has nearly one million fans who have collectively posted tens of thousands of wall posts, videos, photos, and discussion forum messages.

Any Facebook member can become a fan of the PINK Page. Members can post photos, access events, and participate in the discussion forum and wall. PINK then appears under the "Pages" section in the user's profile, and as an ad (if ads have been purchased) or social story in the News Feed when friends log in.

Victoria's Secret advertises PINK through MySpace and Facebook, as well as partnerships with MTV and youth-oriented blogs. According to those who follow the industry, the PINK brand seems to be the fastest-growing line launched in the history of the company.

But Victoria's Secret brand presence and influence doesn't end there. Besides the officially sanctioned PINK Page, there are also over 500 user-created groups dedicated to Victoria's Secret, including over 300 dedicated to the PINK line. There are groups such as *"Obsessed with PINK* by victoria's secret," "I'm addicted to Victoria's secret PINK, But damnit make some bigger bra's!"* and *"Victoria's Secret PINK—at USC!!"* They groups range from having a few members to tens of thousands of members, and play an important role in influencing how people engage with the Victoria's Secret brand on Facebook. In fact, a few dozen of these groups were started in response to an official contest announced on the PINK Page challenging college women to nominate their school to be part of the PINK Collegiate Collection, special-edition styles branded with school colors and logos.

Of course, I created a Facebook Page for this book (see Figure 5.5), where I am posting updates and book events, sharing links, engaging the community in conversation around social networking-related topics, and collecting feedback for the next edition.

Figure 5.5
The Facebook Era *community on Facebook. Become a fan today! www.facebook.com/ thefacebookera.*

In addition to Pages and groups, Facebook also offers what they call "engagement ads," which offer brands opportunities to integrate into other aspects of the Facebook experi- ence—including video commenting, sponsored virtual gifts, in-line event RSVP, and in- line becoming a fan. Chapter 9 provides an overview of what engagement ads are and how they are being used by brands.

For companies that already have stand-alone online communities outside of social net- working sites, the Facebook Connect and Google Friend Connect APIs described in Chapter 2, "The Evolution of Digital Media," might be appealing options for creating bridges to social network communities to take advantage of the loyalty and engagement possibilities outlined in this section.

Brand Appvertising

In addition to ads and communities, social network marketers are also using platform apps to get people engaging with their brands. An increasing amount of time people spend on social networking sites is on using platform apps like games, slideshows, and polls. Naturally, advertisers want to get involved. Apps have another advantage: They tend to be more active and engaging than ad clicks and impressions. Facebook is even considering offering its own branded apps as ad units.

The majority of applications on social network platforms are now branded in some way. As a marketer, you have three options when it comes to platform apps: Build it yourself, commission someone to build it for you, or sponsor an existing app. Very few companies have the right expertise in-house to build these kinds of apps. Widget developers like Buddy Media, Context Optional, and All Widgets provide custom-branded application-building services. For example, Anheuser-Busch commissioned Buddy Media to develop a Facebook application for its Bud Light party cruise so participants could see who else would be on the ship, share photos, and stay in touch afterward. Launch a Package, another custom app, was built for FedEx.

Despite some successes with custom-developed applications, most companies are finding it extremely difficult to know what kinds of apps will take off and are opting instead to sponsor apps that have already proven to be popular with social network members. The leading social network application developers profiled in Chapter 2, including Slide, RockYou, and Zynga, all offer brand advertising slots "for rent" on their apps. Other leaders in this space, like Gigya, Offerpal Media, Widgetbox, and KickApps, act more as middle-man ad networks that connect app developers with advertisers. For example, Gap, Inc., reached nearly seven million users in one month by temporarily sponsoring virtual campaign buttons in RockYou's Pieces of Flair app during the U.S. presidential election. Lookery is another company that used to provide an ad network but now focuses on providing user data-targeting services for advertisers.

Zynga's Texas HoldEm Poker game on Facebook, which has over seven million active users, is another application brands like to sponsor (see Figure 5.6). Facebook members can complete special offers, such as signing up for a free trial of Netflix or joining Jamster's Mobile Content Club, in exchange for virtual poker chips to use in the game.

Figure 5.6
Zynga's Texas HoldEm Poker app lets players earn poker chips by completing special offers from sponsors like Netflix, Free Scholarships for School, the Columbia House DVD Club, and Jamster Ringtones.

Social Distribution

Hypertargeted ads, engagement communities, and branded apps are tremendous innovations—but they become even more powerful when you combine them with social distribution. Especially in today's crowded marketplace—the average American is exposed to over 3,000 advertising messages *each day*—social distribution from customer to customer rather than from vendor to customer is by far the most affordable and effective way for brands to stand out.

Among the social networks, Facebook has been the clear leader in social distribution. Facebook News Feeds, which broadcast members' recent activity to all of their friends, have transformed how messages spread by automating social distribution of information. What would have been isolated incidents before become highly publicized updates on Facebook. The new mantra is don't advertise *to* people, advertise *between* people. Recommendations and referrals from known and trusted friends can be powerful influencers of purchase decisions.

In the preceding chapter, we talked about how trust in sales is transitive. So are brand attention, enthusiasm, and loyalty. Customer X pays attention to and likes your product. Prospect Y pays attention to and likes Customer X. All of a sudden, without you really having a say, you might find that Prospect Y also pays attention to and likes your product! The transitiveness was there all along, but it was harder for Prospect Y to track what Customer X was up to. Facebook News Feeds provide the channel to let people find out and engage.

This section outlines five aspects of social distribution: passive word of mouth, social ads, viral marketing, reaching new audiences, and social shopping.

Passive Word of Mouth

Due to transitive trust and decentralized distribution, word of mouth is the most-effective and least-expensive kind of marketing that exists. To the recipients of such marketing, it feels less like spam if the endorsement is coming from someone they know. For the referrers, providing a recommendation can be a gratifying experience that allows them to provide value, express themselves, and connect with their friends. But prior to online social networks, word-of-mouth marketing was a proactive, inefficient endeavor. People had to really love your product to construct and deliver a message about it. There was a high bar for what kinds of products got talked about—most products weren't so lucky. Even when someone did talk about your product, she might not have told very many people.

Facebook Friend updates have made word-of-mouth marketing easy, thoughtless, and automatic. Every time anyone on Facebook updates a status message, writes on a wall, sends or receives a gift, RSVPs for an event, makes a comment, becomes a fan, or plays a branded game, *people find out*. This dramatically increases advertisers' return on appvertising and community initiatives. For every one person advertisers engage, dozens more can become engaged, and the effect cascades.

To do research for this chapter, I became a fan of Victoria's Secret PINK Page. Without my having to do anything or Victoria's Secret having to do anything, my friends were notified in their News Feed that I had become a fan (see Figure 5.7). Anyone who visited my profile could see this information as well (see Figure 5.8). The same thing happened when I installed the Texas HoldEm Poker app from Zynga. Instead of requiring me to provide a proactive update or endorsement, Facebook enables word of mouth to be passive.

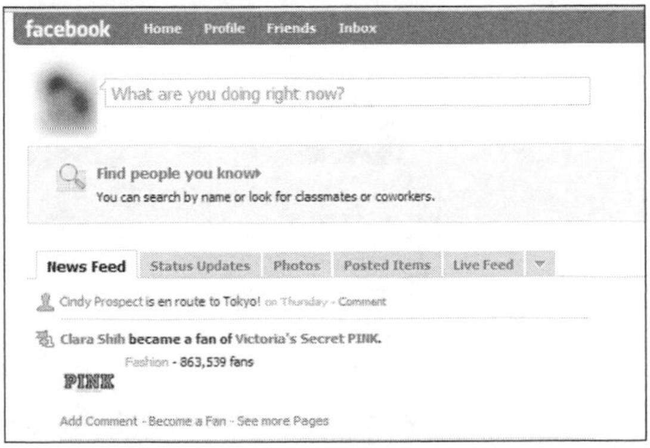

Figure 5.7
My friends received a notification in their News Feed when I became a fan of Victoria's Secret PINK Page.

![Facebook profile screenshot of Clara Shih showing Wall, Info, Photos, Books, Boxes tabs. The wall shows "Clara became a fan of Victoria's Secret PINK. Fashion - 863,541 fans - Become a Fan" with a PINK logo.]

Figure 5.8
Anyone who views my profile can see that I became a fan of Victoria's Secret PINK Page.

Social Ads

In the previous examples, Zynga and Victoria's Secret both benefited from free passive word of mouth, but the effect was temporary. My friends get notified only when I initially install the app, play a game, or become a fan. Although the *update* is passive on my part, to generate the update there needs to be an underlying action I have taken.

Social ads extend the life of these passive word-of-mouth messages by "reusing" fan information again and again to make ads more compelling. Essentially, Facebook members who are fans of a Page are used by the advertising system as "passive endorsers" for the brand (see Figure 5.9). By associating an ad with a Facebook member, brands can, in effect, tap into the social capital between friends to win attention and engagement from new audiences.

Figure 5.9
A social ad from Bonobos.

Advertisers can specify whether they want a particular ad to be social during the campaign setup process. From the perspective of Facebook members, every time they become a fan of a Page, they are implicitly providing consent to allow their name and image to be used to endorse the brand.

The Facebook analytics team has an incredible amount of data about which members have the most influence and result in the most ad clickthroughs. For example, they found that endorsements from women carry more weight with men. The advertising system incorporates a lot of this data to determine which of a Page's fans to use to endorse to whom.

Going beyond passive endorsements, a start-up company named Zuberance is helping brands encourage *active* endorsements by customers. Zuberance has developed a customer referral and incentive management system that allows companies to provide rewards, such as coupons and discounts, for customer-generated leads.

Viral Marketing

Viral distribution is the Holy Grail for many marketers, but it can be extraordinarily difficult to achieve. What makes campaigns viral? Viral campaigns have three components: the message, the medium, and the delivery. First and foremost, the message has to be sticky. In their breakthrough book, *Made to Stick,* authors Dan Heath and Chip Heath outline six principles that explain why some ideas get passed on while others don't: simplicity, unexpectedness, concreteness, credibility, emotions, and stories.

Viral mediums, usually video clips, images, games, software, or even just text, can help explain the idea. For example, if pictures are worth a thousand words, communicating a message through image or video might help make it more simple and concrete while telling a story and evoking emotion.

The delivery is critical, too. Traditionally, popular delivery vehicles include e-mail, instant message, SMS, and phone. The ease of sending and viewing messages and the pervasiveness of the delivery technology can make or break a viral campaign. For example, you would not get very far disseminating a message by fax in a country where most people don't have fax machines—it wouldn't matter that you had a sticky idea. Delivery is where Facebook excels.

Virality depends on network effects, and social networking sites amplify network effects. Online social networking offers an ideal communication environment for sending and receiving viral messages. There are four reasons, explained in the following list—widespread adoption, broadcast format, connections across networks, and longer message life:

- *Widespread adoption.* Like phone, e-mail, and SMS, social networking sites are widely adopted around the world. The nearly 200 million people on Facebook, for example, are a sizable audience for marketers to pursue.

- *Broadcast format.* Instead of being limited to one-to-one (as with most phone calls and SMS messages) or one-to-few (as with most e-mails), social network status messages and wall posts are one-to-many. Broadcasts are also automatic, so messages can be disseminated even when the sender doesn't specify recipients.

- *Connections across networks.* By supporting entrepreneurial networks (as discussed in Chapter 3), online social networking members are likely to have weak ties that bridge across different networks. This is critical for virality—otherwise messages get "stuck" within the same clique groups.

- *Longer message life.* Because Facebook walls capture and display historical information, messages have longer lives and, therefore, additional opportunities to be picked up by others.

For example, the Barack Obama presidential campaign of 2008 brilliantly used social networking sites to deliver its messages to tens of millions of people across the United States. The *messages* were "Hope" and "Change we can believe in." The *mediums* were the "HOPE" poster, official Barack Obama Web site (containing policy papers, blogs, tax savings calculator, event information, and so on), and videos.

Appealing to the right *people* is also very important. In *The Tipping Point*, Malcolm Gladwell describes viral campaigns as "social epidemics" driven by three key kinds of people—*connectors, mavens,* and *salesmen.* The following sidebar explores how online social networking affects each of these personality types.

Magnifying and Accelerating Social Epidemics

According to Gladwell, products and messages spread like viruses across social networks, helped by three kinds of people—connectors, mavens, and salesmen—each with a very particular and rare set of social skills. It is, of course, every marketer's dream for her products to hit a tipping point and become wildly successful in the market.

By offering new tools and channels for connectors, mavens, and salesmen, social networking sites are magnifying and accelerating social epidemics.

- *Connectors.* Connectors are the natural networkers who seem to know just about everyone, maintaining many more times the number of relationships than the average person. Because of their ability to spread messages to a large number of people quickly, connectors are crucial for enabling social epidemics. By supporting weak ties (as discussed in Chapter 3), social networking sites allow connectors to maintain larger networks. Passive word of mouth then helps connectors disseminate messages across their vast networks.

- *Mavens.* Mavens, also called early adopters, are information specialists, such as hobbyists, enthusiasts, and experts who are typically the first to discover new products. People trust and act on mavens' opinions, so smart marketers will engage with mavens as a way to "influence the influencers." Social networking sites then offer an ideal environment for mavens' ideas, opinions, and recommendations. The distribution of these ideas is multiplied when they propagate to connectors in the maven's network.

- *Salesmen.* Salesmen, or influencers, are charismatic persuaders who are able to win others over to their point of view. Whatever the message or their expertise in the product area, they have a certain ability to influence strangers and pass on messages. Social networking sites provide salesmen with means of actively propagating their opinions, such as using Facebook messages, status messages, and wall posts.

Reaching New Audiences

Because you lack brand awareness and traction from an existing customer base, it is very difficult to enter new markets. Not only can it be prohibitively expensive, but it is also impossible to know which new market is the right or best one to go after.

Word of mouth that happens across social networks makes reaching new audiences possible and cost efficient for the first time. As we talked about in Chapter 3, online social networking encourages entrepreneurial networks by offering casual interaction modes and the ability to support a greater number of weak ties. This is good news for marketers. Entrepreneurial networks can help brands build bridges from existing audiences to new ones.

By tapping the existing connections between individuals that cut across different homogeneous networks like region, age, and industry, companies are able to extend their spheres of influence to new, sometimes unexpected markets and reach new pockets of people. For example, Facebook and MySpace helped Barack Obama's campaign recruit unlikely supporters among low-wage, blue-collar workers in Harrison County, Indiana—historically a very Republican region of the country. Obama's advertisements weren't working there. Some campaign staffers wanted to write off this part of the state entirely. But Obama supporters belonging to other networks tapped their ties to individuals in this group and won some impressive support. A few dozen Harrison County residents ended up volunteering for national phone-banking efforts and contributing to the campaign, and Obama narrowly won Indiana in the general election.

Social Shopping and Recommendations

But the possibilities don't end with social ads and brand recommendations. The future of shopping will be social. Already, social network members are starting to engage with specific products and services through virtual gifts, friend recommendations, and e-commerce.

MyListo is an innovator in the branded virtual gift space. Facebook has had virtual gifts for a few years, but most are made-up graphics. MyListo focuses on virtual gifts corresponding to *real products,* like cars, jewelry, and electronics. People find out what their friends want and can send virtual gifts of those things (see Figure 5.10). For some high-end luxury items, like virtual Tiffany's earrings or a virtual Maserati convertible, people are even willing to pay real money to gift those items. Brands, too, can pay for placement of their products, similar to how brands sponsor Facebook gifts today. By encouraging people to engage virtually with real products they want, MyListo cultivates people's desire for these products, increases the chances that people will ultimately decide to buy, and accelerates the buying process. Because the app is social, it also creates an opportunity for friends to purchase the product as a gift, or come to desire the product for themselves.

Figure 5.10
MyListo allows people to engage with products by sending, requesting, and receiving virtual gifts corresponding to real products they want in the offline world.

Another Facebook application, Questa, lets people request and provide trusted recommendations on different kinds of products and services (see Figure 5.11). Questa layers the social graph on top of traditional online product reviews, pioneered by sites like CNET, Epinions, and Amazon.com, to bring transitive trust to shopping. For example, if you are looking to buy an electric toothbrush, you can ask your friends about their experiences with different electric toothbrush products and brands.

Other popular product review applications, such as Books iRead, BrewSocial, and My Camera Gear, focus on providing reviews in specific product categories (books, beer, and camera equipment, respectively).

Figure 5.11
Questa lets Facebook members ask their friends for recommendations on products and services.

Some companies are even hoping to close the deal while the customer is still on the social networking site. For example, Pizza Hut has a Facebook application that allows people to place orders for takeout or delivery without leaving the Facebook Web site. The app automatically figures out which Pizza Hut location is closest to the delivery address and routes the order there. Information about orders placed then gets broadcast to friends via News Feed as well as the person's profile page.

Challenges and Limitations

Of course, we are still in the early days of social network marketing. There are tremendous opportunities and possibilities but also serious challenges and limitations. Yes, Facebook advertising is precise, personal, and social—but so what? Some progress has been made but poor brand fit, poor performance, social network fatigue, nonstandard ad formats, adjacency, and negative buzz continue to be real problems that need to be considered and addressed.

Poor Brand Fit

In many situations, social network marketing doesn't make sense because people don't want to broadcast their affinity for your product. For the most part, it depends on two factors: the product and the site demographic. Certain product and brand categories, such as sports, recreation, politics, movies, books, food, clothing, and celebrities, are ideal because they evoke passion and are used by individuals to express themselves. Products that might be less exciting, more commoditized, embarrassing, and either too personal or too impersonal, such as laundry detergent, tax filing services, medication, and office supplies, are usually not a good fit. Similarly, luxury items such as high-end cars or jewelry might feel like bragging to many people. As a company considering a presence on social networking sites, the best thing you can do is guide your brand in a direction that is exciting but credible. Position your product to stand for something, and customers will want to stand behind it.

Poor Performance

There have been a few runaway viral hits with social network marketing, such as Gap, Inc.'s, experience with Pieces of Flair and T.I.'s MySpace profile, but there have also been a lot of poor-performing campaigns and unmet expectations. No one has figured out the perfect formula yet for overcoming low purchase intent on social networking sites. The best advice is to start small and simple and set realistic expectations. Just like slapping up a Web site and buying AdWords doesn't automatically transform businesses into a success, effective social network marketing requires strategy, testing, and iteration.

Social Network Fatigue

One concern people have about social network marketing is that people are starting to tire of Facebook, MySpace, and LinkedIn. Only time will tell whether people continue to sign up and log in once the novelty wears off.

There is also fatigue around social ads. Some social network members are already beginning to complain that the sites feel too commercial. One danger is that people could get turned off if their experience on social networking sites becomes too inundated with ads and stops being about them and their friends. The social networks will need to balance their monetization efforts against keeping people happy and engaged.

Nonstandard Ad Formats

Because advertising on social networking sites is still so new, no clear standards have emerged yet around ad formats and metrics. A good portion of the over ten billion dollars or so spent each year on online advertising is sold through the large Madison Avenue agencies, which for the most part really have not standardized and are not pushing ad units around Facebook, MySpace, or any of the other social networking sites.

Part of the problem is there hasn't been huge demand because businesses that advertise are still uncomfortable with the new metrics around social network advertising. Because users spend so much time on social networking sites, there are a lot of impressions and some clicks, but these are not necessarily translating to sales at the same rate as traditional online ads. The ambiguity has made many traditional businesses hesitant to buy large ad volumes because they are unsure of how exactly to value social network ads.

But industry pundits aren't concerned. When Google AdWords launched in 1999, it too was a new, nonstandard format not promoted, supported, or understood by the big ad agencies. As the AdWords model proved its effectiveness and gained critical mass over time, it became the new industry standard—in fact, the most successful ever in online advertising history.

The Adjacency Problem

One challenge advertisers face with any type of social media is adjacent placement to questionable user-generated content, such as a sexually explicit MySpace profile page. For example, a brand might not want to be associated with a particular political group or controversial celebrity. The social networks are starting to explore ways to give advertisers more control over where their ads appear. For example, Facebook allows advertisers in the U.K. to opt out of placement next to all groups.

Negative Buzz

The risk in empowering users to define and spread brand messages is that these messages might not always be positive, and brands might have very little control over the aftermath. Many believe the 2005 movie *King Kong* failed to meet expectations at the box office because negative word of mouth that it was "too long, too loud, and overdone" caused many people to not even give it a chance. The Segway scooter is another example of a product that generated a lot of buzz from word of mouth, but it was mostly negative. A reputation of being "funny looking" and "dangerous on sidewalks" did not help sales.

That said, people are having brand conversations whether you are even aware, as evidenced by the over 500 unofficial Victoria's Secret groups on Facebook. Better try to facilitate where it makes sense, reward and provide channels for your advocates, and address feedback from the community than not.

Comcast, a national provider of cable television and Internet services, has experienced this firsthand. Company executives one day discovered to their horror a Facebook group dedicated to negative rants about the Comcast service, "I bet I can find 200,000 people who hate COMCAST!" started by a disgruntled customer (see Figure 5.12). A company executive promptly posted to the wall to try to steer the group in a constructive direction by humbly welcoming feedback and inviting people to engage. As Comcast realized, user buzz about your product, even when it is negative, can be viewed as an opportunity rather than a threat.

Figure 5.12
People will form communities and talk about your product whether you like it or not. Sometimes, the word of mouth is negative. Rather than ignore the problem, Comcast executives decided to try engaging with the "Comcast, We Hate You" community on Facebook and redirect the group toward a more constructive outcome.

In our age of information and transparency, people will talk about your product regardless. The only difference when these conversations occur on social networking sites is that brands gain visibility and have the chance to respond. Instead of turning a blind eye, companies should welcome and respond to feedback from the community. Ultimately, this is real and valuable feedback that could improve your product or service in ways you might never have thought of yourself.

6

"Social networking is becoming social innovation. A new mode of invention and production is in the making."—
Don Tapscott, coauthor Wikinomics

Social Innovation

Innovation—the introduction of a new and useful method, process, product, or service—is the lifeblood of business and, indeed, of civilization. Innovation comes in many forms. This chapter focuses on product innovation, though the ideas presented here can be applied to other kinds of innovation.

There are, roughly speaking, four stages of innovation: generating concepts, prototyping, commercial implementation, followed by continual iteration (see Figure 6.1). Although these are by no means clear-cut or necessarily sequential, most innovations in history have more or less followed this process.

Every stage is an intensely social process between inventors, collaborators, customers, business partners, critics, and others. Therefore, in many ways, innovation is ideally suited for online social networking. In particular, online social engagement transforms the relationship between companies and customers from one-sided "build it and hope they come" to a true partnership model. Armed with information about customers and what they want, companies can feel more empowered to go after new markets. Because their ideas are heard, customers feel more accountable for providing input and more grateful when that input is incorporated in the design of new products. It is a win-win for companies and their customers.

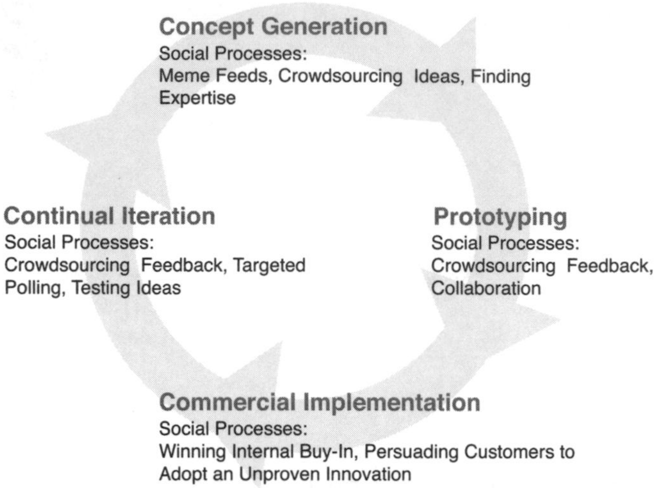

Concept Generation
Social Processes:
Meme Feeds, Crowdsourcing Ideas, Finding
Expertise

Continual Iteration
Social Processes:
Crowdsourcing Feedback, Targeted
Polling, Testing Ideas

Prototyping
Social Processes:
Crowdsourcing Feedback,
Collaboration

Commercial Implementation
Social Processes:
Winning Internal Buy-In, Persuading Customers to
Adopt an Unproven Innovation

Figure 6.1
The cycle of innovation typically follows four stages, each of which contains multiple social processes: concept generation, prototyping, commercial implementation, and continual iteration.

Concept Generation

The first stage in innovation involves creative brainstorming of new ideas and then for-mulation into concepts. Traditionally, ideas have come from designated people within the company, usually product managers. The approach is generally driven from the top down by the company, rather than from the bottom up (from the customer and employee base). Because there just isn't the time or the right tools in place, customer input tends to be more serendipitous than systematic and typically ends up heavily biased toward feed-back from the largest, most vocal customers.

Online social networking turns this traditional approach on its head. By connecting prod-uct managers more closely with internal and external communities, the online social graph facilitates three important bottom-up processes in concept generation: inspiration, ideation, and expertise discovery.

Getting Inspired from Meme Feeds

Sometimes, all it takes to come up with a killer concept is a little inspiration. Talking to customers is a good way to get inspired. Sometimes it is an article that was forwarded to you, something you saw in a movie, or an interesting tidbit you overheard in the hallway that reminds you of something, makes you think about something you wouldn't have otherwise thought about, or helps you see things in a new light.

At the heart of these ideas, thoughts, and tidbits that inspire us are **memes**, a term Richard Dawkins coined in his 1976 book, *The Selfish Gene,* to describe the unit of information representing a basic idea that can be transferred from one individual to another. Dawkins applied evolutionary principles around how viruses propagate and mutate to explain the spread of ideas and cultural phenomena.

How can product managers expose themselves to the right memes to become inspired without feeling overwhelmed?

It's important to have access to both external and internal meme feeds. For external memes, people use Twitter tweets and Facebook status messages to share what they are thinking about, what they are doing, how they are doing, and other memes. It is a blank slate: *"Jill is…"* Jill can type in whatever she wants, and it will get broadcast to her network. Twitter and Facebook feeds have generally done a good job of helping people "digest" the stream of memes that continually flows in from friends. By investing in building out entrepreneurial networks on social networking sites that cut across different homogeneous networks, product managers can increase the chances they will be exposed to radically new thinking.

Product managers can also use Twitter's search to find out what *everyone* on Twitter has said about something. For example, because I'm in charge of product management for the AppExchange at salesforce.com, I looked up "AppExchange" on http://search.twitter.com. There were hundreds of tweets (see Figure 6.2).

Figure 6.2
Twitter search on the term "AppExchange."

External memes are generally good at helping product managers identify problems. Internal memes are often good at helping them find solutions. Other employees are an ideal source of memes. They are probably thinking about a lot of the same problems or at least related problems, often from a slightly different angle, and how to solve them—not to mention, your colleagues share your goal of making the company successful. Memes spread every day in meetings, at the water cooler, and in e-mails that get forwarded to certain distribution lists. Unfortunately, with everything else going on in an organization, the ability for memes to be transmitted isn't as great as it should be. Especially as organizations get bigger, it becomes increasingly difficult to pass memes on. One reason start-up companies are so effective at getting inspired and coming up with new concepts is it is easier to brainstorm and share thoughts with the whole team.

Of course, not everyone has something breakthrough to say all the time, so rarely is having everyone hang out at the water cooler efficient or feasible. Nor does everyone care about what everyone else has to say, so e-mailing the entire company every time someone has an idea is too distracting and disruptive.

Yammer is a meme broadcast tool for individual company networks. It's like Twitter for business. Yammer aims to make organizations more productive through the exchange of short, frequently updated answers to one simple question: "What are you working on?" Any employee who has a working e-mail address in the company's domain (that is, ending in @*companyname.com*) can join and start posting on the company's Yammer page. Colleagues can then discuss ideas, ask questions, post news, and share links.

Unlike an e-mail blast, it is noninvasive. Employees visit Yammer when they have a free moment and have something to say or want to see what other people are saying. Unlike Facebook or Twitter, all the memes are related to work and are visible only to other employees. Some of the memes might be silly or not readily applicable, but at minimum allows the employee to feel better connected to her coworkers and every so often might provide just the right meme for her to make progress on an idea (see Figure 6.3).

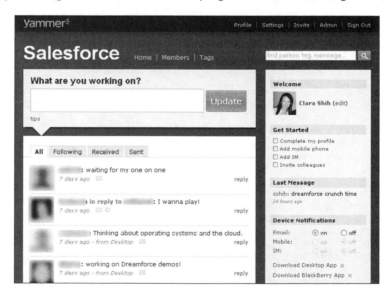

Figure 6.3
Yammer is a status broadcasting tool that allows employees of the same company to answer and view colleagues' answers to a simple question: "What are you working on?" This is salesforce.com's Yammer page.

Crowdsourcing Ideation

In addition to providing us with inspiration, other people are a wonderful source of good ideas. We introduced the notion of *crowdsourcing* in Chapter 4, "Social Sales," in the context of customer support. Product managers can also use crowdsourcing techniques to generate ideas from the community for their products.

Depending on the product and competitive situation, it might make sense to engage with internal communities, external communities, or both. The advantage of internal communities is that your colleagues are often the people with the greatest expertise about your product or service because they live, work, and think about it every day. There could also be a confidentiality advantage if you are concerned about competitors copying your ideas and even beating you to market. The advantages of external communities are that customers and partners can bring new, often more realistic perspectives about your product, not to mention they will feel more engaged, grateful, and loyal that you value their input and are willing to be transparent. In many situations, it makes sense to engage with both kinds of communities but about different topics.

Very few product managers have time to interact regularly with every customer on a one-to-one basis. Crowdsourcing enables one-to-many conversations between the product manager and the community. Here is how it works:

1. *Establish an ideation forum.* The product manager or an online community manager sets up a forum for ideas to be solicited, generated, and collected.

2. *Seed the conversation.* To get things going, the product manager might need to post some initial ideas or ask open-ended questions that get community members to participate. Some product managers have even launched contests for user-generated product ideas to generate a better response.

3. *Encourage customers to interact with one another.* By setting up a strong system of trust, identity, and recognition, product managers can, in effect, encourage participation. A lot of the best ideas will come out of this process whereby customers are sharing their ideas and opinions with one another, and the product manager is in the backseat listening.

4. *Act on results.* When a good idea is suggested, the product manager might want to intervene and ask the community to develop it further. When it is sufficiently developed, it might be time to take the idea and start prototyping.

5. *Reach out to key contributors.* In most communities, a handful of members are the most active and vocal with their ideas and opinions. These are often the mavens or early adopters we talked about in the preceding chapter. Product managers should engage in more in-depth conversations with these individuals to dig deeper and gain even more insights.

Online communities have been around for some time and are starting to be used for ideation. What makes social network communities different? As we discussed in the previous chapter, the online social graph helps involve new audiences and improve the quality of community interaction. Because they are among friends and no one is anonymous, people feel more engaged, more at ease, and more accountable for what they say when they are logged in and participating on a MySpace profile, Hi5 group, or Facebook Page.

As powerful as social network communities are for encouraging customer brand conversations, they can be a lot of work to manage when used for ideation. Unlike marketing, involving customers in the innovation process is not just about making them feel engaged. There is a concrete end goal to find the best ideas and act on them. Often, the hardest part is making sense of the tremendous amount of ideas that can be generated. For product managers, it can be like finding a needle in a haystack.

Tools are being developed to help product managers aggregate, summarize, analyze, and prioritize community feedback. The MyStarbucksIdea for Facebook application (built with Salesforce Ideas) profiled in Chapter 2, "The Evolution of Digital Media," is one example. Instead of having customers post free-form ideas, Starbucks community managers have created structured categories for classifying different ideas. Customers are encouraged to vote and comment on existing ideas; only if they have a truly unique idea that doesn't already exist should they post it. Moreover, every time community members post an idea, vote, or comment, the action is tracked inside the back-end CRM system so that product managers can close the loop if and when the idea becomes implemented.

By providing categories and tying participation back to CRM, Salesforce Ideas attempts to bring structure and analytics to traditionally unstructured user-generated content, making it easier for product managers to sort through the best ideas, take action on them, and even continue to track them through product development, marketing, and sales.

Dell Computer is also using the Salesforce Ideas application to crowdsource ideation. In its first year, Dell's ideation community, IdeaStorm, generated over 10,000 new ideas and half a million votes from the community. These ideas have caused the company to rethink its strategy and go in new, unexpected directions. For example, nearly 100,000 Dell customers rallied together on IdeaStorm to urge the company to include support for the Linux operating system in its hardware—something company product managers had once considered but didn't think the market would demand. Thanks to IdeaStorm, this request got the attention of the Dell product management team, which has been able to accommodate the request and provide a better experience for customers. Dell is also using Salesforce Ideas internally to get suggestions from employees on how to make the company a better place to work and advance their careers.

Finding Answers and Expertise

Beyond inspiration and ideation, concept generation requires finding the right expertise within your company needed to finish baking half-baked concepts. Often, product managers will have a general sense for what areas they want to focus on or what problems to solve but not know where to begin or how to make progress on an abstract concept.

Traditionally, people relied on tacit, anecdotal knowledge about who knows what and who used to work where to track down internal expertise. This is extremely difficult, however, in organizations that are larger, geographically dispersed, or have high employee turnover—the trend most companies are headed in. Also, the desired expertise often lies across organizational and functional boundaries where tacit knowledge and regular communication links are weakest.

Online social networking offers an easier, more systematic way to find experts and knowledge. Public social networking sites like Facebook and LinkedIn are helpful for finding external expertise. Corporate social networking solutions, such as Connectbeam and IBM's Lotus Connections, are ideal for locating internal expertise.

On Facebook and especially LinkedIn, member profiles typically include past employers and roles, projects, and areas of interest and expertise. Using these social networking sites allows product managers to tap not only among their direct connections and coworkers but also friends of friends and extended networks.

How does it work? At the most basic level, you can perform a search for people on social networking sites. Both LinkedIn and Facebook allow you to search based on name, title, location, and keywords.

In addition to people, you can also find answers. LinkedIn Answers is a free service that allows members of LinkedIn to ask and answer professional questions of their networks. For example, here are a few recent questions posted by people in my network:

- *"Attention Flash Developers: What books do you recommend for learning ActionScript? I'm currently using Flash 8."*

- *"Are you aware of company policies which address quota relief for sales reps on maternity leave?"*

- *"Are there any CPC ad marketplaces or aggregators (not tags or feeds)?"*

Community members are motivated to provide answers because doing so builds up their expertise reputation on LinkedIn, which comes in handy when and if they are looking for a new job or project (see Figure 6.4). If they know you personally, answering your question also builds their social capital with you.

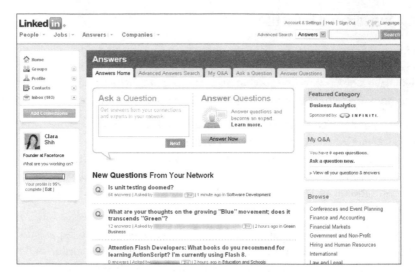

Figure 6.4

LinkedIn Answers allows LinkedIn community members to post professional questions to their networks. People who answer questions can build their reputation by earning points for expertise in the question's category.

In addition to encouraging employees to use public social networking sites to track down external expertise, companies are also beginning to invest in internal knowledge and expertise management tools such as Connectbeam and IBM's Lotus Connections.

Connectbeam builds expertise profiles on every employee based on projects they have worked on, articles they have bookmarked, and information they have posted to enterprise wikis, blogs, and other systems. Product managers can use Connectbeam to search for subject matter experts in the company. In addition, Connectbeam also proactively recommends colleagues with whom to network based on similar expertise, projects, and interests (see Figure 6.5).

Online social networking is helping product managers be more efficient and effective at locating the internal and external resources needed to make progress on their ideas. In particular, expertise discovery solutions like Connectbeam help minimize redundant efforts within companies and allow product managers to leverage past related work done in a particular area of interest.

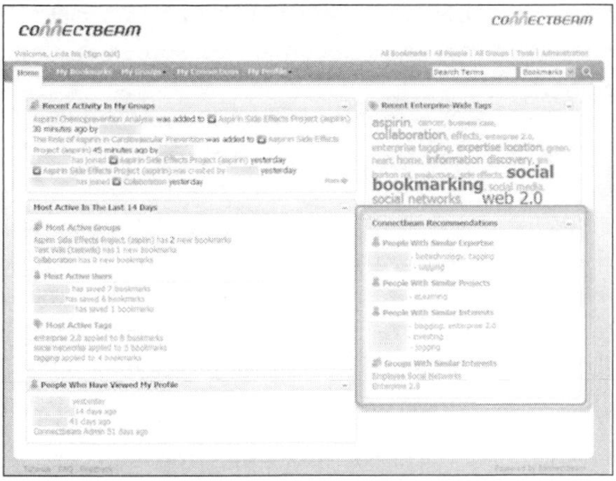

Figure 6.5
Connectbeam is a popular enterprise social networking solution that specializes in expertise discovery.

Prototyping

Prototyping—that is, the rapid development, testing, and iteration of products before a commercial version is created and released to the mass market—is a critical step in the innovation process. In many ways, prototyping is largely composed of concept generation and iteration, which are covered in separate sections in this chapter. Prototyping also requires collaboration and feedback channels.

Collaboration

Successful collaboration is built on trust and mutual commitment. As we discussed in Chapter 3, "Social Capital from Networking Online," social networking sites allow individuals to build better rapport and can, therefore, contribute to a more trusting and satisfying team environment. In particular, three aspects of online social networking make it ideally suited for supporting collaborative prototyping efforts: casual communication and interaction modes for establishing rapport, ability to connect with individuals outside of your networks including different organizations and geographies, and ability to find functional experts and view the expertise of collaboration team members.

In addition to the informal collaboration that takes place on public social networking sites like Facebook and LinkedIn, a number of software companies have emerged in the last few years that provide enterprise collaborative productivity tools. Pioneers in this space include ThoughtFarmer, Mzinga, HeadMix, Socialcast, Small World Labs, and Trampoline Systems. Most of these offer some combination of the following features to help employees work better together: enterprise wikis, blogs, social networks, employee directory, calendars, tag browsing, feeds, document collaboration, employee learning and training, and messaging.

Feedback Channels

The act of prototyping also demands continual feedback from internal and external parties. Sometimes, it might make sense to solicit feedback from the "masses" through crowdsourced ideation communities as described in the previous section. But that typically requires significant lead time and is overkill for prototyping. Often, obtaining frequent, high-quality feedback from an important few stakeholders is much more helpful.

Backboard is a useful social feedback tool that helps people do just this. Backboard allows prototypers to invite feedback and approval on documents, images, and presentations from their LinkedIn, Gmail, and Yahoo! contacts. Reviewers can mark up files to provide feedback using a combination of drawing and text comments (see Figure 6.6). They can also view one another's suggestions and approve different versions of files.

Figure 6.6
Backboard is an innovative social feedback tool for documents, images, and presentations. Product managers and others use Backboard for obtaining frequent, high-quality feedback on concept prototypes.

Commercial Implementation

An important distinction between innovation and invention is that innovation is the successful practical deployment of an idea or invention. That is, innovation is about execution as much as anything else. Having a good idea and prototype are necessary, but not enough.

Execution is a very social process. Successful execution requires both internal buy-in from colleagues and executives, as well as external buy-in from customers, partners, and others. Online social networking can help.

Winning Internal Buy-In

Before focusing on your product's go-to-market plan, you first have to win over the right stakeholders and decision makers internally. Support from colleagues and executives is essential for mobilizing the necessary resources to build the product, secure sufficient levels of marketing investment around the product, and persuade sales reps to talk about the product with customers.

Many of the concepts from Chapter 3 around building social capital are applicable for winning internal buy-in. By cultivating strong and diverse entrepreneurial networks across different departments in your company, you will be better positioned to ask for help, feedback, and support. The flattening effect of online social networks discussed previously means that wherever you are in the organizational hierarchy, executives and decision makers might be more accessible to you than in offline networking situations.

Using communication tools like Twitter, Yammer, or Connectbeam as described in an earlier section, you can broadcast updates about your project and do some internal marketing around your initiative. People can't support something if they don't know about it or don't understand it. This stage of the innovation cycle when you have a solid prototype is an ideal time to engage people broadly across the organization and solicit additional feedback and support.

Finally, nothing provides more compelling evidence to make the case for a new product than demonstrated customer demand. The crowdsourcing techniques discussed earlier, such as ideation communities on Facebook, can provide reliable customer data to back up your internal pitch. Have customers been receptive to the product concept? Was it their idea to begin with? Has the idea received a lot of votes, comments, and attention? Product managers should collect this feedback both in aggregate, as well as a few anecdotal examples, and socialize it within the organization.

Winning over the Market

In previous chapters, we discussed social sales and marketing techniques for winning over customers. This is especially critical for innovative products and services that might not yet have customer trust, proven success, and widespread demand.

The diffusion of innovation theory offers a good way for thinking about how online social networking affects the commercial success of a new product. In his 1962 book, *The Diffusion of Innovations,* Everett Rogers describes how innovation spreads through members of a society following an *S*-curve, initially with a few early adopters, followed by the majority, until the innovation becomes mainstream. By facilitating communication across vast networks, social networking sites accelerate the rate of diffusion for any given product, as shown in Figure 6.7.

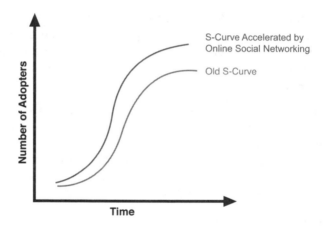

Figure 6.7
Online social networks accelerate the traditional S-curve of innovation diffusion, allowing new products to become adopted more quickly and by more people.

Diffusion research looks at the factors that might accelerate, increase, or decrease the chances a new idea or product will be adopted by members of a culture. According to Rogers, innovation diffusion from an individual's perspective occurs through five stages: knowledge, persuasion, decision, implementation, and confirmation. Here is how online social networking changes each of these stages:

1. *Knowledge.* To accept an innovation, people first need to know about it. The passive word-of-mouth broadcasts that occur on social networking sites, such as Facebook News Feeds, encourage the diffusion of information through an accepted, trusted medium. The medium containing information about an innovation could be a status message, posted link, wall post, or someone becoming a fan of the product's Facebook Page.

2. *Persuasion.* Next, individuals must be persuaded regarding the value and validity of the innovation. Transitive trust across friends plays an important role: Because Person X

endorses the innovation and Person Y trusts Person X, Person Y is more likely to become persuaded in favor of the innovation. As discussed in Chapter 5, "Social Network Marketing," online social networking also makes it easier for influencers to promote their opinions.

3. *Decision.* Individuals then need to make a decision to adopt or reject an innovation. Social networking sites help in two ways. First, they can help advertisers create a sense of urgency and force a decision with time-sensitive campaigns (introduced in Chapter 5). Displaying a timely offer that is associated with a real-world event with an expiration date might accelerate an individual's decision of whether to accept an innovation. Second, for people who aren't ready to decide, social networking sites can help prolong the decision to give the innovation more chances to be accepted. For example, feed stories, including information and products, linger rather than disappearing right away. Also, platform applications like MyListo use virtual gifts and games to prolong engagement with product brands, giving people additional time to make up their minds.

4. *Implementation.* At this point, individuals must carry through with setting up and actually using the innovation. As we talked about in Chapter 4, social network communities help connect novice adopters with others who might be more experienced with the product and might be able to offer help and guidance. The encouragement and support from people you know both accelerates implementation as well as increases the likelihood of success. Figure 6.8 provides an example from the YouTube community discussion board on Facebook.

5. *Confirmation.* Last, but not least, an individual evaluates the results of an innovation she has chosen to adopt. Here again, it might be useful and more enjoyable to reflect on one's experience in the context of a social network community rather than in isolation. Which of an individual's friends also adopted this innovation? What are their thoughts and reactions, and how do they compare with those of the individual?

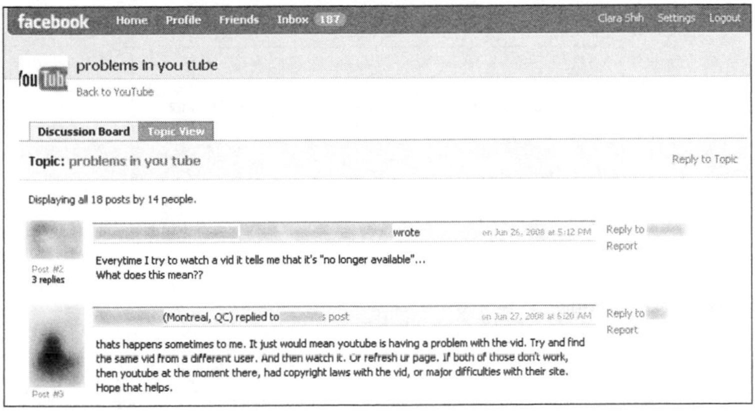

Figure 6.8
An example of a community-led Facebook discussion board about problems using YouTube, Google's video-sharing service. As you can see, a new user encountered a problem during implementation (stage four) in her adoption of YouTube. A more experienced user in her extended network then responded with help.

Continual Iteration

After you've implemented your idea and released the product to market, your ongoing success will depend on your ability to continually respond to customer feedback and iterate. This is especially crucial if you have launched a radical new product, radical new take on an existing product, or you are addressing a new market.

Crowdsourcing Feedback

Similar to the concept generation stage, it can be highly efficient to crowdsource feedback from social network communities such as what Starbucks is doing with MyStarbucksIdea. After all, feedback is just another form of ideation specifically on how to improve existing products. As a product manager, feedback might automatically come to you through these forums you have set up. Otherwise, it is a good idea to solicit feedback by moderating these forums, asking open-ended questions, and even offering rewards for participation if needed.

Polls

Polls are an easy way to get customer feedback on specific product decisions. Once products are out, product managers often find themselves faced with decisions of whether to offer slight variations on the product, such as offering it in different colors, adding or subtracting functionality to create premium and basic versions, and providing a children's version. These kinds of "either/or" and multiple choice questions are perfect for polls. Just about every online social network allows community managers to incorporate polls. Figure 6.9 shows a poll on Gap's Facebook Page.

Figure 6.9
A poll on Gap's Facebook Page.

Transforming Customers into Partners

Online social networking tools can help product managers transform customers into true participant-partners. In the Facebook Era, companies and customers are able to achieve a new level of conversation that is bidirectional and extends across product development, sales, marketing, and customer support. Thanks to the social graph, not only are customers encouraged to engage with your company, but they are also motivated to engage with their friends and colleagues *around* your company, contributing to your sales, marketing, support, and product innovation efforts.

7

Social Recruiting

It's hard to find good people, and it's only getting worse. A growing number of articles in publications like *The Economist* and *McKinsey Quarterly* speak of "the war for talent" and "looming talent shortages" around the world. To make things even harder for employers, people today are switching jobs more often, creating sometimes very sudden staffing gaps that can disrupt company growth and productivity if not immediately backfilled.

As the competition for talent grows, recruiting is becoming an even more vital function than ever, and recruiters who understand how to tap the online social graph will be at a disproportionate advantage. The reality is most people find jobs through someone they know and accept job offers from people they trust. Recruiting through social networking sites takes advantage of these facts, and makes the matching of job opportunities and candidates faster and more efficient.

In many ways, recruiting resembles a sales cycle. The recruiter is "selling" the employer, role, and job opportunity. She has to generate leads and pipeline, and manage candidates through a qualification process that hopefully results in some percentage of successful hires. But, compared with selling a product or service, recruiting is typically more welcomed by the recipient because it is viewed as a mutual win-win situation more of the time.

Because there is a limited supply of good jobs, the ratio of jobs to job seekers is typically low. In contrast, there are far more product advertisements and sales pitches than interested buyers. Recruiting is also far more personal. Accepting a new job is a major life decision. Few goods and services can be classified with the same level of importance. Together, this means that interpersonal rapport between recruiters and candidates is even more important than in sales, and that online social networking tools have the potential to be even more transformational.

This chapter is divided into seven sections. First is an overview of the four most popular social networking sites being used by recruiters and how they differ. Second, we discuss how online social networking makes it easier to source job candidates, including active candidates, passive candidates, college candidates, extended network referrals, and specialized groups. The third section explains how the online social graph brings greater transparency and objectivity to candidate references. Next, we talk about the importance of employer and recruiter reputation on social networking sites. The following section walks through how recruiters can leverage casual interaction modes on social networking sites to stay in touch and sustain rapport. The chapter concludes with advice for job candidates on how they can keep their profiles professional and advice for employers on how to prevent poaching of their employees.

The Best Social Networks for Recruiting

There are four social networking sites that the recruiters I interviewed recommend for different stages in the recruiting cycle and candidates types: LinkedIn, Doostang, Ryze, and Facebook. Depending on your industry, what types of jobs you recruit for, and where you are in the recruiting cycle, one or a combination of these online social networks might make the most sense. Other popular sites, including CareerBuilder, Monster, and Yahoo! HotJobs, are dedicated job sites rather than social networks, and are beyond the scope of this book.

LinkedIn

Started by former PayPal executive Reid Hoffman, LinkedIn is by far the most established professionally oriented network and has already become a standard recruiting tool in many industries. Launched in 2003, LinkedIn now has over 30 million business professionals among its membership across 150 different industries. Member profiles are more or less like a living version of a résumé, which is ideal for recruiters seeking up-to-date information about a candidate. LinkedIn is good for posting jobs, requesting candidate referrals, and making contact when it is explicitly related to a concrete business objective. LinkedIn is generally not used for casual communication, even with professional contacts.

Doostang

Doostang is a much newer and smaller, invitation-only professional network started in 2005 by Mareza Larizadeh and Pavel Krapivin. It has half a million members, mostly recent business school graduates with 5 to 12 years of work experience. Doostang positions itself as a private, exclusive network. I, for one, have Doostang to thank for helping place me in my current role at salesforce.com.

Ryze

Ryze was founded in 2001 by former engineer Adrian Scott. Like Doostang, it has half a million members. A lot of Ryze members are aspiring entrepreneurs and small business owners seeking to hire employees and network with like-minded professionals. It is common for members to introduce themselves with a written biographical narrative and even upload samples of past work in addition to listing employment history. The main focus of Ryze is on business networking, but it incorporates personal elements such as birthday, hometown, and "books I'm reading."

Facebook

Last, but not least, Facebook is emerging as a popular recruiting tool, mainly due to its extensive reach to nearly 200 million people around the world. There are dozens of recruiting applications that have been built for the Facebook platform, including some by popular job sites like Jobster (see Figure 7.1) and Simply Hired. Recruiters already on Jobster and Simply Hired get automatic access and exposure to Facebook members that install these applications into their account. Another popular app, Indeed Jobs, lets people search millions of jobs across thousands of job sites, newspaper classified sections, associations, and company career pages. Many of the apps target specific niches, such as Tax Jobs Worldwide, Jobs in Egypt, and California Library Jobs. Facebook members who install these applications can browse available openings and make their profiles visible to recruiters.

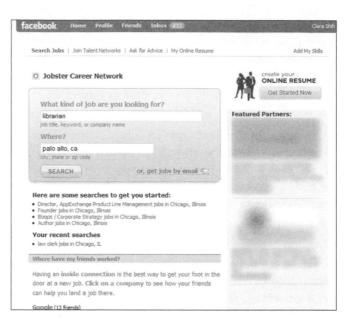

Figure 7.1
Recruiting site Jobster has a popular application on the Facebook platform. Facebook members who install the app can search for jobs in Jobster's database as well as allow recruiters to view their profile information and résumés.

Sourcing Candidates

Hundreds of millions of the best-educated, most qualified job candidates are becoming members of social networking sites like LinkedIn, Doostang, Ryze, and Facebook. Increasingly, smart recruiters are joining these sites too to connect with these individuals and cultivate lasting relationships.

Why do social networking sites attract desirable candidates? One reason could be that high-achieving professionals are more drawn to networking, and that strong networks have contributed to their professional success. Also, these individuals tend to be savvier and more selective about where they work. They are more likely to periodically reevaluate their careers and seek out or at least be open to new opportunities for career advancement.

In the past, one big problem with job boards and résumé submission was résumés would become outdated, sometimes making it difficult to even get in touch with a candidate. Because social network profiles are self-maintained, living documents, they tend to be more accurate and up to date with a candidate's most current experience, qualifications, availability, and contact information. Additional features of social network profiles, such as showing who you know in common, testimonials from colleagues, and profile search capability, makes the recruiter's job easier. These features provide valuable additional insights that allow recruiters to qualify candidates earlier in the cycle and not have to waste their time or the candidates' time when there is not a good fit.

Recruiters typically categorize candidates into active candidate status or passive candidate status. Active candidates are those proactively seeking a job. Passive candidates are those usually currently employed but potentially open to hearing about new opportunities. Online social networking offers different options for addressing each. There are additional nuances for how to best interface with college candidates, extended network referrals, and specialized groups, which we cover in turn.

Active Candidates

Increasingly, people who are actively seeking jobs are looking to LinkedIn and to a lesser extent, Doostang. There are a few reasons people might prefer to find jobs using social networking sites. First, there is a greater sense of trust within one's social network. Job seekers can see exactly how they might be connected to a prospective job and employer, perform better due diligence, and gain tacit knowledge about the people and opportunity at hand. Trust and familiarity are paramount in job seeking; as mentioned earlier, people's careers are a major, intensely personal life decision.

Second, the candidates with whom I spoke complained about the overwhelming number of junk listings on traditional job sites that were irrelevant, redundant, or out of date.

Just like social filtering helps people find the interesting needle in the haystack of information on the Web (as discussed in Chapter 2, "The Evolution of Digital Media"), the social filtering that occurs with jobs and employers on LinkedIn and Doostang can similarly help job seekers narrow down which set of jobs might be relevant, compelling, and realistic.

Finally, often the best way to get hired is to know people inside the company. Not only can they vouch for a job seeker, perhaps just as important they can keep the job seeker top of mind for recruiters and help expedite the hiring process. From the job seeker's perspective, nothing speaks more highly of a prospective employer than people she trusts and respects choosing to work there. Not to mention, the candidate would likely enjoy the opportunity to work alongside people she knows and likes.

The job search is a big investment that requires a lot of time; the modern job seeker doesn't want to waste her time on job opportunities from which she will never hear back. Applying for jobs within her social network is the best way to maximize the odds of getting hired while having greater visibility and influence into the process. By filling out just a few basic fields, recruiters can post jobs to their networks for free on Doostang and for a small fee on LinkedIn.

In the face of competitive recruiting situations, some firms are even advertising on social networking sites, especially to appeal to those under the age of 30. Hypertargeting allows employers to preselect which profiles of people they want to see their ad and customize specific campaigns to appeal to the particular hypersegment. As described in Chapter 5, "Social Network Marketing," ads can be hypertargeted along eight major dimensions: location, sex, age, education, workplace, relationship status, relationship interests, and interest keywords. For example, a library in Louisville looking to hire junior staff librarians might target college-educated people age 22 and older from Kentucky who have a stated interest in "books" and "reading."

Hypertargeting capability is ideal for recruiters, who are generally seeking a very specific set of skills and work experience, education, and location. Starbucks Coffee Company is one employer using Facebook Ads to recruit new employees (see Figure 7.2).

Figure 7.2
A Starbucks recruiting ad on Facebook. An increasing number of employers are using hypertargeted Facebook Ads to source job candidates based on profile criteria such as age, college, work experience, and location.

Passive Candidates

Social networking sites are great for finding active candidates, but they are potentially even more powerful for discovering passive candidates. Many of your greatest potential hires might not be actively looking because they are happily employed. These passive job candidates do not post their résumé on Monster or CareerBuilder, but they do sign up for LinkedIn and Facebook. Why? Online social networks are viewed as strategic places to build long-term, lasting relationships, network, and keep in touch with people you know, rather than tactical places to seek a specific job at a specific time.

Social networking sites have dramatically expanded the talent pool by including passive candidates who were previously not accessible in a systematic way. Instead of waiting for candidates to come to them, recruiters can more easily be proactive about seeking out the exact profiles of people they want. Using advanced profile search, recruiters can specify very precise criteria based on things like past employers, roles, projects, education level, location, and relevant skills and experience to find potential candidates in their network.

LinkedIn Recruiter, shown in Figure 7.3, is a premium service that allows paying sub-scribers to search by title, company, or keywords across all LinkedIn members, not just people in their network. It also includes collaboration tools to allow recruiting teams to group candidates into folders and tag them with comments.

Figure 7.3
LinkedIn Recruiter is a premium corporate recruiting service that helps recruiters identify, contact, and manage passive job candidates.

College and MBA Recruiting on Facebook

University recruiters need to be where students are, and just about every college or grad-uate student these days is on Facebook. There are few better ways to achieve the level of reach at the same cost. More and more, recruiters are using Facebook to provide informa-tion about prospective employers, promote campus info sessions, connect with student groups, stay in touch with interns, and even perform due diligence on prospective appli-cants.

In lieu of or in addition to traditional Web pages, college recruiting teams are setting up Facebook Pages to provide company information and foster communities of recruiters, employee alumni (current company employees who are alumni of the school), interns, and prospective applicants. (In case you missed it, Chapter 3, "Social Capital from Networking Online," explains what Facebook Pages are, and Chapter 9, "Get Your Message Across," walks through how to make one.) Facebook events are used to promote informa-tion sessions, campus talks, and other recruiting events. Events can be associated with a Page, allowing fans to receive updates when event details change or new events are posted. For example, P&G created a Facebook Page for its recruiting efforts at the

University of Dayton (see Figure 7.4). The Page describes job opportunities at the company, invites students to attend an upcoming "Meet and Greet P&G Engineers" session, and introduces a current P&G employee who recently graduated from the university, encouraging interested students to get in touch.

Figure 7.4

Facebook Page for P&G recruiting at the University of Dayton.

Similar to the word-of-mouth marketing scenarios described in Chapter 5, enthusiasm and awareness around employers spreads across the online social graph. When prospective applicants look at your Facebook event page, they can see which of their friends are also planning to attend. When students RSVP for a recruiting event or become a fan of your recruiting page, their friends are notified via News Feed. As mentioned previously, employers can amplify the effects by sponsoring social ad campaigns hypertargeted to the right campus and majors. In-person events and ad campaigns can be timed with the recruiting season or school calendar, such as offering a study break during midterm exam week or placing an ad for résumé submissions a few weeks before on-campus interviews.

Another effective, low-cost strategy used by college recruiters is engaging with campus student groups. Most student organizations have a Facebook group that lists their officers. Recruiters or employee alumni can send a Facebook message to these individuals to say hello and perhaps offer to sponsor or speak at an upcoming meeting. Afterward, the company can follow up with group members by posting the slides presented, related links, and speaker contact information to the group.

Many employers offer summer internships or co-op programs to provide students with an opportunity to work at the company prior to graduation. Facebook is a great way for recruiters and hiring managers to stay in touch after the program ends. By keeping these students engaged with the company, recruiters not only increase the likelihood of successfully hiring them after graduation, but they can also use students as campus ambassadors to find additional candidates. The second-to-last section in this chapter goes into greater detail on using social networks to keep in touch.

Lastly, recruiters and hiring managers are using Facebook and MySpace to check out prospective applicants. Is the candidate's profile consistent with how she has presented herself in interviews and on her résumé? Does this person seem friendly and well balanced? Or is her profile blatantly inappropriate and unprofessional? Obviously, there is a fine line to balance between privacy and due diligence. The last section of this chapter gives advice to candidates on what information to share, when to restrict profile access, and how to manage social network identities.

Referrals from Extended Networks

As we discussed in Chapter 4, "Social Sales," social networking sites allow people to reach far beyond just their immediate networks. For recruiters, the ability to find and contact candidates among friends of friends and greater extended networks dramatically expands the pool of trusted talent.

LinkedIn, in particular, lets recruiters reach *the extended networks of their extended networks.* Instead of only asking *n* people in their extended network whether they would be interested in a job, recruiters can ask those *n* people if they *know* anyone who might be interested in the job (see Figure 7.5), thereby potentially reaching n^n people. Recruiters can further expand their network reach by joining a LION network, described in Chapter 4 in the context of sales prospecting.

Figure 7.5
A request for referral sent to me from a LinkedIn connection. LinkedIn allows recruiters to tap extended networks not only for interested applicants but also for referrals of interested applicants, which has a multiplying effect on how many people within the trusted network they are able to reach.

Silicon Valley start-up company Appirio has taken this concept to Facebook with Jobs4MyFriends, an application it developed that allows businesses to easily tap employees' Facebook networks to source job candidates. Given the high costs of recruiting and the near-universal tendency for many of the best candidates to come from employees, many employers offer some form of referral bonus to employees if the referred candidate ends up getting hired and taking the job.

Motivated by the referral bonus or just a desire to help the company find more good people, employees install the Jobs4MyFriends application into their Facebook account, kicking off a matching process that compares the company's job listings to the profiles of the employees' Facebook Friends (see Figure 7.6). As we talked about earlier, most social network profiles contain relevant information for recruiting such as interests, location, former employers, associations, role, and title. Matches found between job postings and potential candidates are recommended by the Jobs4MyFriends application for referral to the employee. The employee can then decide whether to actually submit the referral.

Say an employee, John, refers his friend Kelly for a business development role at his company. The next time Kelly logs in to Facebook, she will receive a notification that John referred her for this position. If she is interested in learning more about the job or applying, she can go to the candidate application portal, also provided by Appirio. Behind the scenes, John's company can track which candidate referrals came from which employees, and if Kelly eventually gets hired, be able to ensure John receives his referral bonus.

Figure 7.6
Jobs4MyFriends is a Facebook application that lets employees refer friends for openings at their company.

Targeting Specialized Networks

Social network communities and affinity groups are another great source of talent, particularly if you are looking for candidates of a certain background. There are tens of thousands of Facebook groups and LinkedIn groups around company employees and alumni, roles, industries, conferences, and trade associations—for example, the Northeast Black Law Students Association group on Facebook, the Healthcare Management Engineers group on LinkedIn, or the Women Business Owners group on Ryze.

Sometimes, membership and access to these groups are restricted, but in general it seems pretty relaxed. Several recruiters I spoke to for this chapter told me they have never been denied membership into one of these groups when they tried to join. Once in, recruiters can post messages, view members, and reach out to specific group members.

For example, my friend is on the diversity recruiting team at a large engineering company in Ohio. One of the first places he goes to find candidates is the Society of Women Engineers group on LinkedIn. He has brought dozens of welcome job opportunities to the group and successfully hired four group members last year. Every few months, he checks on the group to see who new has joined and browses member profiles to look for potential candidates. His advice is to take extra precaution to respect the group's posting policies and to never send spam.

Reading Between the Lines

Aside from obviously important information recruiters usually look at like experience, education, and current title and employer, there is a lot of subtle information on social network profiles that can be very insightful and valuable. By reading between the lines and "doing their homework," recruiters can tap powerful data to determine candidate fit, opportunistically go after candidates who are likely unhappy, and increase the odds of closing the deal with a candidate:

- *Tenure and stated accomplishments in current role.* Most people specify job tenure on their social network profiles. How long a candidate has been at her current employer is an important indicator of how likely she will be to leave for another opportunity. Based on profiles of past employees at this company, what is the average tenure of an employee? How does this person's tenure compare? If the person is relatively new (less than one year) with few accomplishments to show, the timing is probably not right to try to recruit this person for an immediate opening. On the other hand, you might come across someone whose tenure has far exceeded the company average, with a lot of accomplishments but perhaps not a proportional number of promotions. This person might be more open to being persuaded that another opportunity could be better for career advancement.

- *Organizational structure.* As most recruiters know, titles can vary significantly from company to company. Just like sales reps need to understand the lay of the land of their prospective buyer organizations, recruiters can benefit from understanding the organizational structure of the existing employers of people they are trying to recruit. As we talked about in Chapter 4, poking around on social networking sites can yield valuable information about which departments have the best people and what titles really mean.

- *Mass exodus from a particular company.* Occasionally, companies make poor decisions. Some go out of business. Others flounder and stagnate. Their employees are the people closest to this information, and sometimes we will see a voluntary or involuntary exodus of people from a particular company. In LinkedIn, you can see this activity in the Network Updates section of the home page. In Facebook, this activity is broadcast via the News Feed feature. For example, when I logged in to Facebook last month, I saw three updates from my network saying "so and so has left her job at Company X." If I were a recruiter, now might be a good time to tap Company X's employee pool.

- *Commonality with you.* As in sales, shared personal experience between the candidate and recruiter, such as the same hometown or alma mater, can go a long way in establishing personal rapport. Especially if you are an independent headhunter not affiliated with a particular employer, this rapport can help differentiate you as someone the candidate remembers, likes, and trusts with finding career opportunities.

- *Commonality with company employees.* It is common practice when recruiters are trying to close a candidate on a job offer to introduce that person to employees and executives at the company. These individuals can offer different perspectives on the employer and help persuade the candidate. Recruiters can take this to the next level by looking for commonalities between company employees and the candidate to strategically pair up people and maximize those conversations. We can repurpose a prior example from Chapter 4 to illustrate this point. Say the candidate you are trying to win over is originally from Texas and graduated from Rice University. Among the executives in your company, there happens to be one who is also a Texan and attended Rice. That person rather than a random employee is likely one of the people you want on the phone helping to close this candidate. Especially because whether to accept a job is a very personal and emotional decision, tapping shared experiences even if they are small coincidences can make a big difference.

Candidate References

The shortcoming of traditional candidate references is that they are provided by the candidate, and any rational candidate will only disclose favorable references. As a result, recruiters might be getting a biased view of the candidate.

More Objective

The online social graph can make reference checking more independent and objective. Instead of asking the candidate to supply references, a recruiter can go to LinkedIn and find them herself. For example, the recruiter might want to browse the candidate's LinkedIn contacts, including mutual connections, or search for profiles of people with overlapping tenure with the candidate at a previous employer. Either way, the recruiter or hiring manager for the first time can decide for herself who to tap for an independent reference. As a courtesy, the recruiter might want to ask the candidate for an introduction to this person or at least provide a heads-up that she will be reaching out.

More Accountable

Another type of candidate reference comes in the form of professional testimonials on social networking sites. For example, LinkedIn members can publicly recommend another member. The testimonial becomes part of the member's profile (see Figure 7.7). LinkedIn recommendations are public and last forever until or unless the member removes it from his or her profile. People think twice before agreeing to provide an endorsement, and they think twice about what they are going to say. This introduces a new level of transparency and accountability to these endorsements that private reference checks in the past might not have had. There is a Facebook application, Testimonials, that offers a similar professional testimonial capability.

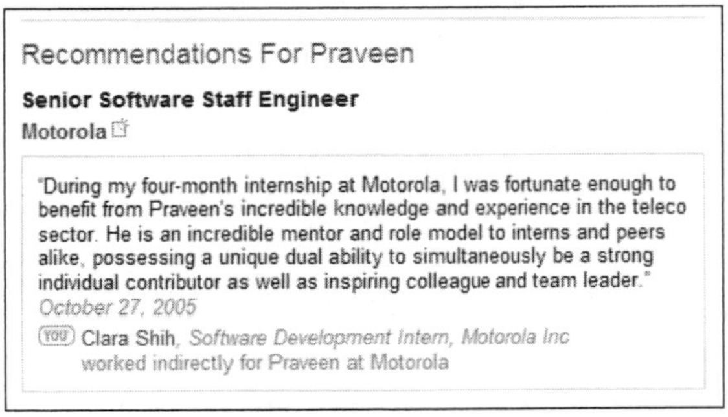

> Recommendations For Praveen
>
> **Senior Software Staff Engineer**
> Motorola
>
> "During my four-month internship at Motorola, I was fortunate enough to benefit from Praveen's incredible knowledge and experience in the teleco sector. He is an incredible mentor and role model to interns and peers alike, possessing a unique dual ability to simultaneously be a strong individual contributor as well as inspiring colleague and team leader."
> October 27, 2005
> (YOU) Clara Shih, *Software Development Intern, Motorola Inc*
> worked indirectly for Praveen at Motorola

Figure 7.7
Profile recommendations on LinkedIn carry more weight because they are public testimonials that can be scrutinized by other members.

Employer and Recruiter Reputation

Online social networking is powerful because it offers bidirectional visibility. Not only can recruiters and hiring managers perform due diligence on candidates, but candidates can also research the hiring manager and other employees, see who they might know who works there, and reach out to learn more. In the competitive landscape for top talent, companies can use social networking to market themselves as desirable employers and recruiters can use social networking to establish credibility.

Market Your Company as a Desirable Employer

With employees switching jobs more often, it is more important than ever for companies to establish their brand as a desirable employer. As we described in the earlier section on college recruiting, some companies are using social network communities and hypertargeted ads to achieve this objective.

Employee testimonials can be another important resource for providing social proof and credibility. I've seen some companies ask select employees to blog about their experience working there. Others encourage employees to be engaged in recruiting communities and make themselves available to share their experiences or answer questions. Many of the techniques we went over in Chapter 5 for marketing products can also be applied to marketing your company as an employer.

Establish Your Credibility as a Recruiter

Especially for independent recruiters or head-hunting firms not affiliated with one particular employer, public recommendations on LinkedIn from successfully placed candidates are a great way to highlight your track record and establish credibility.

In addition to public testimonials, the recruiter can use online social networks to see if she and the candidate have any mutual contacts. As in the sales example, the recruiter could ask these individuals to serve as references.

If the recruiter is really lucky, one of these mutual contacts might even be a past candidate who she successfully matched with a job! Transitive trust happens at two levels for job candidates:

- *Trust in the employer.* Friend X works for Employer Y. Candidate Z trusts and respects Friend X, so Candidate Z is more likely to trust that Employer Y is good. Otherwise, his friend would not be working there.

- *Trust in the recruiter.* Friend X went through Recruiter M and landed a good job that she is very happy with. Candidate Z trusts Friend X and sees she is happy, so he is more likely to believe Recruiter M is qualified.

Because finding a job is so personal and emotional, transitive trust plays an even bigger role in recruiting than in sales. In most cases, there is no single "perfect" or "best" job. There is an inherent level of uncertainty about any new role. Until the candidate actually starts working there, she won't have full information about what her experience will really be like. At a certain point, she needs to make a "leap-of-faith" decision based on trust that this is the right job. Employee references, especially from friends the candidate knows and respects, provide the best information for mitigating the uncertainty.

Keeping in Touch

Despite their greatest efforts, however, occasionally even the best recruiters aren't able to close a candidate. The timing isn't right, the candidate decided to go with another opportunity, a personal emergency is preventing the candidate from relocating—there could be any number of reasons. Prior to social networking sites, it was easy to lose touch with candidates, even those with whom recruiters invested months and even years.

As we first talked about in Chapter 3 and then explored further in the context of sales in Chapter 4, one of the most valuable aspects of online social networking is the ability to maintain more weak ties. For recruiters, this means being able to keep in touch with candidates regardless of whether they were successfully placed.

Recruiters can then revisit those candidates later when new opportunities emerge. Recruiters can also further capitalize on those relationships by tapping those candidates' friend networks for additional talent.

Why would candidates want to keep in touch? As we talked about at the opening of this chapter, most people view recruiting as more mutually beneficial than sales calls. They want to keep their options open in case something happens with their current job or something better comes along. Maintaining relationships with recruiters, especially low-effort weak ties, buys them privileged access to new career opportunities down the road. So more often than not, assuming the working relationship was positive, we are seeing candidates accept LinkedIn invitations and Facebook Friend requests from their recruiters.

Making the Most of Successful Placements

A successful candidate job placement is just the beginning of a relationship. Of anyone, candidates who have been successfully placed feel the most indebted and grateful. These individuals can become a recruiter's greatest allies and advocates. Good recruiters depend on trust and rapport from past placements for future placements, introductions, and referrals to other candidates. They might even get employment and contracting opportunities to recruit at the company who hired the candidate.

One recruiter I interviewed who specializes in placing industrial designers said that because of the high turnover in her industry, nearly half of her placements have been repeat placements. Over the last decade, she has built up a network of artists and designers who trust and look to her every time they are ready to pursue a new full-time or contractor opportunity.

Keeping Lines of Communication Open with Nonplacements

Nonplacements can be equally important for a recruiter to stay connected and continually grow her network. The ability to easily maintain weak ties on Facebook and LinkedIn means that recruiters can take a longer-term view on candidates and not feel like they have wasted any time on candidates, even if things don't work out the first time around.

According to the same design-industry recruiter, she views every rejection as an opportunity to place the candidate in the future and ask the candidate for referrals. Many candidates feel guilty that they turned down an offer from her and are eager to help by referring her to other candidates. Almost always, the designers with whom she works to place into job opportunities know a large number of other designers from school, past employers, and networking in the community.

The following case study profiles another recruiter, Joe, who uses LinkedIn and Facebook to cultivate long-term relationships with younger candidates. It is only fitting that I found and contacted Joe through my extended network on LinkedIn.

Financial Services Recruiting in Chicago

Joe is a Chicago-based recruiter for mainly associate-level positions in financial services firms. Over the last five years, Joe has helped match dozens of recent MBAs and banking analysts with 2–3 years of experience with associate roles in banking, real estate, private equity, and venture capital. As a free agent, Joe's success depends on his ability to network with both employers and candidates. Joe categorizes his candidate network into three types: candidates he has successfully placed, candidates he will successfully place in the future, and people he has just met.

- *Successful placements.* Joe maintains close relationships with his top placements, as they often become repeat job candidates and eventually even clients who employ his recruiting services. With or without online social networks, Joe invests heavily in these relationships, checking in at least once a month and catching up over lunch or dinner once a quarter. Especially in working with candidates who are mostly in their mid- or late-twenties, Joe can use casual interaction mechanisms on Facebook to be more playful and make these relationships feel less businesslike. He sends virtual Facebook gifts for birthdays and other milestones. Joe pokes, bites (with the Zombies application of course), and shares photos of his newly born son with his top recruits. Far from replacing quality face-to-face interactions, Facebook enriches Joe's relationships with this top-tier network with more casual but also more frequent and personal interaction.

- *Candidates he is still working on placing.* Generally speaking, Joe's relationships with "candidates in progress" tend to remain more professional. Most communication occurs via more traditional means such as phone or e-mail. According to Joe, he prefers to prove his capability as a competent recruiter before trying to establish more personal relationships with people. However, in situations where a candidate drops out of the process because another opportunity emerges that was not sourced through Joe, Joe adds the candidate to his LinkedIn and Facebook networks to maintain the relationship. Joe benefits from having instant access to the individual's social network to find additional talent, as well as potentially working to place this individual in the future.

- *People he has just met.* For new candidates that Joe has met maybe just once or twice, it used to be up to chance and timing (a combination of the candidate's immediate availability and Joe's pipeline) whether he would make an effort to stay in touch. With online social networking, the cost of establishing the connection is so low that there is almost no downside to doing so. Joe might or might not ultimately end up working with a particular candidate, but with each connection he receives a free option but not obligation to reach out in the future.

In every case, online social networking has enriched the reach and perpetual value of Joe's network. Perhaps it is the secret to his success.

Alumni Networks

Company alumni are another powerful but often overlooked source of talent and new business opportunity. No matter how great the working relationship between employer and employee, it is almost inevitable in this day and age that people eventually move on. Instead of rebuffing this natural phenomenon, employers could stand to gain from accepting it as the reality of doing business in the modern day and try to make the most of it.

Despite choosing to move on, most corporate alumni view former employers in a positive light. They did after all choose to work at the company for some period of time. Therefore, company recruiters can rely on these alumni just like they might current employees for referrals and access to their LinkedIn or Facebook contacts. With such heavy competition in the market for top talent, companies should not overlook the very people they invested so heavily in to develop and who very likely still feel loyal to their former employer.

Recent retirees are proving to be an unexpected, indispensable source of talent for many American employers. The rising wave of baby boomer retirements has left some employers suddenly short-staffed, particularly in areas requiring deep domain knowledge where newer hires aren't as able to contribute due to lack of experience. As the following case study shows, some companies like Dow Chemical are using online social networking to reengage retirees to help fill the gap.

Additionally, company alumni are a great source of new business opportunities, such as potential partnerships and generating leads for prospective customers. Alumni know their former employer's product or service better than anyone else and are likely to be an advocate in their new role. Consulting firms such as McKinsey & Company have long known this and have gone so far as providing updates on where alumni end up and actively engaging them in everything from conference speaking engagements to recruiting events.

My Dow Network

To address sudden workforce gaps from a wave of retiring boomers, Midland, Michigan-based Dow Chemical Company turned to online social networking. Using corporate social networking software from SelectMinds, Dow created "My Dow Network," an online community for Dow alumni, retirees, and current employees. Anyone with a Dow employee ID number from the last seven years can register for the site.

My Dow Network has taken off, boasting thousands of members just several months after launching. People are signing up to network with current and former colleagues, renew old friendships, stay abreast of the latest developments within Dow, and explore new full-time and contractor opportunities. Dow benefits from staying connected to its cumulative talent pool, tapping special skills and knowledge from experienced alumni, facilitating knowledge transfer across different generations of employees, and fostering a more-inclusive, diverse work environment.

From new moms who take time off to retirees with domain expertise, most alumni are grateful and enthusiastic about the opportunity to reconnect and reengage. According to one retiree Jeff Schatzer, "One of the great losses of retirement is the severance of ties that had such meaning. [My Dow Network] is one way to reestablish those ties. After three years of retirement, it's heartwarming to know that people think of me, that they have a comment for me, or want to share some news with me."

Not surprisingly, those alumni who have returned to Dow as consultants or employees are proving to be more affordable to hire and ramp, more productive, and less likely to leave for another company.

Advice for Candidates

For someone who wants a job or wants to keep a job, the need for social networking has never been greater. The tenure for C-level positions average less than two years. New hires, especially at the top, are being asked to hit the ground running and produce quick results. With more jobs going overseas, fewer guarantees about employment, and rising competition for the top jobs, people need to take full advantage of online social networks to strategically and opportunistically develop their careers. Many of the concepts from Chapters 3 and 4 on social capital and social sales, respectively, apply to candidates trying to "sell" themselves for certain roles internal or external to their company.

For job seekers, social graph information available from searching and browsing on LinkedIn and Doostang can help line up informational interviews and uncover tacit information about prospective employers and what it's really like to work at a particular company. Job seekers can learn a great deal about interviewers, hiring managers, and prospective colleagues. Because online social networks allow people to maintain a greater number of weak-tie relationships, job seekers might discover in their expanded networks that they know people at the company where they want to work and then use those relationships to get their foot in the door.

It's important to keep in mind, however, that it works both ways. It's becoming increasingly common practice for hiring managers and recruiters to perform due diligence on candidates via social networking sites (they used to just Google candidates). It is a good idea to keep Facebook, Friendster, and MySpace pages PG-13 if not G, and if you must post photos from a bachelor party in Las Vegas, at least create different profile views and Friend Lists for professional contacts versus college fraternity brothers. Chapter 11, "Corporate Governance and Strategy," includes a more in-depth discussion on how to manage your professional identity on social networking sites.

How to Protect Against Employee Poaching

The unprecedented access provided by online social networking is tremendously empowering for recruiters and job candidates, but can be worrisome for employers. Poaching is not a new phenomenon. Employees of reputable firms are constantly being sought after—these individuals are prescreened and know the company's best practices, so their experience is highly valued by others. What makes online social networking potentially scary is that now, recruiters can be very systematic about their poaching.

Employers might want to be careful about creating employee communities on social networks unless they are properly moderated and watched over carefully to prevent poachers from joining. Some companies have instituted internal policies about what employees can and cannot disclose about the organization and their role in public forums, including social networking sites. Other recruiters I know follow tacit rules of engagement that focus their efforts on active candidates and make them less aggressive about pursuing passive candidates, especially from outright competitors.

Ultimately, employers need to do three things. First, be aware that poaching is a reality. Second, have backfill plans ready to be mobilized in case a mission-critical role is suddenly left vacant. Most important, invest in creating a great workplace environment so that employees won't want to leave!

III

Your Step-By-Step Guide to Using Facebook for Business

8

Engage Your Customers

With the conceptual frameworks from Part I, "A Brief History of Social Media," and the functional overviews of social networking in Part II, "Transforming the Way We Do Business," behind us, the remaining chapters are meant to be an action-oriented guide on how to get started. Before doing anything else, you first need to come up with a strategy for your company's social network presence. You need a place to drive people *to* before you invest in ads to drive them there (Chapter 9, "Get Your Message Across") or have sales reps and recruiters making contact.

Having a presence on social networking sites allows you to do two very important things: Engage existing customers and engage prospective customers on these sites. Depending on the nature of your product or service, customers could already be seeking you out. Perhaps some have already taken the initiative to create an unofficial group about your brand to discuss, rant, and rave about it with friends. Prospective customers too often want a way to engage with others about your product in an unbiased environment before engaging with you.

This chapter has three sections. First, we walk through how to come up with your brand strategy and objectives for online social networking. How would you ideally want your brand to be perceived? Which new audiences do you want to reach? Are they on Facebook, MySpace, or Orkut? What are your goals? Improving customer satisfaction? Market research? Finding early adopters to help define the future of your product? Is your priority to upsell existing customers or find new customers?

Next, it's time to do some due diligence to see what unsanctioned communities and conversations have sprung up around your brand and products. What are people saying? Who is doing the talking? Who is listening and reacting? Should you participate?

The chapter concludes with how to build social network communities to achieve your objectives while taking into consideration existing brand conversations. The keys to success include appropriate use of brand personas, integration with existing social media investments such as blogs, and coming up with creative techniques to differentiate your brand and keep people coming back.

Start with Clear Strategy and Objectives

As with any investment you might be considering for your business, you should always start by determining your strategy. What are your goals? What is your budget? Here are some common objectives guiding many of the early business forays into engaging on social networking sites:

- Conducting market research, such as identifying trends and recruiting early adopters for more in-depth focus groups

- Improving customer satisfaction by providing opportunities for engagement and customers helping one another

- Promoting additional products and services to existing customers

- Expanding into new markets

- Encouraging word-of-mouth marketing

- Recruiting new employees

- Establishing or evolving your branding and positioning

Take the top two or three goals and use these as the basis of your strategy and decision making. When coming up with the prioritized list, it might be useful to score goals not only based on importance to your business but also whether social networking is uniquely positioned to contribute to a goal.

For example, because of their expansive reach across different regions, age groups, and other segments and their capability to target specific segments, social networking sites are a great place to test and expand to new markets. Think about not just where you are but where you want to go. Perhaps your business sees an opportunity to expand from adults to a children's offering, or a new region, industry vertical, or audience personality type.

Measuring Success

After you've decided on high-level goals, it is useful to define metrics around these goals to help define what success means, determine the appropriate level of investment, and measure value to the business. For example, here are some possible annual metrics and targets that correspond to the objective areas in the preceding list:

- Identify X new trends. Recruit focus group of Y early adopter 14–18-year-olds to help us understand the teen market and design the next generation of our product.

- Improve customer satisfaction scores by X. Decrease customer support call center volume by Y percent.

- Increase existing customer average spending X more dollars this year.

- Acquire X number of new customers in a new region, such as Taiwan and Hong Kong.

- Achieve X responses to our word-of-mouth campaign and Y conversions into sales.

- Source X number of candidates for the recruiting department.

- Rebrand company as X, as measured by a customer survey on how they perceive our brand. Increase our Net Promoter Score by 1.

Start with a modest level of investment. Set realistic goals and expectations. It probably took several iterations to arrive at your current Web site strategy. Coming up with an optimal social network presence will require the same kind of learning by doing. Starting off overly aggressive can set companies up for disappointment down the road and cause people to burn out or quit.

Always Think from the Customer's Perspective

To be successful over the long term, the foundation of all of your strategies and tactics needs to come back to the customer. Why would they want to engage? What are their incentives, motivation, expectation, and thought process? Generally, you can tap into one or a combination of these reasons:

- To express strong emotion. Perhaps they are overjoyed, overwhelmed, or frustrated. Your product has really been a positive or negative in their life.

- To improve your product with constructive feedback.

- To define their identity to be associated with your brand.

- To feel important in helping others answer questions.

- To benefit from selling peripheral goods and services, like a vendor selling iPod cases on the iPod group page.

- To meet new people.

- To bond socially with friends over the experience of using your product.

At the end of this initial planning exercise, you should have a strategy that you are ready to execute:

- Prioritized list of objectives including time frame, metrics, and targets

- Value you expect to bring to your business

- Level of resources you are willing to commit (might even be able to calculate expected ROI)

- Means and frequency by which you will evaluate progress

- The person in your organization who will be responsible for carrying out this initiative

Find Your Unsanctioned Communities

Before establishing your own official community, it's a good idea to first research what people are already saying about your company and find out who is doing the talking. The blogosphere never sleeps, and in our age of online media and an increasingly mobile, connected world, someone somewhere could be talking about your company or product at any time of day. It used to be enough to create Google Alerts around your brands and related terms. Google Alerts send an e-mail notification when new articles, blog posts, or other Web content appear that mention the keyword or phrase for which you set an alert.

Increasingly, though, these conversations about your brand aren't happening out in the open but rather within the confines of social networking sites. What you learn might surprise you. For instance, Victoria's Secret executives were pleasantly surprised to learn over 500 unofficial groups had sprung up around their brand on Facebook, as profiled in Chapter 5, "Social Network Marketing." It's important to tie the input from these unofficial mediums back to your overall social networking strategy. You might need to tweak your initial assumptions and priorities based on this new information.

First, you need to research whether any unofficial communities have emerged around your brand and products. Next, evaluate and try to summarize what people are saying. You can then decide whether it makes sense to respond. Sometimes, it's best to not respond and let the community initiative thrive on its own. The detailed steps described in this chapter focus largely on Facebook, MySpace, and Hi5 because they are the top three sites, but the concepts apply to other online social networks as well.

Step 1. What Communities Have Emerged Around Your Brand?

Search for your company and product names on each of the top social networking sites listed in the appendix. For many of these, you will need to register for an account before you are allowed to search, but for a few like Friendster and MySpace, anyone can search.

Say you represent Sanrio Co., Ltd., the Japanese character company that created the popular Hello Kitty character. Searching on Hi5 returns over 50 unsanctioned community groups, such as "mE gUStA cHoKoCaT i ToOs LoS DiBuJiToS D SaNrIo !" and "I love sanrio." The groups range from a few members to hundreds of members. Of these dozens of unofficial communities, only one appears to be negative, "muerte a KiTTy," which means "death to Kitty" (presumably Hello Kitty) created by a member in Honduras.

Searching on MySpace returns over 7,200 results, including the "Hello Kitty Sanrio Fan Club" group, which has 4,000 members. There are other groups, such as a profile page created by the local Sanrio retail store in Copenhagen, as well as the "sanrio luver" video channel, the "Serena loves Sanrio" user photo album, and user profile pages of people who talk about Sanrio on their profile (see Figure 8.1). (You also get a random mix of user profiles of people who happen to have the last name "Sanrio" and just have to ignore those.)

On Facebook, there are over 100 Sanrio-related community groups like "鍾意 sanrio系列精品的人就入黎啦,""iHeart My Melody" (My Melody is another popular Sanrio character), and "Hello Kitty is My Homegirl," some with tens of thousands members (see Figure 8.2).

Around the world, in different regions, friend groups, and social networking sites, people are talking about Sanrio's character brands. Most of these conversations are favorable toward the brand, but some are not. In either case, Sanrio executives need to be aware of these conversations. If your business is smaller or perhaps has a less distinct name, you might not find any unsanctioned communities—but it can't hurt to look. You might be surprised.

Figure 8.1
MySpace returned over 7,000 results for "Sanrio." Compared with Hi5, the average group size is much higher.

Figure 8.2
Facebook has over 100 unofficial Sanrio groups.

Step 2. What Are People Saying?

Now that you've found your unofficial communities, you next need to analyze what people are saying about your brand. This might be easy to do if there are only a handful of communities, but if there are hundreds or even thousands, you might want to do some sort of prioritization exercise based on number of members, or specific geographic regions, subbrands, and other angles that might be of particular importance to your business.

With potentially tens or hundreds of thousands or more of conversation threads, comments, and posts, how are you supposed to make sense of it all? One way is to come up with a list beforehand of issues and questions that are important to your business, and categorize relevant statements accordingly. As you go through the set of comments, you might be inspired by something you see to add to this list. Here are a few examples:

- Do most people view our brand favorably or negatively?

- What are the words most commonly used to describe our company or product?

- Are people describing or using our product in ways we did not expect or encourage?

- Are certain segments, such as a particular geographic region, age group, or school, particularly enthusiastic or negative?

- Who are the founders of the group? What motivates them?

- Who or what influences this group? Is it one of the group officers, members, or an external source such as a blog? There is a lot you can learn by clicking into the user profiles of community members.

Hi5 groups are centered around a community message board. You can view the most recent or most active topics, and search on keywords that appear in posts. MySpace groups offer two ways for members to engage: discussion forums and bulletin boards.

Forums are similar to Hi5's message boards. Bulletin boards let members make announcements, such as share news about the product. People can reply directly to the person who posted the bulletin but are not able to modify it or publicly reply.

Facebook groups are a little different. They not only display who founded the group but also allow that person to specify officers and admins to help them manage the community. In addition to a discussion board and posted items (similar to MySpace bulletin boards), there are default sections created on the group page for photos, videos, and wall, which are unique to Facebook. By putting these sections here, Facebook is encouraging group members to create a more interactive and engaging community experience.

Another good way to listen to unofficial brand conversations is to check on Twitter. Chapter 6, "Social Innovation," described how product managers can use Twitter search to get inspiration for product concepts. Twitter is a becoming an essential tool for marketers, too. Go to http://search.twitter.com and type in your phrase of interest (for example, company name or product name). This will return every instance that the phrase has appeared in tweets going back a few months (see Figure 8.3). You can subscribe to an RSS feed for these search results to automatically receive alerts whenever there are any new tweets about your brand.

Figure 8.3
Tweets about me, mostly referring to this manuscript.

For popular phrases and keywords, Facebook also provides a useful analysis tool called Lexicon. Lexicon tracks the frequency and sentiment of a particular keyword (like your brand) across Facebook wall posts, status messages, and comments (see Figure 8.4).

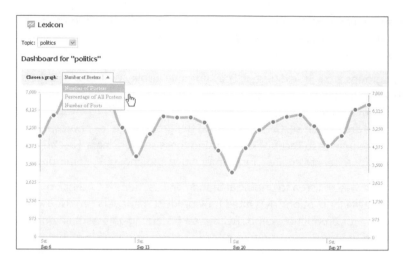

Figure 8.4
Lexicon is a keyword frequency and sentiment analysis tool that looks across all Facebook wall posts, status messages, and comments.

Lexicon measures *frequency* in three ways: the number of posts in which the keyword appears, the number of Facebook members who have referenced the keyword in a post, and what percentage of all members reference this keyword. *Sentiment* reflects the percentage of posts referencing a keyword that are positive versus negative. For example, the phrase "I love *X*" would be categorized as positive for *X*, and "I hate *X*" would be categorized as negative. Sentiment scores range from 0 to 100 percent, with an 80 percent score indicating that 80 percent of the sentiment is positive and 20 percent is negative. The data is charted over time, so you can analyze trends and see the impact of certain events such as a marketing campaign or big news. Marketers can also slice and dice the data by gender, age, and geographic location, as shown in Figure 8.5.

Today, Lexicon's keyword coverage is limited to only terms that appear with high frequency, as well as the brand names of select top, mostly Fortune 1000 advertisers who pay for the premium service. Especially if you are a big brand name or seeking to become one, Lexicon can be a powerful tool for gauging your relevance in people's everyday interactions. Even if you are not, Lexicon can be harnessed to understand trends. What memes, phrases, or even other brands are people talking about or using to express themselves and socialize? Perhaps these are the themes you should incorporate and examples you should follow in your campaigns and branding efforts.

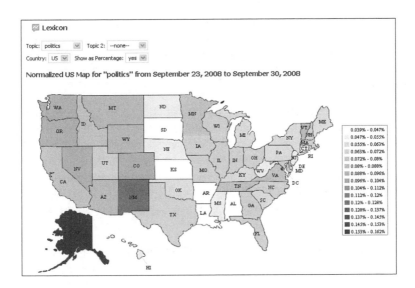

Figure 8.5
With Lexicon, marketers can slice and dice data along different dimensions, such as geographic location (by state, in this case).

Step 3. Should You Participate?

Now you are in the loop about what people are saying, but should you do anything? Well, it depends on the size and nature of the community. If it's a tight-knit group of close friends, your participation could be very intrusive. If it's a large community comprised largely of strangers coming together around your product, your participation could be welcome. Are the conversations positive, constructive, or purely negative about your brand? Could you and are you willing to take action on people's suggestions? Based on the answers to these questions, one or a combination of different participation styles and strategies might make the most sense: official public response, unofficial public response, proxy response, private response, and response through another channel.

- *Official public response.* As you might recall, Chapter 5 concluded with an example of a Comcast executive who joined the "Comcast, We Hate You" group on Facebook and responded to complaints from the community. This might not have resolved the issue completely, but demonstrated that Comcast cares and wants constructive feedback.

  Sometimes, an official company statement made in the form of a posted photo, video, link, or reply to a message board post can be a good way to respond to suggestions and constructive feedback when the online social community is large and composed of at least some members who do not know one another. The response should always include acknowledgment of the important role played by the community, sincere thanks, and either clarification of facts or commitment to action as a result of the feedback. The response should come from someone credible, usually a company executive who works in the aspect of the business receiving feedback, and include opportunities for community members to follow up with that individual through the online social network. Company executives might want to create user profiles for this purpose that are separate from their individual personal profiles and allow PR or customer service staff to reply on their behalf.

There are certain scenarios for which the official public response is not a good idea. If the community is small and composed of people who all know one another, a sudden unexpected post from an outsider could feel invasive. Similarly if members are just expressing themselves in their discussion board messages and there really is no constructive action to be taken, a corporate response is unnecessary and out of place. Finally, if action could be taken but there is no commitment by the company to do so, responding might only serve to annoy community members because no one likes lip service.

- *Unofficial public response.* For certain products and audiences, such as a particular age group, geographic region, or role, a response might be more effective coming from someone other than a company executive. For example, a young employee who recently graduated from college might be better able to relate to a community of teens or college students. An employee in your Bangkok office or if you don't have one, an employee of Thai heritage, might be the best representative of your company to respond to feedback from a Thai group on MySpace. Because these responses are from someone other than an executive, they can be crafted to sound more informal and are often perceived as being more credible.

- *Proxy response.* Taking this one step further, sometimes the best person to respond to community criticism isn't someone inside your company at all. It might make sense to ask a trusted customer to respond on your behalf. This can be the most credible option because it is an unbiased third party rather than you coming to your defense or tooting your horn. The risk here is that if community members suspect in any way that you have "planted" someone, your company could lose a lot of credibility. Another drawback of the proxy response is that it could get lost in the series of community posts, whereas a company response might stand out and receive more notice.

- *Private response.* If a community member has expressed strong feelings or suggested an idea but failed to engage other community members, a public response might not be warranted. In this case, if you are to respond at all, you might want to do so privately by sending a message directly to the individual and engaging on a one-on-one basis. It is like clicking "reply" instead of "reply all."

  Private response is also a good option when you have identified early adopters, influencers, and thought leaders within a community and want to engage further through, for example, a more in-depth survey, interview, or focus group.

- *Response through another channel.* Sometimes, your best response might be through another channel. Tapping into unsanctioned communities in listen-only mode can help drive your strategy elsewhere, such as how you think about TV and radio advertisements, new product and feature development, and targeting new audiences.

- *Sit back and just listen.* Sometimes, it's best to sit back and just listen. People create and join these unofficial communities in the first place because they want an unbiased place where they can share information and validation about your product from people they trust. Especially when customer conversations are neutral, positive, or advisory, it is in your best interest to let these happen organically without intervention. For example, if customers are helping each other with questions and issues, your participation could stifle this free and wonderful resource.

Whatever you do, you must tread carefully and respect the autonomy, tacit rules, and culture of the community that has been created. The community might be around your product, but it is not a community you can dictate or control. If anything, you should take what you learn from these unsanctioned communities and conversations and use them to refine or even reshape your online social strategy.

Define and Establish Your Presence

Armed with the full context around your strategy and priorities as well as what side conversations people are having about your brand, you are ready to establish your official social networking presence.

Why should companies invest in a social network community? Your customers and prospects—hundreds of millions of them—are on social networking sites. Increasingly, they are looking for you there, for example to share their experiences using your product, ask for advice, or learn about other products. Directed engagement not only allows you to influence your brand and take it in new directions, but it is also an efficient and cost-effective way to improve customer satisfaction and create channels for your customers to do word-of-mouth marketing on your behalf. As we talked about in Chapter 5, doing so on social networking sites means you are catching people when they are among friends and comfortable.

There are several important aspects of establishing a social network presence. First, marketers need to evaluate which social network or social networks make sense for their product. Next, marketers should consider using a persona to represent their brand. Personas can be effective for helping people relate to brands that might be harder to understand or become passionate about. Third, social networking initiatives should tie back to and incorporate existing social media efforts, such as blogs and wikis. For certain products, marketers can help drive additional online engagement by forging closer ties to offline purchases or building unofficial guerilla communities in place of or in addition to the official one. This section also includes a sidebar that walks through how to set up a successful Facebook Page.

But Which Social Network?

With hundreds of social networking sites out there, it is easy to get distracted or over-whelmed. Especially at the outset, it's not a bad idea to focus your efforts on one or two sites where you've identified your most valuable audiences spend time. Many marketers are concentrating their efforts on Facebook and MySpace because of their extensive reach and sophisticated advertising tools that support techniques like hypertargeting and social distribution. But the other social networks are catching up and innovating in their own ways.

Ultimately, your product niche and target audience should drive the decision of where you invest. Each site has its pros and cons, unique culture, and demographic. For media and entertainment, it is likely MySpace. For most English-speaking countries, it is Facebook. For India and Brazil, it's Orkut. For many other non-English speaking countries, such as Thailand, Peru, and Greece, it is Hi5 and Friendster. Social networks are also seg-mented by age. Often younger audiences start on one site and later "graduate" to new sites as they grow up. For example, a child might start on Club Penguin and then move onto MySpace in her early teen years, myYearbook during high school, Facebook during college, and then during her professional years join LinkedIn and later TeeBeeDee. Marketers need to tailor their advertising efforts and messages to the unique culture of each social networking site. The appendix at the end of this book provides an overview of the top sites, their niches, and key stats.

For sites that don't make your short list, you might still try to periodically pay attention to what's being said, but take more of a backseat. You can be more *laissez-faire* about these communities and conversations while still offering audience members opportunities to engage if they so choose. The key here is to rely more on zealous community members to take the lead on these sites, or if that is inadequate, link to more active forums you might have elsewhere.

Use of Personas

Especially if your product or positioning isn't particularly sexy, for example if you are the low-cost provider of something, even satisfied customers might not want to publicly associate themselves with your brand. Personas, or fictional characters created to tell a story and convey a certain voice, can help. Some personas are used to make otherwise dull brands seem cool and fun. In other situations, personas are used to make it easier for people to relate to what your product or service helps them accomplish.

Persona marketing has been around for awhile but is given new meaning in the context of online social networks because customers can "befriend" and interact with the per-sona. Instead of interfacing with a vague brand entity, interactions feel more personal and emotional.

The Jack in the Box page on MySpace, described in Chapter 5, does a good job of persona marketing. Instead of making the page about the restaurant (which might not be that exciting), marketers created a funny, sarcastic biography and voice for their persona, Jack Box, that incorporates facts about the restaurant. For example, Jack in the Box was started in San Diego, which is Jack's hometown. The persona serves as a proxy for the restaurant that uses humor and storytelling to bring the brand to life. It fits perfectly with the profile metaphor on MySpace that lets people add Jack as a connection just like they add other friends. People love Jack. They leave comments for him. They write poetry. They send messages.

People love Jack Box but don't necessarily relate to him. The other kind of persona marketing seeks to create believable characters who reflect the same cares, concerns, and values as your customer, who feel your customer's pain. What motivates this person? What keeps her up at night? What are her goals and how does your product help her achieve them?

What are the personas that make sense for your brand? What is their voice? What do they blog about? What story would you tell about them using biography, photos, and video? How do they interact with friends and fans? If you've never done persona marketing before, MySpace and Facebook can provide a good forum for trying it out.

Your Official Community

As Chapter 5 described, MySpace brand profiles and Facebook Pages are reserved for use by the brand. Only the official representative of the artist, business, or organization is allowed to create the official community. Anyone else who wants to start an unofficial community must use groups, detailed in a later section, to do so.

The following sidebar guides you through how to set up a Facebook Page.

Setting Up a Facebook Page

Your Facebook Page is your brand's official social network community. It should represent what your company is, who you are serving, why they should care, and where they can go to learn more or take further action. When people become fans of your Facebook Page, their friends are notified via News Feeds. If they click on the story, they are taken to your Facebook Page. Pages are also often used as the landing page for social ads. There are eight simple steps for getting started:

1. *Register for a Facebook account.* To create a Page or buy ads, you first need a personal account.

continues...

2. Create a new Page. Most products and services fall under the "Brand or Product" category. If you are a smaller business focused on a specific locale, you can select the "Local" option, which Facebook has defined mostly for services businesses catering to a particular city. The last option is for artists, bands, and other public figures, such as politicians and celebrities (see Figure 8.6).

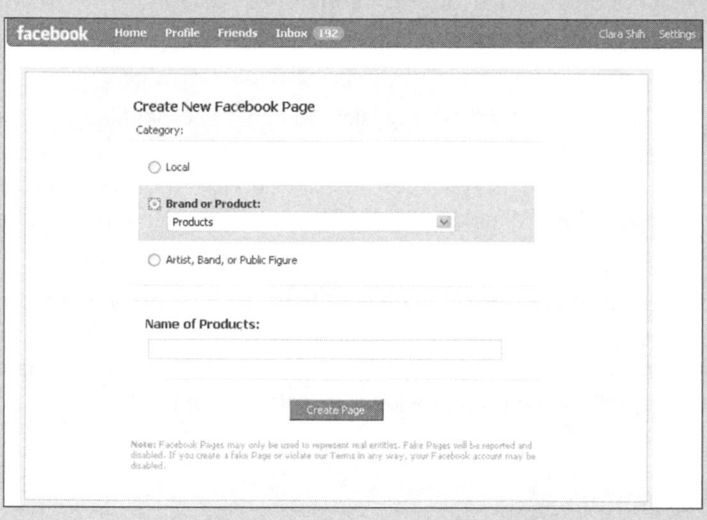

Figure 8.6
Once you have come up with a strategy and your set of content, actually creating a new Facebook Page is fairly straightforward. Just specify the name and type, and Facebook will generate a page template with blank sections for picture, description, wall, photo, video, and notes.

3. *Upload a picture, provide basic information, and customize the look and feel.* Use a large, high-resolution logo for your picture. Grainy pictures look unprofessional. Next, provide basic information about your brand, such as when it was founded, a link to your Web site, company overview, mission, and list of products. To make it more entertaining and stand out, it's not a bad idea to also include interesting facts such as celebrity customers, funny quotes, and brand trivia. Last, but not least, you can use Facebook Markup Language (FBML) to customize the Page's look and feel using HTML and Flash. You might want to make this consistent with your brand look and feel elsewhere. Some companies choose to purposely create a completely different look and feel to bring fresh perspective to the brand.

4. *Add engaging content, platform apps, and opportunities for interaction.* Before you make the Page public, seed it with interactive content and apps, such as polls, petitions, games, contests, slideshows, and surveys, to inspire engagement. Platform applications can be added to Facebook Pages just like they are added to a person's profile.

In addition, you should write a "welcome" message on the wall, post relevant links, seed discussion board topics by posing open-ended questions (like "what are your thoughts on X?"), upload photos, and add a Note (similar to a blog entry). If you already have an external blog, you can have updates stream into your Page by adding your blog feed into the built-in Notes application.

When you are ready, publish the Page so that it becomes public, shows up in search results, and becomes viewable by others.

5. *Recruit early fans.* Make sure to become a fan of your own Page, and ask your employees, friends, and acquaintances to do the same. It's important to seed the Page with a critical mass of fans before going out to the public and recruiting new people. You want people being exposed to your brand or Page for the first time to feel like it's dynamic and in high demand.

6. *Promote your Page to get more fans.* You can help promote your page using Facebook Ads. Another popular technique is to include a link to your page in your e-mail signatures, Web site, blogs, and other customer or prospect touch points so they know where to find you on Facebook.

7. *Moderate the community by periodically updating content and responding to posts.* At least once a week, refresh content with new surveys, contests, videos, photos, articles, and announcements. Hopefully, you will have developed these for other channels such as your Web site. You can reuse them here. Less frequently, you might want to check out new platform apps to add and switch out old ones. Respond where appropriate to user generated content, such as wall posts and forum messages, especially if someone asks a question that has not received a response. Dynamic content is best at keeping users engaged, so select content that is timely, recent, and preferably multimedia.

People will keep coming back to your Page only if you give them reasons to do so. If your Page is stale, you will lose people's attention and potentially even hurt your brand. Set the right expectations for your community according to the high-level strategy you developed, and then make sure you follow through on the commitment.

8. *Consider different Pages for different audiences.* Just like you might create multiple landing pages in traditional online marketing to tailor your message to specific audiences, you might consider creating multiple Facebook Pages. There are trade-offs to maintaining more than one Page, so it might not make sense in every case. If you do decide to support multiple Pages, keep in mind you can reuse elements across Pages, such as streaming blog updates, video, and apps.

Integrate with Existing Social Media Initiatives

The biggest challenge of any community is how to keep it dynamic. Social network communities can be a great opportunity to reuse a lot of the assets you have developed elsewhere. Consider your Facebook Page or MySpace profile as additional channels for these social media assets. For example, you can set up the Notes application in your Facebook Page to automatically stream the RSS feed from an external blog directly into Facebook. Your brand's Facebook Page in effect becomes another window for customers into your company, products, and vision. Instead of starting from scratch, you can get more mileage out of your existing investments. Not only does this save you time, but tying back to existing initiatives also creates a greater sense of cohesiveness across all of your customer touch points.

This is good news for many companies. Sixty-two percent of Fortune 500 companies, for example, report that they have at least one customer-facing blog. Instead of expecting customers to come to you and read your blog, you might win broader readership by bringing your blog to them on Facebook.

Offline Bridges

Another way to drive traffic and increase engagement is to create bridges to your customer's offline interactions with your product. Ganz, a toy company based in Canada, has pioneered a successful online-offline model with its Webkinz line of stuffed animals. Every Webkinz toy comes with a special code that allows the owner to access the Webkinz virtual world Web site and claim the virtual version of his or her pet stuffed animal. In the virtual world, users can play online games such as trivia, send and receive virtual gifts, create and share virtual television shows, chat, and participate in contests for prizes (see Figure 8.7). Unlike a traditional toy sale, the purchase of a Webkinz stuffed animal is just the beginning of a long customer engagement.

The Webkinz virtual world is not a pure social networking site the way we have been describing in this book so far. As the target audience is children ages 5–13, Webkinz is less about networking and more about virtual interaction. But the model is breakthrough and could potentially be applied more broadly to online social networks. The bridge from offline to online has proven very successful in building brand loyalty, not to mention creating ongoing engagement and marketing opportunities for upselling and cross-selling.

Some social networking sites are starting to take notice. In 2008, Hi5 acquired PixVerse, a virtual world company, to quickly introduce virtual world functionality into its social networking service. Second Life, already described in Chapter 1, "The Fourth Revolution," is another popular virtual world used by over 15 million people. Hi5 and Second Life have yet to link these virtual worlds with physical goods, but it seems like there might be an interesting opportunity to do so, like what MyListo is doing with virtual gifts of real products (see Chapter 5).

Figure 8.7
Webkinz has a virtual world with virtual toys that correspond to real-life toys.

Unofficial Communities

Last, but not least, you might want to consider creating unofficial social network communities with Facebook, MySpace, or Hi5 groups. For example, unofficial communities are good for guerilla efforts when you want to be incognito or try something drastically different. They can also be more credible because they are assumed to be of and by the people instead of controlled by your company. In case efforts are not successful or something controversial gets posted, your brand is held less accountable because it wasn't officially sanctioned and sponsored.

There are drawbacks, however. Because it doesn't have the official endorsement of your brand, people might take it less seriously and put less faith in its accuracy. There are also limitations on how much you can customize the page; for example, you cannot add platform applications, use HTML and Flash, or stream blog updates into groups. Some companies are exploring using a mix of official and unofficial communities to define their overall social network presence.

9

Get Your Message Across

As we introduced in Chapter 5, "Social Network Marketing," online social networks allow advertisers to achieve new levels of precision and social distribution with hypertargeting and word of mouth. Hypertargeting provides marketers a way to hone in on very specific audience segments who are most likely to be interested, reducing the number of wasted ad impressions. Hypertargeting techniques can also be used to tailor custom campaigns to make ads feel more relevant and personal to the people viewing them. Passive word-of-mouth broadcasts across friend groups and the social graph multiply the distribution effects of these campaigns. Word of mouth also brings the credibility and personal touch of social filtering to marketing messages; social ads feel more like endorsements from friends.

This chapter walks through how and when to hypersegment your audience based on your product, customers, and goals. We discuss best practices around using hypertargeting to optimize campaigns, including how to reduce variance when you are testing new ads. We then devote the second half of the chapter to discussing the pros, cons, and how-tos around the four aspects of social network advertising: targeted ads, appvertisements, Social Actions, and Facebook engagement ads.

For the sake of brevity, the examples and step-by-step instructions in this chapter are largely geared toward Facebook. Among the online social networks, Facebook has the most sophisticated and comprehensive set of advertising tools. For example, engagement ads are unique to Facebook. Hypertargeting thus far is available only on Facebook and MySpace. Only appvertisements, that is sponsored branded apps, are available on a majority of social networking sites (any social network that supports a platform). That said, we are still in the early days of social network marketing. It is probably just a matter of time until the other social networking sites come up with similar hypertargeting and engagement advertising capabilities, or their own innovative ad capabilities that harness the unique power of the social graph.

Hypersegment Your Audience

Facebook Era advertisers have an unprecedented ability to target ads based on very specific demographic and psychographic audience criteria, such as gender, age, education, workplace, relationship status, relationship goals, interests, and location. Using data about individuals' self-stated attributes and preferences, advertisers can focus their efforts on the highest-impact audiences and tailor messaging to make ads more relevant.

The hardest but most important aspect of hypertargeting is choosing the right hypersegments. The flexibility to target along so many dimensions can be overwhelming for new advertisers. The trick is to find the two or three criteria that matter most about your product. These criteria vary by product. For example, relationship status ("engaged") and gender ("female") might be most important in ads for wedding planning services but have no bearing on ads for digital cameras.

Ultimately, finding the right hypersegments comes down to what about people makes them more or less likely to be interested in your product. Over time, as you discover more about the audiences interested in your product, the effectiveness of your hypersegments should improve. Finally, hypersegmented campaigns can also be used to refine campaign analysis by reducing variance, particularly for smaller ad runs.

What Matters Most About Your Product

To take advantage of hypertargeting, you first need to hypersegment your audience along the key dimensions that matter for your particular product. Not surprisingly, the most often used dimension is interest keywords because that is all-encompassing. Here are other ways you can think about each hypertarget dimension:

- *Sex (Male, Female).* Gender is especially important in retail ads. If your product is meant for a specific gender, for example women, you might want to consider using two ad segments: ads appealing to women about your product and ads targeting men that talk about your product as a great gift for women.

- *Relationship Status (Single, In a Relationship, Engaged, Married).* This is mostly useful for anything related to dating and relationships, such as books, dating services, bachelor parties, couples vacations, engagement rings, wedding planning, and couples counseling. Relationship status is also correlated with lifestyle, and certain lifestyles might be more amenable to your product or service. For example, a married person might be more likely than a single person to be interested in ads about income tax filing services or purchasing a home in a good school district.

- *Relationship Interest (Male, Female)*. This is used for products and services related to dating and matchmaking. For example, groups and services targeting the lesbian, gay, bisexual, and transgender (LGBT) community can reach this audience by selecting the same gender in both the Sex and Relationship Interest fields.

- *Age (Age Range)*. Age is pretty self-explanatory, but note it is increasingly common practice for social network members to either not specify age or make something up, especially for those out of college. By specifying an age range, you are implicitly (often unintentionally) leaving out these individuals.

- *Education (College Grad, In College, In High School, or All)*. Education can be an imperfect but useful proxy for age. It is useful because almost all Facebook members specify their education; that is, how they get associated to their school network. For example, it's probably safe to assume that most college grads are over 22, most people in college are between 18 and 22, and most people in high school are between 14 and 18 years of age.

- *Workplaces (List of Employers)*. This is useful if your product or service is specially geared toward a particular industry, location, or company. For example, if your product targets fast-food workers, you might specify *McDonald's, Burger King,* and *Wendy's* under Workplaces. A restaurant in a particular city might target ads for its business lunch to employees at surrounding companies. Finally, advertisers might want to use employer information to make their ads seem more relevant, even if their product isn't actually specifically meant for employees of that company. For example, the same restaurant might make an appeal, "Calling all Company X employees!"

- *Location (Country or City)*. This is an important dimension to use if your products and services are only offered in certain geographic areas. Facebook allows you to specify location at the country or city level.

- *Interests (free-form keywords)*. Based on Facebook's analysis, interest keywords, which encompass profile fields such as favorite music, books, movies, and job title, are for many products and services generally the most effective hypertargeting dimension.

The dimensions are even more powerful when used in combination. One helpful aspect of the Facebook advertiser tool is that as you are going along specifying criteria, it automatically tells you what the size of the audience segment is that you have selected. If this is too small, you might want to relax on your criteria a bit. If this is too large, try specifying narrower criteria or more criteria dimensions.

The obvious way to segment is to look at what kinds of audiences you have had the most success marketing to in the past, and try to look for certain patterns that emerge. A new, Facebook-Era segmentation method is to brainstorm what kinds of people *might* be interested in your product. Perhaps in the past, it was too expensive or not possible to reach these people. Hypertargeted ads provide the perfect opportunity to test many different messages on many different audiences until you find something that sticks.

Tie Back to Your Goals

Of course, anything you do should be tied back to your social networking strategy developed in Chapter 8, "Engage Your Customers." Work backward from your goals. Is your primary focus new customer acquisition? Or do you have plenty of customers but need to upsell and cross-sell them on new products? Here are some goals for which hypertargeting works particularly well:

- Reach new audience segments, such as a new age group, region, interests, and college attended.

- Test new messages and see what resonates.

- Think global, act local—similar to how Bonobos, Inc., has global sales and operations but tailors its campaigns to each school and hometown sports team fans to make its products feel more personal and relevant.

- Upsell or cross-sell existing customers on additional products and services.

- Learn about your customer base and what factors most heavily influence interest and purchase decisions.

If your campaigns aren't performing to your expectations, try different copy or altering your hypertargeting strategy. Table 9.1 highlights common issues advertisers face with hypertargeting and suggested ways to address them.

Table 9.1 COMMON ISSUES WITH HYPERTARGETED AD CAMPAIGNS AND SUGGESTIONS ON HOW TO RESOLVE THEM

If you have this problem...	... then consider doing this
Not enough impressions	Try adjusting your targeting to be less restrictive by reducing the number of dimensions or increasing the number of acceptable values.
Low clickthrough rate	Create smaller hypersegments to pinpoint who is clicking and who isn't. Make ads more personal and specific based on what you know about the audience. Test different calls to action.
Low sales conversion	Make sure your landing page is consistent with your ad and similarly customized for the hypersegment. Try using limited-time offers to create a sense of urgency.
Campaign performance worsening	Your ads are probably stale. Refresh campaigns with new ad copy and images.
Consistent low performance in a particular hypersegment compared with others	You might want to consider cutting this hypersegment out altogether and focus your efforts on more responsive segments.

If you have more complex campaign requirements or are in an advertising-crowded market, a number of companies, such as Lotame, specialize in providing social media ad analytics and helping companies design effective hypertargeted campaigns.

Reduce Variance

Another important use of hypersegments is in testing. By specifying very narrow homogeneous dimensions, you are reducing the presence of confounding factors that could be affecting your campaign. In effect, you are creating a controlled experiment that gives you more insight into what campaigns work and why. The "variable" you change is the ad.

For example, a poorly performing campaign could actually be more nuanced: Perhaps the ads perform extremely well with single women between 30 and 35, but extremely poorly with everyone else. Before, there was no way to dig deeper. Now, advertisers can be very scientific about their campaigns and audience segments.

Choose Your Media Strategy

After you know *what* you want to say and to *whom* you want to say it, it's time to decide *how* you want to say it. At a high level, there are four aspects of social network ads: targeted ads, appvertising, Social Actions, and engagement ads. Depending on your product, audience, and campaign objectives, one or a combination of these might make the most sense.

Targeted Ads

Targeted ads on Facebook consist of a heading, body text, and an optional picture. They appear in two places: designated ad space in the right column of the Facebook screen (Figure 9.1) and News Feeds (Figure 9.2). Placement is based on ad performance, your specified ad budget, and whether you have elected a CPC or CPM payment model. CPC, or cost per click, allows advertisers to pay for the number of clicks generated by their ads. CPM, or cost per thousand impressions, lets advertisers pay based on how many times their ads have been viewed. The "Creating a Targeted Ad on Facebook" sidebar walks through how to set up a targeted ad campaign on Facebook.

Figure 9.1
Facebook Ad in the designated ad space. Ads here can be either CPM or CPC ads.

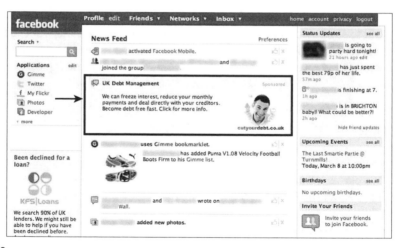

Figure 9.2
News Feed ad. Only CPC ads appear in the News Feed. To avoid annoying users or polluting the Facebook experience, it is Facebook policy that the News Feed contain at most one ad.

Creating a Targeted Ad on Facebook

There are four steps to creating targeted ads on Facebook.

First, you have to decide where you want to drive ad clickthroughs (see Figure 9.3). Is your landing page on Facebook or external to Facebook (for example, a lead capture form on your Web site)? If you are an admin of a Facebook group, Event, application, Page, or Marketplace listing, you can create targeted ads that link to it.

Figure 9.3
You can drive ad clickthroughs to a group, Event, application, Page, or Marketplace listing on Facebook, or to an external landing page, such as a lead-capture form.

Next, you have to create the ad itself. Based on the hypersegment you have identified, come up with custom ad copy that will catch your audience's attention. What's important to this particular segment? What do you know about them (that is, what have you selected for) that you could use to make the message more personal? What have they bought in the past? What are they likely to want to buy in the future?

Keep the ad text simple and be specific. Avoid compound sentences. Use simple language and good grammar. Especially if your objective is brand recognition, you should include your company or product name in the ad title or body (see Figure 9.4).

The most important thing you can do is to provide a compelling call-to-action that encourages users to click on your ad. It should be clear from your ad copy exactly what you expect them to do and how they will benefit from going to your landing page. Use strong action-oriented phrases such as *buy, sell, see, order, register,* and *win.* Improve customer engagement and likeliness to click by making messages feel more personal and meant for them specifically.

Uploading an image is optional but highly recommended. Facebook's data shows that ads with an image perform much better than ads without. The maximum image size is 110 pixels wide by 80 pixels tall, so you will want to create or resize your ad image accordingly. Without special consideration, text in images in particular can sometimes become distorted and hard to read.

You also have the option to include Social Actions with your ad. Social Actions display which of your friends is also a member of the group, fan of the Page, or confirmed to attend the event being advertised. Social Actions are covered at greater length in a later section.

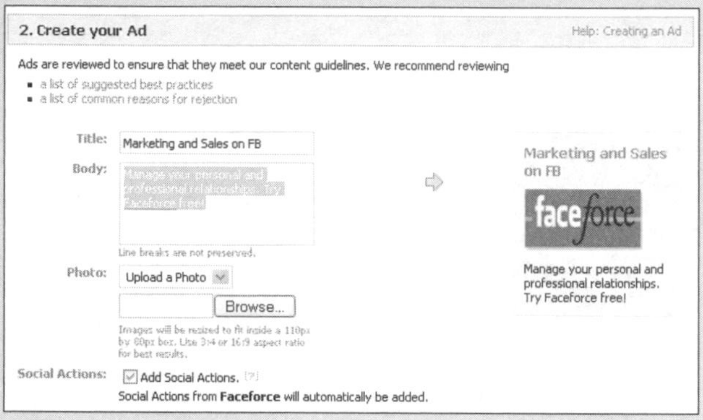

Figure 9.4
The four most important things to keep in mind when creating your ad: Keep it simple, customize the message to your hypersegment, create a clear call to action, and include a picture.

Step 3 is to specify the targeting parameters. As mentioned earlier, Facebook provides an estimate of hypersegment size; that is, how many of its members fit the criteria you have established? Depending on your ad budget and desired reach, you can tweak the parameters to expand or narrow down the addressable audience for your ad campaign, as shown in Figure 9.5.

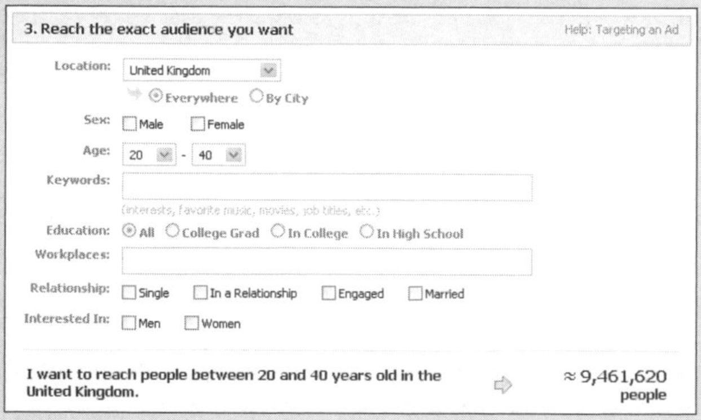

Figure 9.5
Facebook advertisers can hypertarget along eight different dimensions: location, gender, age, interest keywords, education level, workplace, relationship status, and relationship interest. At each step, advertisers can see how many Facebook members fit the criteria specified thus far.

The final step is to decide on the ad pricing model. You have two options: CPC or CPM. With CPC, advertisers pay per click. Your ad will appear in the News Feed, ad space, or both. With CPM, you pay for impressions. CPM ads on Facebook appear in the ad space slots only. Many advertisers find CPC appealing because they are paying for performance only. When ads are not clicked on, the advertiser essentially gets a brand impression for free. On the other hand, CPM can deliver impressions more cheaply when clickthroughs don't matter. Without the pressure of having to generate a click, CPM ads might also tend to be flashier and contain more information.

In either model, you specify a daily budget (you will never get charged more than this amount per day), maximum bid (either for each click or for every thousand impressions), and schedule, as shown in Figure 9.6.

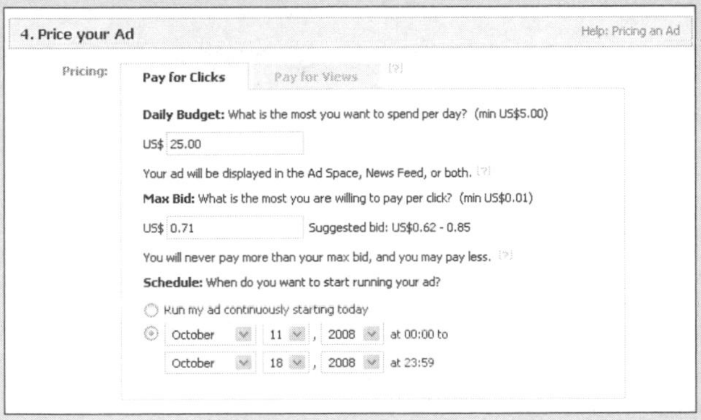

Figure 9.6
The fourth step is setting your daily budget, maximum bid, and schedule for your ad campaign.

For your first few campaigns, start small. Tweak and test your campaigns with different hypertargeting criteria and values. Compare your cost to performance ratios for CPM versus CPC. Be creative. Try different messages out. Run ads for two weeks, and then assess their effectiveness. What was the clickthrough rate? What was the conversion into sales? Which hypersegments perform the best? Learn from your tests and keep trying new things.

Brand Appvertising

Apps are the new ads. Platform apps are another way to encourage audiences to engage with your brand. The idea is that people tend to spend more time on apps—such as playing games, looking through slideshows, and taking surveys—than traditional advertising, so apps might provide more lasting and memorable interactions with your brand.

As discussed earlier in the book, the biggest successes in social network appvertising we have seen have come from brands working with already-popular applications rather than trying to build their own. It's just too hard to know what new apps will take off. If you are willing to make a substantial sponsorship investment, you can work with the top app developers—for example, RockYou, Slide, and Zynga—to advertise within one of their apps (see Figure 9.7). This is what large brands like Netflix and Gap, Inc., have done to reach big audiences quickly.

Figure 9.7
Advertising by an IQ quiz app in RockYou's Pieces of Flair application. For larger brands, RockYou also sells dedicated brand campaigns that run for a specified duration of time.

To sponsor more niche apps or to get help distributing your own brand widgets, you can go through ad networks such as Offerpal Media, and Gigya. Increasingly, advertisers are also using user profile data-targeting analytics tools such as those offered by Lookery to run more sophisticated hypertargeted campaigns (see Figure 9.8).

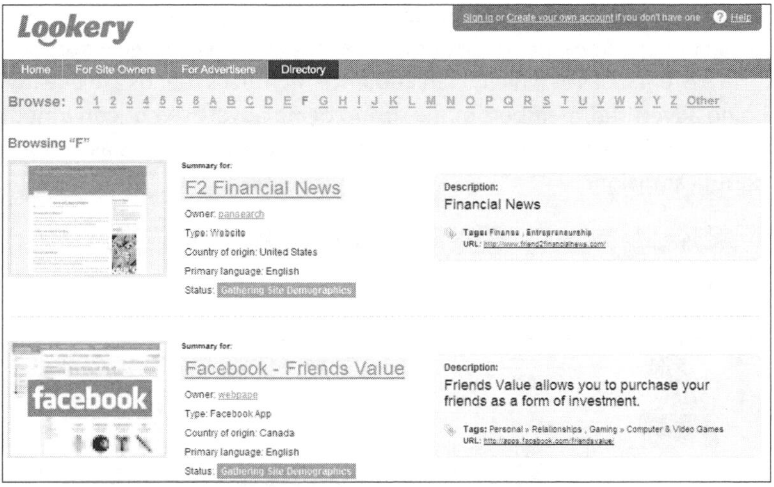

Figure 9.8
Lookery's directory of ad network publishers, including Facebook apps, for which they have demographic data. Lookery specializes in analytics hypertargeting tools for advertisers to reach precise audience segments based on demographic profiling and usage behavior.

How do advertisers determine which apps, if any, are a good fit? The app developers and ad networks have pretty good data around the profiles of people using their apps. Depending on your goals and budget, the networks also vary in terms of ad models, ranging from CPM and CPC to CPA (cost per action).

Social Actions and Social Stories

The social distribution of News Feed broadcasts provide a powerful amplification effect for targeted ads and brand appvertisements. Every time an audience member engages becomes an opportunity for several of his or her friends to become engaged as well. People pay more attention when they see their friend's name. Two things happen. First, social filtering occurs. People are curious about what their friend found interesting and compelling enough to act on. Second, people might choose to engage with the ad as a means of engaging with their friend. If the ad is promoting an event, people might choose to RSVP because they see their friend is planning to attend. Advertisers, in effect, can tap into the social capital between friends and friend groups to win higher engagement levels.

Facebook's ad system serves Social Ads that combine Social Actions from your friends— such as a purchase of a product or review of a restaurant—with an advertiser's message. This enables advertisers to deliver more tailored and relevant ads to Facebook users that now include information from their friends, so they can make more informed decisions. No personally identifiable information is shared with an advertiser in creating a Social Ad.

When advertisers choose to associate Social Actions with a campaign, ads are shown that combine Social Actions from friends with the advertiser's message (see Figure 9.9). Facebook's ad system looks at which of an audience member's friends are already fans of the Page being advertised, members of the group being advertised, or confirmed attendees of the event being advertised, and in effect uses those individuals as endorsers in a word-of-mouth campaign.

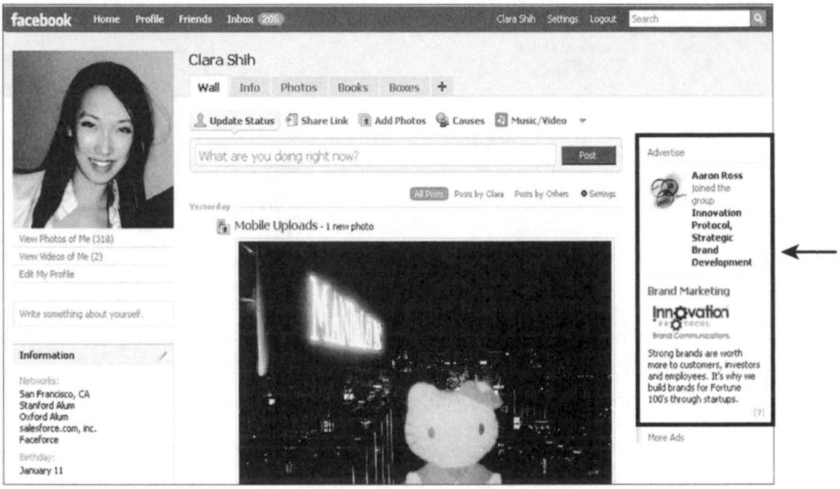

Figure 9.9
Social Actions automatically bring word-of-mouth marketing to your ad campaigns. For example, this ad for the Facebook group, "Innovation Protocol, Strategic Brand Development," also tells me one of my friends is already a member of this group.

The equivalent of Social Actions occurs in appvertising, too. Games, polls, slideshows, and other platform applications encourage people to invite friends to install the app, sometimes using invites sent as a way to accrue points and status in the app. App engagement is social—in games, for example, you can see which of your friends is playing the game, see how your score compares, or directly challenge friends head-on in live games (see Figure 9.10). By default, every time you install or use an app, this shows up as a feed story on your profile and on your friends' News Feed updates about you.

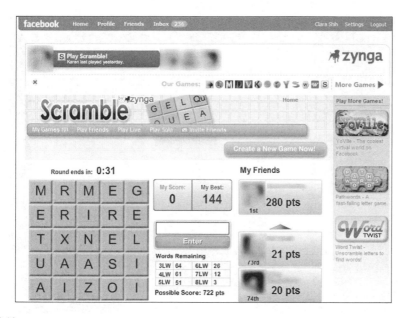

Figure 9.10
Social engagement on Scramble, a game by Zynga.

Last, but not least, social stories can be enabled for external apps that plug into Facebook using Facebook Connect. As we discussed briefly in Chapter 2, "The Evolution of Digital Media," some apps use the Facebook Connect API to bring the social graph to an external Web site and conversely to broadcast actions taken on the external Web site back to user profiles and News Feed updates within Facebook. We talked about the Red Bull Web site in Chapter 2. Citysearch, a popular restaurant and nightlife review site, is another good example of how an external Web site is using Facebook Connect. On the Citysearch site, I can see which of my Facebook Friends are also members of Citysearch and which restaurants they have reviewed. When I write a restaurant review on Citysearch, I am given an option to publish the review to Facebook (see Figure 9.11). If I agree, the review appears on my profile as well as in my friends' News Feed updates about me (see Figure 9.12).

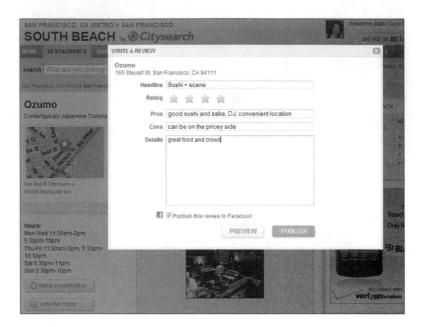

Figure 9.11
Citysearch uses Facebook Connect to bring the online social graph to its Web site. When I wrote a restaurant review on Citysearch, it asked if I want to publish the review to my Facebook profile and my friends' News Feed updates.

Figure 9.12
My friend's News Feed containing a story about my Citysearch restaurant review.

With Facebook Connect, users have to provide explicit permission for any action from external Web sites to be published back to Facebook. Facebook Connect has been a welcome improvement on Beacon, Facebook's earlier attempt to incorporate external Web site activity into Facebook feed stories. Beacon, which publishes external feed stories without explicit user permission, generated a privacy outcry when it launched in autumn 2007.

With sophisticated privacy setting options, Facebook members can now control whether they appear in Social Actions and which platform apps or Facebook Connect sites are allowed to generate feed stories on their profile. As a result of the increased trust, the social aspect of targeted ads, appvertisements, and external Facebook Connect applications has become a welcome and valuable part of the engagement experience on Facebook that can also greatly benefit advertisers.

Engagement Ads

In addition to click ads and apps, Facebook is also exploring what they call engagement ads. Engagement ads were designed to offer advertisers minimally invasive ways of inserting their brands into everyday Facebook interactions. The thought is that if there are opportunities for people to engage with brands without disrupting their primary mission on social networking sites—that is, expressing themselves and socializing with others—then they will be much more likely to take advantage of these opportunities. Targeted ads, in contrast, are disruptive in the Facebook member's experience. Clicking on an ad drives the user away from what she was previously doing without giving the user a chance to socially engage.

Facebook has developed four models of incorporating advertising into social behavior that people are already doing: in-line video commenting, sponsored virtual gifts, in-line event RSVP, and in-line becoming a fan of a Facebook Page.

Video commenting takes the viral nature of entertaining videos popularized by YouTube and combines it with the Facebook Friend graph and feed stories (see Figure 9.13). For example, MTV purchased a video ad on Facebook of Britney Spears opening the 2008 Video Music Awards. Users could view and comment on the video completely in-line, without clicking to another page. This generated awareness and participation while offering members an opportunity to engage with friends.

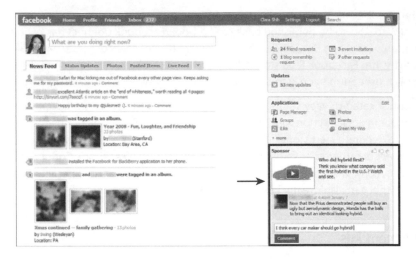

Figure 9.13

Video commenting ads are ideal for promoting popular media, such as music videos, movie trail-ers, and TV shows. They encourage viral marketing by offering people a way to react and engage with their friends on the video.

Sponsored virtual gifts are a second engagement ad model. Virtual gifts have become a popular way for Facebook users to exchange social capital, express affection, and build rapport, such as for birthdays, special achievements, and other milestones. Brands now have the opportunity to sponsor virtual gifts so that instead of costing the sender $1, they are free. The brand benefits not only from the sender and recipient having engaged with the brand, but also from the resulting social feed stories that get propagated to both sender and recipient's networks. For example, Wendy's, a popular fast-food restau-rant, sponsored a branded virtual gift to spread the word about its new "flavor dipped" sandwiches (see Figure 9.14). Sponsored virtual gifts can be a fun, visual, and memorable form of word-of-mouth awareness for your product or brand.

Figure 9.14
Wendy's, a fast-food chain, has sponsored a virtual gift to virally spread the word about its new line of "flavor dipped" sandwiches.

The last two engagement ad models are in-line event RSVP and in-line becoming a fan of a Facebook Page. The rationale for these is that people are much more likely to participate if it's easy for them to do so. Being able to RSVP or become a fan in-line without clicking to another page minimizes the amount of effort required by the user to engage (see Figures 9.15 and 9.16).

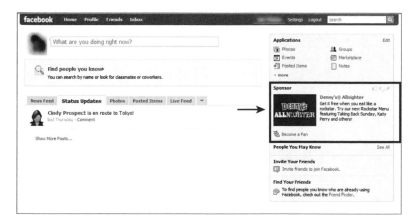

Figure 9.15
Engagement ads on Facebook allow users to become fans of Facebook Pages with one click, without leaving the page they were on.

Figure 9.16
Engagement ads on Facebook also allow users to RSVP and leave notes for advertiser-sponsored events in-line without leaving the page they were on.

10

Build and Manage Your Relationships

Whatever your job or industry, you can start using and benefiting from online social networks as personal relationship management tools. Even if you aren't in sales or recruiting *per se,* at some point in your career you will be buying or selling something. Maybe you will need to sell yourself as a job candidate for an open position or as a domain expert for a project. And you just never know.

But it isn't just about social capital. Building deeper relationships with your colleagues, customers, and business partners outside of work can make your job more enjoyable and fulfilling. The first step is to establish your personal presence on these social networking sites, not unlike how you established your company's presence in Chapter 8, "Engage Your Customers." Next, find friends who are also on these sites and add them as connections. There are a number of different modes of casual interaction with which you can strengthen your relationship. You can also use online social networking to supplement offline networking, establishing better weak-tie relationships. With your personal economy of social capital set up, you will then be in an ideal position to do more favors for others as well as tap your network for favors like finding prospective customers, job opportunities, and expertise.

Setting Up Your Facebook Account

My friend Larry half-jokes that if you are not on Facebook then you don't exist to him. He is a medical student with very little free time, and he expects his friends to find him and contact him on Facebook. The only birthdays, e-mail addresses, and phone numbers he remembers are the ones listed on Facebook. When he is planning a party, invites go out only to people he is friends with on Facebook because he uses the Facebook Events application. Larry is perhaps a little extreme but illustrates where social norms for the future might be headed. There are four steps to setting up a Facebook account: creating a profile, finding friends, organizing contacts, and managing your social network identities.

Step 1. Create Your Profile

In this day and age, people are increasingly seeking one another out on Facebook. It is, of course, up to each individual to determine how much or how little information about herself or himself to provide. Regardless, the important thing to keep in mind is that individuals must take control and responsibility for their identity on social networking sites, even if that means turning on the most strict privacy settings and sharing very little about themselves. For those willing to share more, being on social networking sites opens up a new ability to connect, interact, and bond with people from different spheres of your life.

The first step is to register for a new Facebook account. You will need four pieces of information: name, e-mail, gender, and birth date. (You can choose to hide this later.) Ideally, sign up with an e-mail address belonging to an exclusive domain, such as a company or school that can vouch for your identity. It is possible to sign up for an account using an e-mail address from a public service like Gmail, but for security reasons Facebook requires account owners with unverified public e-mail addresses to take extra steps when trying to add new friends, send messages, or take just about any action on Facebook. They just want to make sure you are not an automated spam robot.

Although Facebook purposely made the sign-up process as easy as possible by minimizing the number of mandatory fields, it is generally in your best interest to provide more information about yourself beyond the required name, e-mail, gender, and birth date. A photo can really help people remember who you are. Maybe you don't want to share religious and political views, but certainly things like hometown, favorite movies and books, and a link to your blog are good low-risk ways to help people get to know you while staying professional and not offending anyone.

Step 2. Find Friends

Because the social aspect of Facebook is so important, the registration process takes you through three optional steps that each tries to help you find more friends. First, you will have the opportunity to import contacts from your e-mail and instant messenger accounts (see Figure 10.1). Next, you will be asked to specify your high school, college, and company. Not only will this information be added to your profile, but Facebook will then find profiles of other users who went to those schools or work at the same company and suggest them as friends for you. In the last step, you are asked to specify your city to join the corresponding Facebook. This allows you to view profiles of other members of the city network and conversely to have your profile be viewable by them.

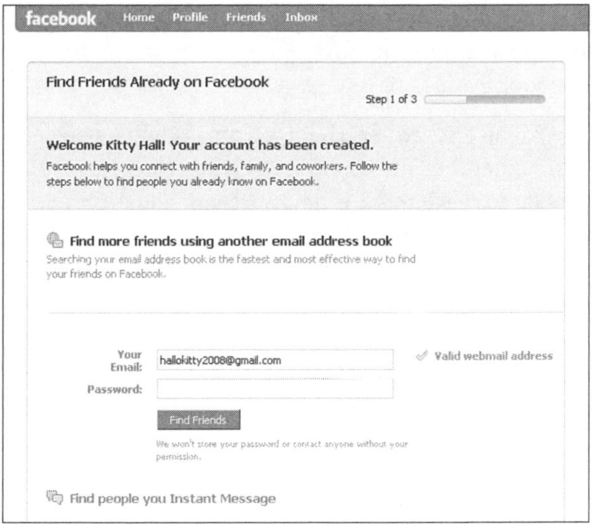

Figure 10.1
There are three steps in the Facebook new account registration process, all with the purpose of helping you establish friend connections. Step 1 is to import your e-mail and instant messaging contacts.

Step 3. Organize Your Contacts

Of course, we all carry multiple identities. We might be a salesperson or CEO or engineer by day, but we are also fathers, sisters, friends, classmates, neighbors, church leaders, intra-mural athletes, customers, and the list goes on. All of these various facets of our lives come together and comprise who we are. Certain social networking sites might focus on any given specific aspect of our lives—LinkedIn for recruiting and business development, MySpace for music, Ning for Kennedy High School in New Orleans, Louisiana—but even in these scenarios, any person might wear multiple hats. On LinkedIn, you could be a recruiter seeking candidates, but later on be looking for a job for yourself or want to find new clients for whom to recruit. Accordingly, you need to define a different social net-working profile presence for each of your identities.

Just as your business segmented its marketing audience and catered a brand message to each segment in the previous chapter, you should also "segment" your relationships and cater what information you share with each group. Using Friend Lists on Facebook, you can create custom profile views for different groups of friends. Friend Lists help you organize and manage relationships in three ways. First, they provide context of how you know someone. Especially for weak-tie relationships, it can help to have reminders of how you met someone, through whom, and so on. Second, Friend Lists allow you to customize information shared and thereby your personal brand for each group. So, you might share your job history, blog posts, and newborn's photos with coworkers but reserve the bachelor party videos from Las Vegas for your college friends. Finally, Friend Lists also function as "distribution lists" of sorts when you are sending a Facebook message (though you are restricted to at most 20 recipients at a time) or inviting people to an event using Facebook Events.

You can define new Friend Lists either when you are adding a new friend or by clicking on "Make a New List" under the Friends tab (see Figure 10.2). How you define your lists, including how granular to make them, is up to the individual, though a good rule of thumb is between three and ten. Less than that, and you are probably either sharing information with some people you shouldn't be or you aren't sharing enough with some people and thereby missing an opportunity to bond. More than that, and it becomes confusing to remember and manage. For example, I have twelve Friend Lists. This is higher than typical, probably because I spend more time on Facebook than the average person (or so I tell myself while I am writing this book). Here are the lists I use:

- Family

- Grade School Friends

- High School Friends

- Stanford Friends

- Mayfield Fellows

- Oxford Friends

- Former Google Coworkers

- Salesforce.com Colleagues

- Faceforce User

- Met at a Conference

- Soccer Team

- Never Met

It's not that you are being secretive or two-faced by exposing different parts of your identity to different groups of people. Rather, the reality is that each of us juggles multiple facets of our lives, and prior to Facebook Friend Lists, it was hard to capture these different nuances in our online identity. It is not appropriate, relevant, feasible, or considerate to share everything with everyone. Just like you have boundaries in real life between work and play, family and acquaintances, adult and child, it is natural too to want to set boundaries in our online social networks. Think of it as tagging your relationships or creating different folders for the different people in your life.

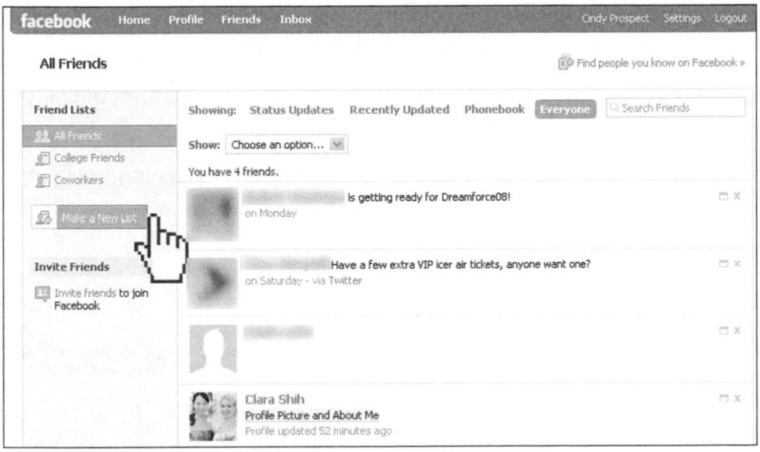

Figure 10.2
To define, view, and manage Friend Lists, click on the Friends tab. Once you create a new Friend List, you can associate any of your contacts with the list.

Step 4. Manage Your Identities

You can customize what is visible to each Friend List across ten different dimensions (see Figure 10.3). What you show to whom depends not only on what kind of content and information you have chosen to provide to Facebook, but also what about you *others* are adding to their Facebook accounts. For example, even if you have uploaded no photos to Facebook, it is possible that your friends have uploaded photos and tagged them of you. If you do not set the proper privacy controls (or if you are not even on Facebook to begin with), you implicitly forgo the right to keep photos tagged of you private. Similarly, others could tag you in videos, write on your wall, and send you Facebook gifts, all of which would show up on your profile by default. There are ten categories of information available on Facebook for which members can specify different visibility options:

- *Profile.* Full-size profile picture and networks.

- *Basic Info.* Gender, birthday, hometown, relationship status, relationship interests, political views, and religious views.

- *Personal Info.* Activities, interests, favorite music, TV shows, movies, books, quotations, and "about me" section.

- *Status Updates.* For example, "Kelly is… [fill in the blank]." These updates appear on the member profile page and are broadcast to the member's friend network via News Feed.

- *Photo Albums.* Note you can specify different privacy settings for each photo album you upload.

- *Photos Tagged of You.* Photos you or friends have uploaded to Facebook that are tagged of you. Note that you can untag yourself from any photo.

- *Videos Tagged of You.* Videos you or friends have uploaded to Facebook that are tagged of you. Note that you can untag yourself from any video.

- *Friends.* List of who your friends are and list of mutual friends (from the perspective of someone viewing your profile).

- *Wall Posts.* Persistent public messages left for individuals on their profile page walls, a space designated for showcasing chronological activity of a Facebook member.

- *Education Info.* School, major, and optional graduation year.

- *Work Info.* Employer, position, and dates.

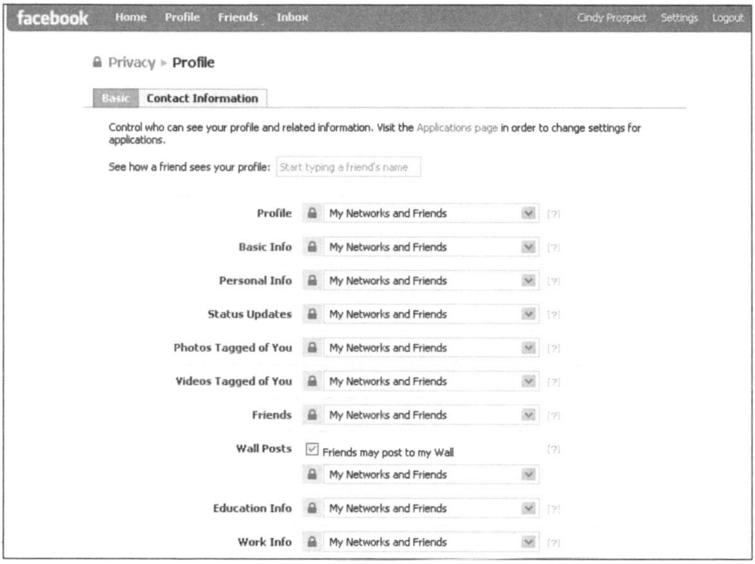

Figure 10.3
There are ten categories of content and information on Facebook. For each of these, you can specify privacy controls over who gets to see what. By default, your information is visible to your networks only, including friends of friends.

Facebook privacy controls also allow you to control what is visible to people on Facebook who aren't your friends. Specifically, you may choose to expose certain information to My Networks and Friends, Friends of Friends, or Only Friends (see Figure 10.4). For instance, you might not want to share your profile with everyone on Facebook, but you might feel comfortable sharing with anyone from your alma mater or other network. Privacy settings are important for business professionals interested in social networking. By strategically sharing some personal information, such as a photo of their newborn, while hiding other information, people can show a softer side and build emotional rapport with colleagues while protecting their corporate image and reputation.

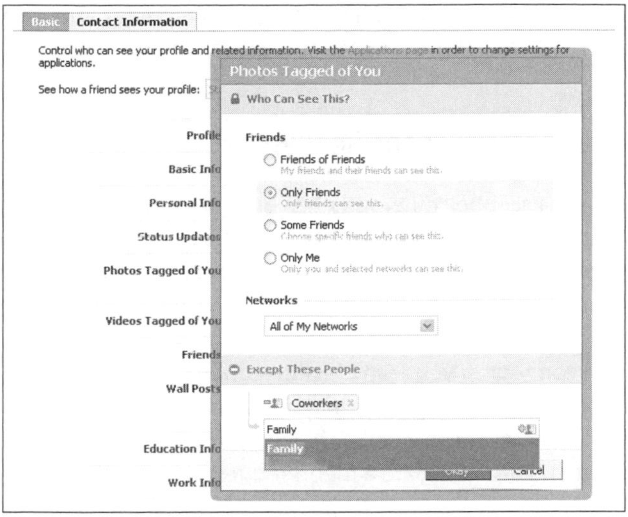

Figure 10.4
Facebook has sophisticated privacy settings, even allowing you to specify at the level of a photo album who does and doesn't get to see certain kinds of information about you. For example, you might not want your professional colleagues to see certain uploaded photo albums and photos taken by others tagged of you.

Interacting on Facebook

After you are set up on Facebook, get in the practice of logging in at least once a week to keep your profile up to date and build everyday social capital. Occasionally, opportunities might arise to supplement offline networking or fulfill requests from others for favors. You might also find yourself in the position to ask something of others.

You will find that over time, your experience on Facebook will become more fulfilling as the number of friends you have and your interaction history with each friend grows.

Keep Your Presence Fresh

Think of your Facebook profile as your Internet directory entry, which you should periodically refresh. If you move to a new city, change jobs, get a new cell phone number, or develop a new interest, you should update your profile to reflect this. But keeping your presence fresh goes beyond just this. Because the appeal of Facebook is largely from social news about your friends, actions you take and updates you provide, such as a new status message, new links or photos you've posted, photos tagged of you, comments you've made, and gifts you have given or received show up as updates on your profile page Mini-Feed and on your Facebook Friends' News Feed when they log in. So, the more active you are on Facebook, the more you (in the form of updates about you) will appear to your Facebook Friends, thereby increasing the probability of ad hoc interaction.

When to Initiate or Accept a Friend Request

Because everyone uses Facebook differently, has different privacy thresholds, and might or might not be using nuanced privacy controls with Friend Lists, it is hard to generally define when it is acceptable to initiate or accept friend requests. That said, the Facebook Friend is emerging as a new kind of more casual relationship and it is, therefore, becoming perfectly acceptable to add people as friends whom you have just met, especially if you know people in common. If you aren't feeling confident about making a request, one good way to test the waters is to send the individual a short, casual Facebook message, then gauge based on her response whether it seems like she would want to stay in touch—or better yet, she might initiate a friend request with you.

What if someone has requested to be your friend whom you don't really know? As always, you have three options: reject, confirm, or don't respond. Not responding can be a polite way of rejecting a request. The requestor is effectively put on hold. If he sees you on someone else's Friend List or searches for you, he sees a message from Facebook "Friend Requested" and can't take action until you have rejected or confirmed. If you reject ("ignore request" in Facebook lingo) someone, he won't get actively notified, but if he ever sees you on someone else's Friend List or searches for you, he will be able to request you as a friend again. The final option is to confirm the request but then just put that person on a "Limited Profile" or other custom Friend List with restricted ability to view and interact with your profile.

As we discussed in Chapter 3, "Social Capital from Networking Online," Facebook allows us to capture value among a new set of lower-commitment, weak-tie relationships by filing them away as options we can exercise and explore later. Of course, creating an interesting profile and establishing Facebook Friendship with these fringe individuals is the first step in building social capital. Casual Facebook interactions are the next step.

Build Everyday Social Capital

Frequent, high-touch interaction like phone calls, sending a letter, hanging out, instant messaging, or even e-mail are not only time consuming and difficult to sustain across many friends, but they also require a base level of rapport to feel socially acceptable. For example, if you do not know someone very well, it can feel awkward and out of place to send them a birthday card or suggest having dinner together. Facebook opens up the world of casual interaction with communication modes that are easy, playful, and spontaneous. Most popular are Facebook wall posts, messages, pokes, and gifts. But a number of third-party developed applications and games built on the Facebook platform have also emerged that people are increasingly using to interact with one another and build social capital.

Facebook was able to create a new relationship category for Facebook Friendship by introducing new modes of casual interaction on the site. There are three components that make this work: passive notification, active classification, and communication media.

First, Facebook provides visibility into what's happening with your friends and reasons to get in touch with notifications and reminders.

- *Friend visualizations and news feed reminders.* Every time you refresh your profile page, home screen, or view your Friends tab, a different set of friends are shown. On any given site visit, you are reminded of and updated with news from just a few Facebook Friends, but across multiple visits you eventually get coverage across all of your friends with lightweight, unintrusive reminders and visualizations. If a particular name, profile picture, or status message piques your curiosity, you can click through onto that person's profile page for a more detailed update. These notifications do not feel intrusive because you are only shown a few at a time, and they are passively broadcast to you by Facebook rather than an individual.

- *Birthday reminders.* On the home page is displayed your list of friends who have birthdays today and tomorrow. You can then click through to wish them a happy birthday with a Facebook message, Facebook wall post, and Facebook gift.

- *Status and incentives to encourage interaction.* How many friends you have, public wall posts, gifts received, and comments made about you are all displayed on your profile and serve as reinforcements and incentives to publicly pronounce your fondness for others by writing on their wall, giving them gifts, and making comments about their photos and notes. They, in turn, feel compelled to return the favor.

Second, Facebook offers different ways to categorize friends so that you remember how you met, it's easier to look them up later, and you can tailor what information about you is visible to them.

- *Friend Lists.* Although Facebook initially offered predefined categories only, users wanted more control and granularity over classifying their connections. In response, Facebook introduced Friend Lists to help users organize their networks. Friend Lists serve not only to help users remember, search, and filter connections, but also to limit who gets to see what on your profile. For example, it might make sense to share the Las Vegas bachelor party photo album with your list of college friends but not with coworkers.

- *Search and filtering by network and friend type.* Because Facebook is organized around networks, you can search and filter among your friends by college, high school, work, regional criteria, categories predefined by Facebook (such as housemates, travel buddies, family members, relationships, and coworkers), and categories defined by you via Friend Lists. There are a variety of situations where this is extremely useful. For example, if you are moving to a new city, for example New York, you can search for all connections that belong to the New York network and potentially have a great starting point for looking for jobs, friends, and an apartment. Another example could be a fund-raiser you are organizing for your high school alumni association. Rather than notify your entire network on Facebook, you might want to target just your friends from high school.

After you have both a motive to communicate and method for finding with whom you want to communicate, Facebook offers several ways to interact with your friends.

- *Facebook messages.* Our communication arsenal has evolved and expanded to become more casual over time, from in-person visits to letters, telegraphs, phone calls, e-mail, and then instant messaging. Facebook messages are the next step in this evolution. It is standard to omit the opening greeting and closing signature and use incomplete sentences, abbreviations, lowercase only, and so on because expectations are lower. Messages are especially well suited for fringe relationships that you don't want to escalate too early with an e-mail or phone call, which might feel too formal, premature, uncomfortable, or inappropriate, like you are overstepping social bounds. Messages are also great for reaching out to strangers, especially those in your network, because people are much more likely to reply if they see you know people in common and can get to know you (or at least about you) through your picture and profile information. The automatic linking of the message to your profile also saves you from having to introduce and explain yourself in the message; you can just cut to the chase. On college campuses across America, Facebook messages are the preferred means of communication. E-mail, I am told, is reserved for "grown-ups," such as parents, professors, and prospective employers.

- *Facebook wall posts.* One of the most interesting features of Facebook are wall posts, publicly broadcast messages that appear not only on the recipient's profile page "wall" but also via the News Feed and Mini-Feeds. These are most commonly used for congratulating, wishing happy birthday, and other news worthy of sharing, although some people just like to publicly announce everything they have to say.

- *Facebook pokes (see Figure 10.5).* What is a Facebook poke, really? Is it friendly, romantic, funny? I don't think anyone really knows. The mystery makes it fun and playful. It's an easy way to call attention to yourself or let someone know you are thinking about them without the stress of thinking of what to say or expecting a reply.

- *Commenting.* Every news item on Facebook can be commented on, which drastically increases the opportunities for engagement. For example, you might want to comment if a friend posts a photo, updates their status message, changes their relationship status to engaged, or joins a group.

- *Games and other platform apps (see Figure 10.6).* And when you don't have anything at all to say, Facebook games and other social apps come to the rescue. In addition to the standard interaction options offered by Facebook, other companies have developed social applications on top of the Facebook platform that allow users to do things like throw virtual sheep, send virtual cupcakes, give a virtual hug, and play Scrabble with their Facebook Friends.

Together, these three components—visibility and notification, ability to organize connections, and casual ways to interact—have remarkably come together to define an entirely new class of interaction.

Figure 10.5

No one really knows what a Facebook poke means. Generally, it is a casual, playful way to interact with someone without having anything to say. The Facebook etiquette is to poke back or to respond with a Facebook message or wall post.

Figure 10.6

In addition to Facebook messages, gifts, wall posts, and pokes, a number of platform apps and games have emerged that allow people to playfully interact with their friends on Facebook. Send Cupcakes, an application developed by Jeffrey Hoffman Yip, is a prime example. It allows users to send premade cupcakes or to design their own and send them to friends.

It is good Facebook etiquette to send a message, Facebook gift, song, cupcake, or at least write well wishes on the wall for birthdays, engagements, weddings, and baby arrivals, but the continual stream of Facebook Friend feeds such as posted links and updated status messages also provide good and frequent opportunities to interact.

Supplement Offline Networking

Facebook interactions are great for building casual rapport, but they are most powerful when used in conjunction with offline networking efforts, such as due diligence and networking at conferences. Over the last decade, it has become an expected part of the due diligence process to search on Google for anyone you are considering as a job candidate, business partner, hiring manager, and the like. Today, it is also becoming standard practice to look people up on Facebook. Even if privacy settings prevent you from seeing the full profile, you can often at least see how you are connected, from which you could then conduct further due diligence by talking to the individuals you know in common.

Facebook is also ideal for networking at conferences and other professional events. If the organizers have created a Facebook Event for RSVPs, usually you can browse through the list of invitees. Maybe someone you have been wanting to meet will be there, or you come across others with whom you realize you would like to network. You could send a Facebook message before the conference to introduce yourself and arrange a meeting. Similarly, you can use Facebook to follow up and start to form a closer relationship with someone you met at the conference. Your photo and professional information will help people remember who you are and the context in which you met. Your other information that you decide to share, perhaps where you are from and photos of your children, will help people get to know you better if they so choose. Increasingly, business cards are becoming more of a formality—sometimes, putting a face to the name makes all the difference.

Last, but not least, you can also join Facebook networks corresponding to your real-life networks, such as city, workplace, school, or region. Workplace or school (high school, college, or university) networks require e-mail addresses from that domain. For example, to join the salesforce.com network on Facebook, I need to provide my work e-mail address. Facebook will send me a verification e-mail to that address, and once I click on the link inside the e-mail, then Facebook takes it as proof that I, in fact, work at salesforce.com and allows me access to the other members in the network. This can be a good way of quickly finding people you know so that you can make friend requests without searching on individual names. It is also helpful for getting to know more people in your company or school, especially those whom you might not normally run into while at work.

Asking for and Providing Introductions

Introductions to people are one of the most valuable aspects of Facebook. In the offline world, it is basically impossible to comprehend and navigate the complex web of who knows whom, so only a small fraction of the time do you know the right person to ask for an introduction. With Facebook, LinkedIn, and Visible Path, you can see exactly how you are connected to someone and likely how your friends in common know this person. Using profile search, it is also easy to find people to whom you would like to be intro-duced (see Figure 10.7). In the offline world, you might not ever know that these people exist and are only a couple degrees away from you. For most business networking, the important search criteria are company, position, networks, and location.

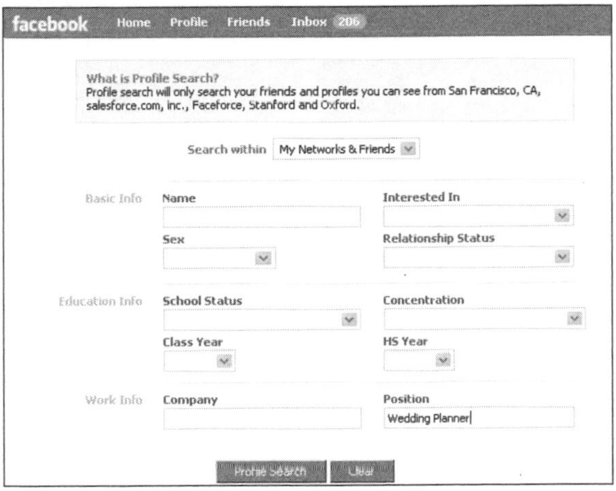

Figure 10.7
The profile search on Facebook allows you to search your network along a number of different cri-teria, including company and position, networks, school attended, and geographic location. It is a useful tool for finding people with whom to network.

When people ask you to be introduced, all else being equal it is also much easier and probably more compelling to provide the introduction. Say Person A has asked you for an introduction to Person B. First, a Facebook message feels more friendly versus professional and utilitarian, so Person B is more likely to respond. Second, rather than having to provide all this context about Person A, you can rest assured that Person B will view Person A's Facebook profile for herself as well as see who else they might know in common.

As we uncovered in Chapter 3, the cost of a favor to the grantor is generally significantly less than the value gained by the person receiving the favor. Facebook lowers the barriers to asking and receiving favors, and is especially well suited for when the favors are requests for introductions. Once you have established a good network and accumulated social capital on Facebook, it will become an invaluable tool for you to find prospective customers, business partners, employees, consultants, and hiring managers, and to help your friends do the same.

11

Corporate Governance and Strategy

At this point, you should hopefully have ideas for how you see online social networking potentially improving various aspects of your company. Successful adoption of online social networking for business, however, requires careful planning and execution. For one, you might have sensed it is hard work keeping tabs on the various initiatives, communities, and subcommunities across different social networking sites. The ability to engage with more individuals from your customer, partner, and employee communities for recruiting, product development, sales, and marketing is powerful, but significantly increases the workload involved in any of these areas. If you are serious about enterprise social networking, it might be a good idea to assign dedicated resources at least initially to rolling out and measuring the success of your social initiatives. Regardless, it's important to start small and test your ideas before making substantial investment on any particular initiative.

Whatever your company size or industry, though, it is also imperative that you consider corporate governance and compliance. Web 2.0 and social networking technologies, in particular, enable unprecedented levels of openness and transparency that can be transformational for business, but there are also new risks that you must address and try to mitigate. First, you will need to decide on which technology model or models to employ, such as whether to go with an open network like Facebook, which anyone can join, or a closed network like a specialized Ning network, which would be limited to your community only. What you decide here will affect user adoption, engagement, cost and ROI, and ultimately the success of your initiative. It is generally a good idea to engage your legal and IT departments earlier in the cycle so that you don't end up in a reactionary situation where there has been a blatant violation in company policy and any social networking initiatives are banned altogether. Your colleagues in those departments can likely help you figure out the right processes and policies around issues like privacy, intellectual property, and confidentiality.

Choosing the Right Network Model

At a high level, companies have two technology options for how they want to run their networks: creating groups and communities on open networks such as Facebook or creating closed private networks using services like Ning or other community software. There are pros and cons to each approach. Open networks benefit from better user adoption because customers, partners, and employees are already using many of these online social networking services in their personal lives. But going this route also presents new risks around privacy, security, and intellectual property. Closed networks, on the other hand, offer more control and focused interaction among community members, but at the expense of lower adoption and engagement. For many CIOs in particular, going with closed networks might be tempting, but in so doing, they might miss out on the very aspect of online social networking that is so transformational: the collective social graph. As we discussed in Chapter 3, "Social Capital from Networking Online," Metcalfe's Law tells us that the value of a social networking site goes up exponentially with the number of members. It is precisely the reach, openness, and transparency of public social networking sites that make them so compelling.

Although companies might want to adopt internal social networking tools such as Connectbeam and Thoughtfarmer (both introduced in Chapter 6, "Social Innovation"), these should be in addition to, not instead of, the greater opportunity of plugging into sites where employees can access and cross-pollinate ideas with customers, partners, and others outside of the company. What does this mean for companies? Well, CIOs will need to take extra precautions to address issues around compliance, security, and governance. Social networking providers will need to continue rising to the challenge with more and better features that address enterprise requirements. Facebook's partnership with salesforce.com is a good example of this starting to take place. By bringing a trusted corporate standard around security, privacy, reliability, availability, and compliance to a traditionally consumer model, the partnership is helping make strides in addressing valid IT concerns and providing CIOs peace of mind about implementing social networking for the enterprise.

Cross-Boundary Collaboration

The value of open social networks lies in the collaborative nature of innovation. Much of innovation, as opposed to invention, takes place *across*—not within—boundaries. Memes cross-pollinate into new industries, communities, and applications. Homogeneous teams seek people with complementary skills that take their ideas into new directions, unlocking their full potential. To succeed, companies need to collaborate externally with customers and partners.

This is not to say boundaries aren't important, just that in the Facebook Era, boundaries become less black and white. Certain interactions and information flow across boundaries that were too difficult or costly before but are now easy and expected. For one, online social networking makes it cost effective for the first time for businesses to approach and cultivate with individual customers. Using sites like Facebook and MySpace, community brand managers can reach many people at once as well as quickly identify who the leaders and influencers are in the community. Two additional areas where online social networking has facilitated cross-boundary collaboration are recruiting and business development. It is much easier than ever before to source job candidates and subject matter experts and to collaborate with business partners. This is all only possible with an open network model composed of homogeneous groups, employers, and industries.

User Adoption

Ultimately, the success or failure of enterprise social networking initiatives is largely an issue of change management. The other advantage of leveraging existing open social networks like Facebook is that there is already high adoption by a large and growing number of individuals. Especially in organizations that employ any number of young people, we are seeing pressure put on the employer and older employees to adapt. "Younger employees" can be loosely defined as individuals who were born after 1975, who have grown up with e-mail, mobile phones, and social networking in their personal and academic lives, and expect these technologies to be available in their professional lives. Empowering employees with social networking technologies in the workplace is helping companies both attract the best and brightest young talent as well as get the most out of these individuals once they become employees.

Today, we are witnessing an interesting phenomenon where there are three to four generations in the workforce, from people who have never used a computer before to so-called "digital natives" who don't know what life is like without. One successful strategy we have seen in bridging this generational divide has been to use younger employees as reverse-mentors. It is a great way too to provide access for these newer employees to more senior managers and executives.

Industry Standards and Portability

With the hundreds of social networking services and platforms that have emerged in the last several years, corporations and individuals who want to adopt these technologies are faced with another difficult challenge around data portability. Many in the industry are calling for standards around social data to accommodate the large number of these heterogeneous open networks. As we briefly introduced in Chapter 2, "The Evolution of Digital Media," OpenSocial was developed (originally by Google) as a set of open source APIs that help make social graph data and applications portable to the extent possible across different social networking sites.

The goal of OpenSocial is to allow social applications and data to transcend the boundaries of different Web sites and particular social networking sites. It is an interesting idea with a large number of participating vendors but will only work if steps are taken to define the data visibility and security rules across applications on each site.

For the software developers building applications for these social networks, instead of having to build a different version for each site as they did in the prestandards world, they can now more or less get away with building and maintaining one that will run across any OpenSocial-enabled site. For people like you and me who are members of these social networking sites, this means we can have a more unified view of and experience interacting with our friends on different sites.

Bob Bickell, a startup veteran and thought leader in the social networking space, has coined the term "federated social graph" to refer to all of an individual's contacts and connections across every site on which they might have friends. Here is an example: Kelly is signed up and has friends on MySpace, LinkedIn, and a swimming enthusiasts' Web site— all of which have enabled the OpenSocial standard. Before, all of these worlds were separate, even if there was overlap among Kelly's friends across each of these respective sites. With OpenSocial, interactions Kelly has with apps on one site can "carry over" to the next time Kelly goes to another site. Kelly, of course, can maintain separate friends on three sites because she wants to show them different facets of her identity; by granting access to different OpenSocial applications on different sites, Kelly can continue to define boundaries that are important to her. More than ever before, Kelly, rather than MySpace, LinkedIn, or another site, owns and is in control of her profile information and friend data.

Identify Key Risk Areas

Enterprise social networking requires a certain degree of openness to work and to succeed, but this introduces new risks around privacy and security, intellectual property, and misrepresentation by employees. After you have selected a network model, the next step in instituting proper corporate governance around these technologies is to honestly assess where the key risks might be. At the end of the day, it is more important to be aware of and manage risk rather than try to avoid risk altogether because that is costly, frustrating, and impossible. The optimal level of risk is not zero; risk is something we in business manage all the time. This is just a new context to which to apply risk mitigation.

Identity, Privacy, and Security

The biggest security risks around enterprise social networking are generally not related to technology. They involve identity and privacy. There is a wealth of personal information about individuals available on social networking sites. To establish their identity and build rapport with their friend connections, people are for the most part very forthcoming with personal data such as date of birth, education, employment history, and the like. But especially without the right privacy settings in place, members of online social networking sites could become easy targets for identity theft. Seemingly harmless pieces of information such as your hometown or pet's name are often the same kinds of security questions used by other sites, such as banking sites, to verify your identity.

Another smaller but growing problem that exists even if you haven't signed up for any online social networking sites is other people posing as you. Arguably, not being on these sites increases the likelihood that this could go on for awhile before anyone noticed and you found out. Earlier in Facebook's history, people needed to have a valid private-network e-mail address, such as *@umich.edu* to sign up and be associated with a private network. That is no longer the case, so we all need to be extra careful about fake profiles, phishing scams, and whom we share information with and whether they are who they say they are.

Intellectual Property and Confidentiality

The second big risk area for businesses around social networking is safeguarding intellectual property and confidentiality against competitive or malicious threats. Sites like Facebook and MySpace remove a lot of barriers for interacting with customers and others in the community at large for productive activities such as marketing, sales, product innovation, and recruiting but also expose your business to the risk of data being shared with the wrong people. Table 11.1 calls out the top issues to consider *before* you embark on enterprise social networking.

Table 11.1 CONFIDENTIALITY PITFALLS OF ENTERPRISE SOCIAL NETWORKING

Business Area	Major Threat	How to Mitigate
Sales	Sales reps at competitor vendors target your contacts.	Only accept friend requests from people you know and trust. Adjust privacy controls to hide visibility of your friend connections.
Marketing	Negative buzz in your social community gets publicized by competitors.	This is unavoidable and exists to a lesser degree on pre-Facebook Era sites. If there are consistent instigators of negative feedback on your social communities, spend time investigating who these people are. Maybe they are competitors you should kick out.

continues…

Table 11.1 CONTINUED

Business Area	Major Threat	How to Mitigate
Human Resources	Your organizational structure is revealed to company outsiders; top executives easily targeted by headhunters.	Though some HR departments have tried instituting corporate policies to limit what company-related information employees disclose on their profile, this is difficult to justify and enforce on employees' personal profiles.
Product Innovation	Product plans and ideas put forth are visible to competitors.	Limit participation to a select group of trusted individuals instead of making it an open free-for-all.

Finally, there is an issue to keep in mind around who owns data and content related to your brand when these are generated from interactions that occur on sites like Facebook or MySpace, such as on a Facebook Page. Though Facebook does not explicitly lay claim to this content, technically speaking, it belongs to Facebook or whichever site on which the content is created. For this reason, it is recommended that any content or information that requires clear ownership and confidentiality that you do choose to publish to social networking sites appear via a platform application you commission for this purpose rather than through the out-of-the-box mechanisms provided by the site.

Employees Misrepresenting Your Brand

Last, but not least, the openness of enterprise social networking can increase the opportunities for your employees to speak out of turn and potentially misrepresent your brand to customers, partners, and the public at large, either purposefully or inadvertently. For the former, you could imagine, for example, a disgruntled former employee who was fired might attempt to retaliate by saying negative things about your company on public forums in Facebook. For the latter, a common example involves employees who carelessly or unknowingly post inappropriate public photos on their Facebook profile, which then reflects badly on your company. As we discuss in the next section, it is imperative to involve the appropriate stakeholders in your company so that they are aware of and can help mitigate the risk involved.

Partner with Legal, IT, and PR

Whether you are in sales, marketing, product development, or recruiting, the new Facebook Era risks around enterprise social network underscore the need for partnering with legal, and if you have it, IT to come up with the proper strategy and precautions. The challenge is that legal and IT departments are by design typically averse to change. Yet business environments change quickly. The most important thing you can do is get buy-in from top-level executives around your social initiatives and try to rally your counterparts in legal, IT, and PR around the business objectives. Together, you will best be able to identify the risks that are the greatest threat to your business and come up with the set of policies and plan to mitigate them.

Update Company Policy

If your business is like most, there should be company policy governing offline activities and likely online activities like e-mail, instant messaging, and surfing the Web. There should be policies, too, governing what's permissible around use of social networking technologies by employees and questions for which you will need to weigh the benefits against risks. Will you make social networking mandatory, like e-mail and mobile phones have become in many companies? Or will you leave it voluntary only for employees who want to use these new technologies? Will you require employees use their personal social networking accounts to interact on behalf of the company with customers, or are both you and they better served with separate dedicated profiles and accounts? Do you have systems in place for when employees leave your company to ensure they no longer have access to your social networking systems and assets?

Where it gets tricky is what employees do in their own time with their personal social networking profiles—the line becomes blurry between what affects your brand and business, versus what is none of your business.

Training and Education

Of course, company policies mean nothing if your employees don't understand and play by them. Training and education are a nontrivial and important part of corporate governance. Update your new hire orientation curriculum to include mention of both the advantages and risks of social networking. Talk about it at your next company all-hands meeting.

For example, you might want to make employees aware about the security threats of public social networking sites like Facebook. To minimize this security risk around identity and privacy, employees should scrutinize what kinds of information they share on their social networking profile. Employees should assume that anything they disclose could become public knowledge. As a general rule of thumb, they shouldn't accept connection requests from people they don't know, especially if they don't know anyone in common or something seems "off" about the requestor's profile. Last, but not least, encourage your employees to carefully think through their privacy settings (urge them to establish Friend Lists to control visibility of their information, as discussed in the previous chapter) and share the minimum amount of information necessary to still achieve the company and their individual goals of being on the social networking site. This is an important and active step employees must take because by default, the privacy settings on Facebook and MySpace are relatively open.

Tony Hsieh, CEO of online shoe retailer Zappos, trains every new call center employee on the appropriate use of Twitter. This has encouraged employees to become active users of social media while supporting Zappos' brand and mission, which is highly motivating and mutually beneficial for everyone.

Reconciling Grassroots Initiatives

Particularly given its newness, enterprise social networking to date has largely taken the form of grassroots initiatives driven by individual people or departments. As social networking permeates your company, at some point it makes sense to develop a cohesive, company-level strategy. Though it requires some coordination effort, eventually reconciling across disparate grassroots campaigns can reduce cost and confusion, and ultimately improve the effectiveness and risk management of your initiatives.

12

The Future of Social Business

Online social networking for business is still a nascent and rapidly changing field. Even in the short course of writing this book, it has been difficult to keep up with the new vendors, user interfaces, jargon, and new possibilities that seem to emerge every day. Specific vendors and technologies might indeed come and go—Six Degrees, for one, is long gone but left an important legacy. And there almost certainly are many new players yet to emerge still in this space.

What is critical isn't the specific technologies of today but rather the general shift in mind-set toward an increasingly socially networked world. To adequately prepare, we must completely rethink our relationships, interactions, and business strategies. Just as the Internet fundamentally changed nearly every aspect of our personal and working lives, so too does the social graph represent a radical step that is already beginning to permeate many important areas of our lives. With the social networking revolution, we are brought closer than ever before to becoming people-centric instead of technology-centric. The online social graph allows our relationships and business goals, rather than technology limitations, to drive business strategies and decisions. Indeed, the online social graph at its best becomes invisible, fully ingrained into our online and offline tasks, transactions, and interactions. It makes our Web interactions and experiences at once emotional, interesting, and trusted.

The Innovator's Dilemma

Reaching this ideal will take time. You might recall in the early days of the World Wide Web, people weren't quite sure what to make of and what to do with the new capabilities. As is typically the case in digital revolutions, the first Internet generation (what we call Web 1.0) merely applied pre-Internet concepts to a new medium. It was linear thinking. Company Web sites were just online versions of the company brochure. A phone call was the predominant call to action.

It wasn't until nearly a decade later that we began to realize and then slowly tap into the unique attributes of the Internet to do things that simply were not possible prior to the Internet: search engine marketing, user-generated content, automating manual business processes in Web applications, and allowing people to interact with those applications. It took a generation of visionaries, early adopters, and believers to make Web 2.0 a reality. In the process, companies came and went—Netscape, CompuServe, Webvan, Napster, Pets.com, to name a few.

Nor should you expect that the kings of today's era will reign in tomorrow's era. More likely, the kings don't see it coming, don't *want* to see it coming, or see it coming but can't get organizationally aligned around doing anything about it. This is a classic example of the *innovator's dilemma,* a concept introduced by Harvard Business School Professor Clayton Christensen to describe the inability of most large companies to embrace radically new technologies because they are disruptive to the existing business. Look at what happened to Eastman Kodak, the dominant player in photography for many decades. As the digital photography revolution was unfolding in the late nineties and into this century, Kodak was still seeing the vast majority of its profits come from its slowly declining but still extremely compelling print film business. This was a lucrative business in which Kodak had made its mark originally and was continuing to dominate. Though it quickly became apparent by the late nineties that digital cameras were overtaking traditional film cameras, Kodak found itself unable to adapt. The organization itself and all of the business momentum were built on the print film foundation. Kodak did not want to change its model, because by encouraging digital photography, it would be cannibalizing and accelerating the demise of its core business in print photography. We might be seeing this same phenomenon with the Internet Era kings and social networking revolution.

Don't let this happen to you. Eastman Kodak is an enormous, cash-rich company. It was able to adapt to the digital camera revolution by making a number of strategic acquisitions. Most small- or medium-size businesses can't afford to follow this approach. Pay careful attention to the emerging social networking trends in your industry around sales, marketing, recruiting, and innovation. Or better yet, blaze the trail for your industry and establish a lasting competitive advantage for your business.

The ROI of Social

Understandably, a large number of you are focused on ROI and might feel frustrated that there has been no clear and quantifiable data around the ROI of enterprise social networking initiatives. The best parallel I can draw here is to rewind ten years to the early days of the Internet. It was as hard if not harder then to calculate the ROI of having e-mail and a company Web page. The Internet was changing rapidly. (It is, of course, still changing!) Many businesses chose then to wait before going online. This was a mistake, especially for small businesses. Across almost every industry, new players emerged with more efficient, lower-cost models driven by the Web. Their competitive advantage was magnified as these new companies shaped and innovated new online models for their respective industries. Those who waited lost.

So, what is the ROI of the social graph for business? What is the ROI of the Internet for business? This is the wrong question to ask. It is too broad of a question to adequately answer. The ROI depends on your business objectives and *how* social networking is being used to achieve them. The ROI in the sales context could be based on how many business contacts a rep can maintain, increased close rate on deals, and heightened ability to upsell and cross-sell. For marketing, ROI might be measured via clickthroughs and views as is common today in advertising, or maybe a new metric of engagement is more appropriate. As social networking technologies continue to evolve and our ability to tie social initiatives back to impact improves these next few years, ROI will become much more quantifiable and standardized.

Social Trends

So what does the future hold? Only time, of course, will tell, but important trends are already taking shape. There are fewer numbers of new social networking sites emerging. The online social graph is becoming better integrated with other emerging technologies, such as video and mobile.

First, there appears to be a consolidation of social networking services. This is thanks in part to standardization initiatives, such as OpenSocial, but also owes largely to the network effects governing online social sites. Network effects mean large sites get larger and small sites get smaller much more quickly. Therefore we should expect that over the next several years, clear winners and losers will emerge.

Second, social networking services are becoming more technologically sophisticated. As compelling and revolutionary as the early days of the social networking revolution have been, the interaction possibilities on sites like Facebook and LinkedIn have been limited at best, largely around asynchronous, low-fidelity communication. The future will bring the power of the online social graph to the cutting edge in information and communication technology, such as real-time interactions and tighter integration with mobile devices. For example, the social graph could enhance GPS-based location systems on mobile phones. What if people could share their real-time location information with

Facebook Friends? Someone using Google Maps on a mobile device could then see which of his or her friends are in physical proximity. Another area that might benefit greatly from enterprise social networking services is video- and Web conferencing. What if in real time, people on a video or Web conference could see one another's profiles and mutual contacts? This might help establish greater rapport, especially among groups of people who are geographically dispersed and might not have ever met face-to-face.

What the Future Means for Doing Business

As enterprise social networking and social networking more generally become the norm, we will see a sociological shift in people's behavior toward relationships and interactions. First, more value than ever will be placed on social capital. People who are well connected will be disproportionately favored. They will be more empowered than ever before to accumulate and exercise social capital. Organizations, relationships, and the experience of buying something will all change dramatically.

Enterprise IT Goes Social

As lines of business owners shift toward a more social strategy, IT departments and technology vendors will similarly incorporate more social media and social networking in the applications they provide. As discussed in the previous chapter, CIOs will need to balance the benefits of plugging into the online social graph with the risks of not being able to have complete control. WorkLight, a New York- and Israel-based start-up company, has been a pioneer in bringing social technologies to the enterprise. WorkLight provides a software platform that brings enterprise software applications into Facebook and other traditionally consumer experiences such as iGoogle, desktop gadgets, and the iPhone to improve efficiency and user adoption. WorkLight's technology ensures that the enterprise data displayed is secure, relevant, and timely.

A customer example often cited by WorkLight is a manufacturing company that needs to manage inventory across different locations, run marketing promotions, and respond to distributor feedback. With WorkLight, the company's employees, distributors, and suppliers are able to view the information and interact with the business processes relevant to them in a secure fashion behind the corporate firewall. For example, information such as oil prices, competitors' actions, even weather, can all be pushed to the right stakeholders directly inside Facebook and other sites that are already being routinely accessed by these individuals (see Figure 12.1).

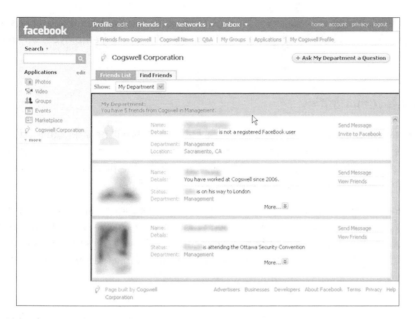

Figure 12.1
WorkLight's solution for enterprise social IT allows companies to publish data and business processes to Facebook and other traditionally consumer sites to make employees more productive.

As mentioned earlier in this book, Facebook is also making a big push for the enterprise. It has partnered with salesforce.com to create Force.com for Facebook, a set of developer tools that makes it easy to build Facebook applications on Force.com's enterprise cloud computing infrastructure. Executives from both companies believe this will pave the way for a new generation of applications on Facebook oriented to business and productivity. The MyStarbucksIdea application and Appirio's Jobs4MyFriends recruiting application previously profiled were both built using Force.com for Facebook. And of course salesforce.com itself is investing in making its Web applications more socially aware and better integrated with the various social graphs, such as our Service Cloud initiative discussed in Chapter 4, "Social Sales."

At a more fundamental level, business professionals are recognizing a growing disparity between the powerful, easy-to-use Web applications they use at home versus the unwieldy, outdated systems they use at work. Gartner Research calls it "IT consumerization."

Flatter, More Productive Organizations

Enterprise social networking fosters greater openness and transparency within organizations as well as beyond organizational boundaries. Within organizations, employees on the whole will have stronger informal ties and know one another better outside of just work, resulting in more productive working relationships. There might tend also to be less hierarchy because online social networking services start everyone on equal footing with an equal voice.

Recruiters and hiring managers will have powerful new tools at their disposal to source expertise as well as cultivate and manage human capital among employees on an ongoing basis.

Stronger Communities

In general, we should also expect that offline communities will be strengthened—for example, tenants in an apartment building, parents at a school, members of a religious organization. Online social networking offers community members greater opportunities for finding mutual interests and interacting with one another.

A big reason why this works is the notion of "divide and conquer" applied to the socialization of large groups. If there are only three tenants in your apartment building, three families in your school, or three members of your church, it is easy to get to know everyone. But as that number increases, community members invariably feel more anonymous and less accountable because it is simply not realistic to develop close relationships with every other member of a large community.

Online social networking alleviates this problem in two ways. First, it facilitates fringe relationships and makes them socially acceptable, as we discussed in Chapter 3, "Social Capital from Networking Online." But in addition to this, profile and friend information about community members also provide valuable context for people to quickly find common ground with specific individuals and subgroups within the community. Let's revisit the school parent example. Using online social networking, a family might be able to establish a baseline connection that wasn't previously possible with all or a large number of other families with children at the school. But then this family can further narrow down from the list to find individual families they want to forge closer ties with—perhaps, the ones living on the same street, or whose children play the same sports.

More Small Businesses

By reducing the cost of working across organizational boundaries and making transactions more fluid, enterprise social networking further democratizes who can start and run a business. We will see the continued trend of a growing number of smaller businesses as the cost and hassle of transacting goes down.

This is especially true in the area of sourcing human capital, and scaling up or scaling back capacity. Instead of having to hire dedicated people for every function as in a traditional business, small business owners today have greater flexibility for sourcing talent "on demand" as needed. For product development, they can crowdsource, as discussed in Chapter 6, "Social Innovation." Online social networks make it affordable and approachable for businesses to form more personal relationships with individual customers and communities.

Greater Collaboration Across Organizations

As organizational boundaries become less rigid, we will see greater collaboration take place across different organizations. Salesforce to Salesforce is a prime example of how this might play out. It's a neat idea: Instead of a social network of *people*, Salesforce to Salesforce is a social network of *companies*. It allows companies to easily share data such as leads, opportunities, accounts, contacts, and tasks with their suppliers, vendors, partners, and customers that also use Salesforce.

In a social network of people, the primary interactions might be exchanging messages, writing on someone's wall, or referring a friend for an open job requisition. In a social network of companies, the interactions center around sharing data and workflow that cut across disparate organizations. How does it work? It is surprisingly similar to how Facebook or LinkedIn operates. First, the company can send and accept connection requests, much like a Facebook Friend request or LinkedIn connection request (see Figure 12.2). Next, the company decides what kinds of data they want to share—perhaps leads, opportunities, contacts, or something else (see Figure 12.3). On the receiving end, companies can choose what updates they want to receive from which connections. Once those preferences are set up, the connected companies can easily collaborate with one another without the traditional headache of integration and manual back-and-forth coordination.

Here's an example: Company X uses Salesforce to Salesforce to share leads with its indirect channel partners and introduce approvals around any joint selling opportunities. Company X also automates workflow to adjust orders to its vendors for raw materials based on customer demand downstream. Lastly, Company X provides customers with real-time visibility into its order fulfillment process and the ability to log customer support cases. Just as the people-centric social networking discussed throughout this manuscript helps facilitate interactions and transactions between individuals, Salesforce to Salesforce makes interactions and transactions between companies easier and more efficient with this innovative new conception of an online social network.

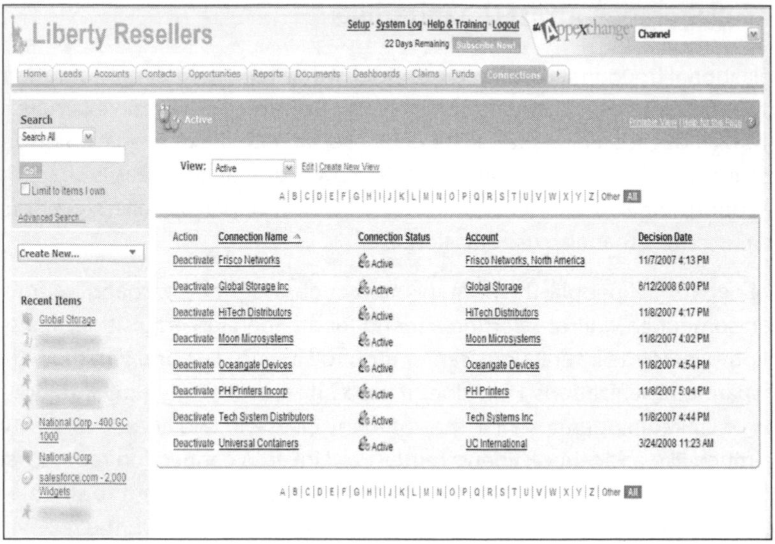

Figure 12.2
Salesforce to Salesforce is an online social networking service for companies. A company, such as Liberty Resellers in this case, maintains a set of connections with partner companies, such as vendors, suppliers, channel partners, and customers. Companies can make and accept connection requests just like an individual would on LinkedIn or Facebook.

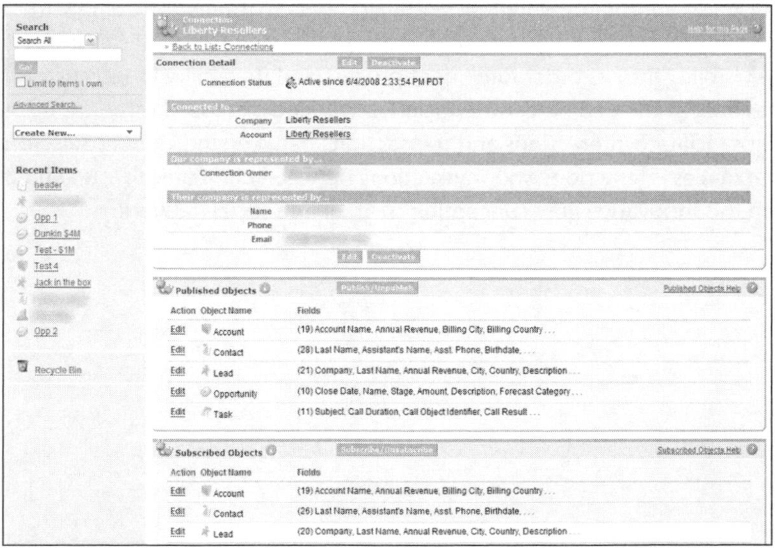

Figure 12.3
With Salesforce to Salesforce, companies can choose to share certain data and workflow, such as accounts, contacts, leads, opportunities, tasks, or custom data, by publishing these to specific connections. On the receiving end, companies can subscribe to the data that has been made available by their connections.

Friends *Forever?*

The sociological transformation won't just affect organizations, they will touch us individually. For one, the nature of relationships will change. Young people today in particular will have the ability if not tendency to keep in touch with every person they have ever known or met. If there is an upper limit on our capacity as humans to maintain relationships, does this mean we will be less open to meeting new people? Especially through adolescence, hasn't it been a godsend to be able to "start over" at summer camp or when entering a new school or grade? As we talked about in Chapter 3, already there has been a small number of people who have committed so-called "Facebook suicide"—that is, deactivating their account—to avoid awkward encounters with people from their past. Only time will tell what will happen to our relationships as a result of online social networking.

Final Remarks

We are very lucky. Not only do we get to witness one of history's most profound technology and sociocultural revolutions, we also get to shape it, live it, and directly experience it across many aspects of our personal and professional lives. What exactly the future holds is anyone's guess, but where we are now with online social networking is similar to where we were in the late 1980s with the Internet. We don't know specifics, but we do know it will be big, whatever your company size or industry, and whether you are in sales, marketing, product development, recruiting, or another business function.

Just as then, there are both extremes—the naysayers who believe this is a passing fad, and the yea-sayers who are eagerly jumping on the bandwagon and committing substantial resources without thinking through their business strategy and objectives. This book was meant to appeal to the vast majority of us who are in-between to help real companies with real customers understand the transformation that is under way and how they might adopt specific online social networking strategies to run a better business and become more competitive. Good luck, and see you on Facebook! I invite you to stay in touch and join the conversation as together we invent the rules of this new era: http://www.facebook.com/thefacebookera.

Snapshot of Top Social Networking Sites, March 2009

The following provides an overview of the top social networking sites, including a brief description, major markets served, number of reported registered users, screenshot of the profile page, and global Alexa Page Ranking for the top ten sites. Alexa rankings are made based on Web traffic data from Alexa's browser toolbars and integrated sidebars.

Facebook

Markets Served: Global

Year Founded: 2004

Active Users: Nearly 200M

Global Alexa Page Ranking: 5

Facebook is the largest and fastest-growing online social networking site in the world. In addition to its large audience, Facebook also has some of the most sophisticated advertising tools at the time of this book's publication. Advertisers can take advantage of features like hypertargeting to focus campaigns on very specific audience segments and feeds to promote word-of-mouth marketing.

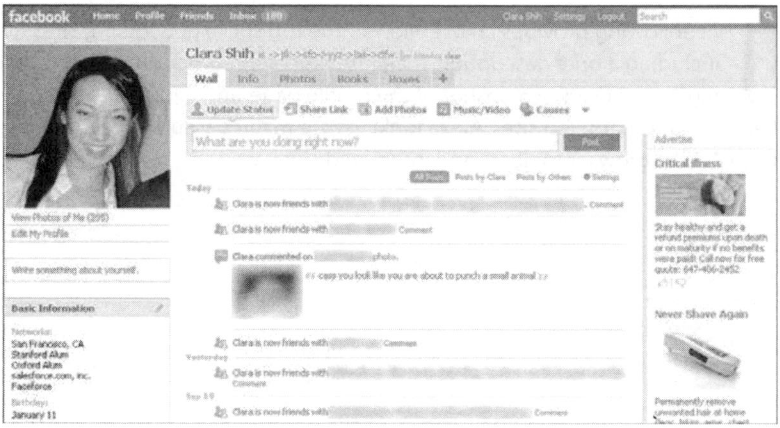

Figure A.1
Facebook, the biggest online social network.

MySpace

Markets Served: Global, especially United States, Canada, Europe

Year Founded: 2003

Active Users: 110M

Global Alexa Page Ranking: 7

MySpace, owned by Fox Interactive Media, is a popular social networking site among teens and adults around the world. MySpace is well known as a media and entertainment destination. Many musicians, comedians, filmmakers, and other celebrities have profiles on MySpace to promote their work and connect with fans. Similar to Facebook, MySpace has sophisticated advertiser tools that offer hypertargeting capabilities.

Figure A.2
MySpace, the leading online social network for media and entertainment.

Hi5

Markets Served: Global, especially non-U.S. countries like Portugal, Cyprus, Romania, and many Latin American markets

Year Founded: 2003

Active Users: 60M

Global Alexa Page Ranking: 17

Hi5 is a popular and fast-growing social networking site with a strong following outside of the United States. Early on, Hi5 aggressively pursued audiences in Latin America, Europe, and Asia by translating its site into 23 languages. Internationalization continues to be a core part of Hi5's strategy.[1]

---

1. Image could not be included at the time of publication.

Friendster

Markets Served: Global, especially Asia

Year Founded: 2002

Active Users: 60M

Global Alexa Page Ranking: 42

Friendster was a pioneer in online social networking, establishing a strong foothold in the United States and other major markets as early as 2003. It has since been overtaken by Facebook and MySpace in many English-speaking countries but remains very strong in Asia. For example, it is the #1 social network in Singapore, Malaysia, and Indonesia. According to Friendster, in Asia, it is more than double the size of any other social network.

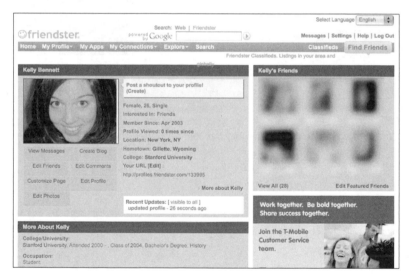

Figure A.3
Friendster, an early pioneer in online social networking. Today, it is the most popular social network in Asia.

Tagged

Markets Served: Mostly teenagers

Year Founded: 2004

Registered Users: 70M (no data available on number of active users)

Global Alexa Page Ranking: 99

Tagged is a newer social networking site that was designed with special consideration for teenagers. For example, profiles of anyone under 16 are blocked from view by members over 18. Tagged encourages brand advertising through contests and sweepstakes, as well as polls, home page ads, and sponsored profiles. Most Tagged members are in the United States, although it is also generating a strong following in international markets, including Qatar, Kuwait, and Kenya.

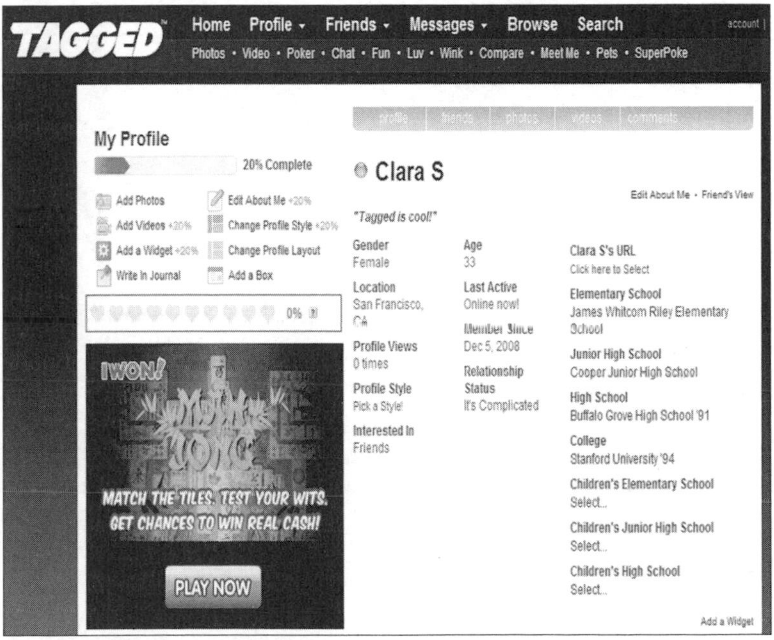

Figure A.4
Tagged, a newer social networking site meant for teens.

Orkut

Markets Served: Primarily Brazil, Paraguay, and India

Year Founded: 2004

Active Users: 25M

Global Alexa Page Ranking: 76

Orkut, owned by Google, started out as an invitation-only social network that gained early traction among the technology community. Orkut was open to the public in October 2006. It has become the most popular social networking site in Brazil, Paraguay, and India. In fact, in 2008 Google decided to relocate Orkut management and operations to Brazil to better concentrate on these markets.

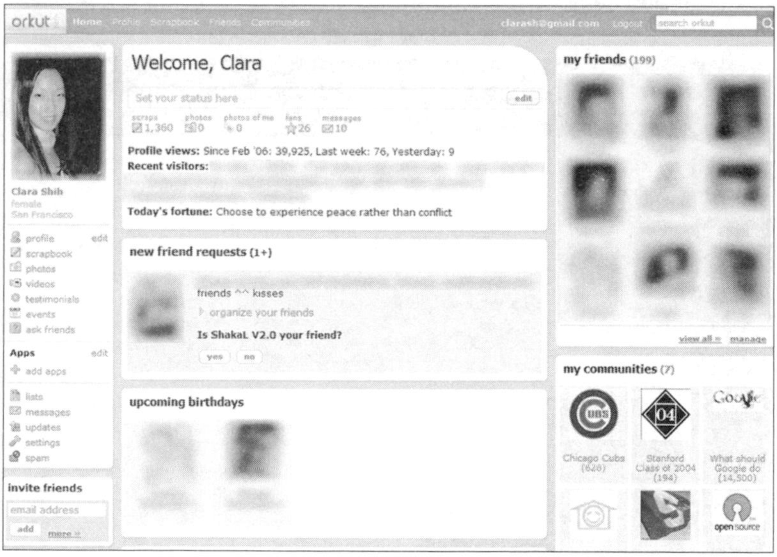

Figure A.5
Orkut is the most popular social network in Brazil, Paraguay, and India.

Bebo

Markets Served: Primarily United Kingdom, Ireland, New Zealand, and Pacific Islands

Year Founded: 2005

Active Users: 22M

Global Alexa Page Ranking: 97

Bebo, owned by AOL, is a popular social networking site in select international markets including Ireland and New Zealand. It has followed MySpace's strategy of creating a platform to promote media and entertainment. For example, the Bebo Open Media Platform allows content providers to distribute media to the Bebo community.

Figure A.6
Bebo is a popular social networking site in Ireland, New Zealand, Pacific Islands, and the United Kingdom. Bebo and the Bebo logo are trademarks of Bebo, Inc. AOL and the AOL Triangle Logo are registered trademarks of AOL LLC. Used with permission.

LinkedIn

Markets Served: Professional

Year Founded: 2003

Active Users: 23M

Global Alexa Page Ranking: 190

LinkedIn is the biggest business social networking site. Over two-thirds of its 30 million registered users are active on the site. In addition to its free social networking service, LinkedIn offers premium paid corporate solutions for recruiters to access profiles of potential job candidates.

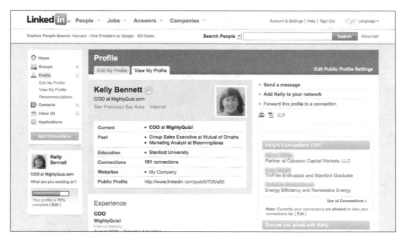

Figure A.7
LinkedIn is the leading professional social network.

Xanga

Markets Served: Mostly teenagers, especially popular in Asian markets like Hong Kong

Year Founded: 1998

Registered Users: 40M (active user numbers not available)

Global Alexa Page Ranking: 319

Xanga is one of the oldest social networking sites and still one of the most popular social networks in Asia. Blogs, including weblogs, photoblogs, audioblogs, and videoblogs, are at the center of Xanga profiles. Recently, Xanga growth seems to have flatlined due to competition from newer social networking sites as well as blog hosting sites like TypePad and Blogger.[2]

2. Image could not be included at the time of publication.

Xiaonei 校内网

Markets Served: China

Year Founded: 2005

Active Users: 9M

Global Alexa Page Ranking: 165

Xiaonei, which has a very similar look and feel to Facebook, is the biggest social network in China. Xiaonei is officially sanctioned by the Chinese government, which in contrast has frowned upon citizens submitting personal information to American social networking sites like Facebook. Following the strict Internet policies of the Chinese government, Xiaonei members are required to register with their actual names and identities, and are liable for any content they post.[3]

In addition to these more detailed overviews of the top ten social networks, the following table provides quick stats on the remaining top twenty social networking sites.

Table A.1   OTHER POPULAR SOCIAL NETWORKING SITES, IN ALPHABETICAL ORDER

Name	Markets Served	Number of Registered Users	Global Alexa Page Ranking
Badoo	Global, especially Europe	13M	209
Classmates.com	Primarily United States	50M	572
Cyworld	Primarily South Korea	21M	213
Doostang	Global, invitation only	500K	40,732
Hyves	Primarily Netherlands	4M	167
Mixi	Japan only	18M	69
Netlog	Primarily Europe	36M	67
Ning	Global	Not available	199
Odnoklassniki	Russian-speaking countries	10M	41
Skyrock Network	France	15M	44
Twitter	Global	2.2M	624
Yahoo! 360	Shut down in October 2007	—	—

3. Image could not be included at the time of publication.

Index

Facebook Ads Free Trial

facebook

$25

FREE $25 FACEBOOK AD CREDIT WITH BOOK PURCHASE

Valid first-time book purchases by first 10,000 readers qualify for a free $25 credit that can be used for Facebook Ads. Visit **www.thefacebookera.com/facebookadpromo** to access your coupon code. Limit one offer per reader and per purchase, new Facebook advertisers only. Additional details are available on the offer registration Web page.

Promotional Terms:

The promotional coupon code and the advertising credits of USD $25 are valid only for purchase of advertising through Facebook's online advertising system. Advertisers will be charged for incremental cost of advertising that exceeds the promotional credit. Advertisers will need to suspend their ads if they do not wish to receive additional charges beyond the free credit amount. Subject to ad approval, valid registration, and acceptance of the generally applicable Facebook Advertising Terms and Conditions: www.facebook.com/terms_ads.php. The promotional coupon code and advertising credits are non-transferable and may not be sold or bartered. Offer may be revoked at any time for any reason by Facebook. One promotional code per new advertiser. Must be a new advertiser.

Facebook is a trademark of Facebook, Inc.

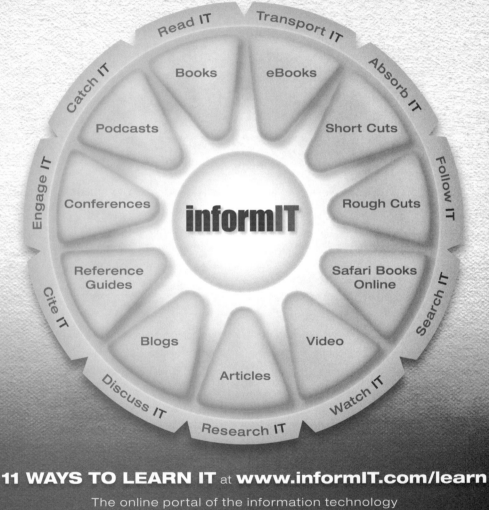